Karma's Child

Karma's Child

THE STORY OF INDIAN CINEMA'S ULTIMATE SHOWMAN

SUBHASH GHAI

with **SUVEEN SINHA**

HarperCollins *Publishers* India

First published in hardback in India by HarperCollins *Publishers* 2024
HarperCollins *Publishers* India, Cyber City,
Building 10-A, Gurugram, Haryana – 122002, India
www.harpercollins.co.in

This edition published in India by HarperCollins *Publishers* 2025

2 4 6 8 10 9 7 5 3 1

Photographs on pages 1 to 13 of the insert courtesy of
Whistling Woods International
Photographs on pages 14 to 16 of the insert by Soumik Kar

P-ISBN: 978-93-6989-867-1
E-ISBN: 978-93-6213-726-5

Typeset in 11.5/16 Adobe Caslon Pro
by HarperCollins *Publishers* India Pvt. Ltd

Printed and bound at
Thomson Press (India) Ltd.

MIX
Paper
FSC FSC® C010615

This book is produced from independently certified FSC® paper to
ensure responsible forest management.

'All autobiographies are lies'

— GEORGE BERNARD SHAW

Contents

Foreword by Subhash Ghai ix

1. Promise 1
2. Destiny 9
3. Becoming a Writer 22
4. Becoming a Director 30
5. *Kalicharan*: Arrival 38
6. *Vishwanath*: Director's Triumph 51
7. *Gautam Govinda*: The Parting 57
8. *Krodhi*: The Wrath 66
9. *Karz*: The Debt 74
10. *Vidhaata*: The Maker 91
11. *Hero*: A Musical Odyssey 106
12. *Meri Jung*: The Battle 123
13. *Karma*: The Extravaganza 131

14. *Devaa*: The Magnum Opus that Was Not to Be 144

15. *Ram Lakhan*: The Small Big Film 156

16. *Saudagar*: Clash of the Titans 173

17. *Khal Nayak*: The Anti-Hero 195

18. *Pardes*: The Home and the World 210

19. *Taal*: The Symphony 226

20. *Yaadein*: The Disconcerting Memories 245

21. *Kisna*, *Yuvvraaj* and Beyond 254

22. Whistling Woods: A New Innings 264

Afterword by Suveen Sinha 271

Subhash Ghai's Filmography 280

Index 282

Foreword

BY SUBHASH GHAI

The first time I looked through the viewfinder of a movie camera was when I became a director and was taking my first shot for *Kalicharan*. However, in a manner of speaking, I have always looked at the world through a sort of viewfinder that's in my head. I have found myself observing the events around me and the people involved in them—including myself—as if I am an observer, looking through a viewfinder. It is like I have been watching this great drama of life unfold before my eyes and while I am a part of it, I am also slightly detached; affected by the happenings around me, but not quite consumed by them.

This, I feel, is what led me to write plays in college—narrating scenes from a third person's point of view. It is what led me to become first a writer and later a filmmaker. It helped me keep my head while scaling the highest heights, and helped me bounce back from the lowest of lows.

Trust me, I have had some lofty highs and I also hit rock bottom more than once. But through it all, I never stopped trusting in tadbeer. I don't know if tadbeer has an exact corresponding word in English. Effort, perhaps. As opposed to taqdeer, fate.

You would have got a whiff of the taqdeer/tadbeer tussle while watching *Vidhaata*, in which Dilip Kumar's character believes in tadbeer, in contrast to his friend, played by Shammi Kapoor, who believes in taqdeer. But that is not all. With *Vidhaata*, I demonstrated how I could use tadbeer to make a successful movie without a reigning big star. That was the time no big star wanted to work with me and I was on the brink.

Countless stars are born in our film industry and just as many fade away; some never to be heard of again. That is the story of this city of dreams. What you have in the book that you hold in your hands, written so well by Suveen Sinha and published by HarperCollins, is the story of how a young man came from nowhere, how he faced the challenges that confronted him, and what he experienced on his way to becoming what he became. This book is the story of the Hindi film industry the way it unfolded before my eyes from the 1960s till today.

I have tried to tell the truth about everyone: my friends, family, colleagues, the film industry, and above all, about myself. Through this book, I speak to everyone who is curious about the relationship filmmakers have with their films, while mirroring life on screen and also entertaining the audience.

When I put my eye on the viewfinder to look at my life, I see that I have had an exhilarating journey. Every day has been filled with excitement as I have imagined characters, screenplays, got into editing, sound designing, marketing and every other facet of filmmaking to be able to bring to you the stories I wanted to tell. In the process, I have made many friends, lost a few, and created Mukta Arts and Whistling Woods International, both of which are my pride and joy.

I have indeed been blessed.

With *Karma's Child*, I hand my viewfinder over to you—and true to the viewfinder approach, this memoir is written in the third person.

1

Promise

In the fledgling India of the 1950s, dehydrated copper sulphate, commonly known as blue vitriol, was easily available in kirana stores, packaged as Neela Tota (Blue Parrot). Towards the end of that decade, a teenage Subhash Ghai emptied a sachet of Neela Tota in a cup of water and drank it. He had decided he could take it no more.

Life had changed drastically for Subhash in the last few years.

Subhash was born in Nagpur on 24 January 1943 at his maternal grandfather's house. His father, Krishan Dayal, was a dentist in Peshawar, now in Pakistan. As was the custom of the time, Subhash's mother went to her father's house to deliver her first child and stayed there for a few years.

Subhash was a happy child in Nagpur, and thoughtful in a childlike way. One day, when he was three, he disappeared from view. His grandfather was a lawyer with a thriving practice. They lived in a house with half a dozen rooms. Subhash could be found in none. Finally, after an hour's search, with Subhash's mother at the edge of a full-blown panic, the child was found in one of the bathrooms.

Relief surging in her heart, his mother asked what he was doing.

'I was thinking,' said Subhash, holding his forehead in his palm.

'Thinking about what?' his mother asked.

'I was thinking,' said the toddler, 'that one day we all have to die.'

Despite herself, his mother burst into laughter. They had all gone to listen to a guru's sermon the day before and had been discussing the broader issues of life and death at mealtimes. The child had indeed been listening.

In the 1950s, after India had been partitioned, Subhash's father moved to Delhi and rented a house in Shahganj, behind Ajmeri Gate. He found a place in Khari Baoli to open his clinic. His wife and children joined him in Old Delhi soon after.

Subhash was in the fourth standard at the time. He moved from Nagpur's Bishop School, run by Christian missionaries, to a school run by the Delhi Municipal Corporation at Ajmeri Gate. A year later, in the fifth standard, he moved to Sanatan Dharm Higher Secondary School. This was a school for children of middle-level government servants. However, in the year he was at the municipal school, Subhash had forged friendships he was not ready to forego. His after-school-hours companions continued to be his mates from the municipal school: sons of tonga drivers, rickshaw pullers, halwais and handymen. Amar Nath, the tonga driver's son, was the hero among them. He had learned to control the tonga at an early age and took his mates for a ride through town every Sunday, his father's day off.

With the passing of years, the group of friends became crazy about movies and would often bunk school to go to a show. Subhash would go back to the theatre again and again while the same movie was playing. Not for a repeat watch—he didn't have enough money to spend on second and third viewings—but to stand outside the door to listen to the soundtrack. He also began to spend long hours at the homes of his friends, sometimes spending nights with them. This was better than spending time at home. Anything was. Home had become a battleground.

Both of Subhash's parents were from educated and well-to-do families. His mother was a graduate, rare for a woman in India in those days, and modern in her thinking. His father was a chauvinist man from Peshawar. Never the twain did meet. Neither of them was a bad human being, they just happened to be very different kinds of people who had ended up getting married to each other.

In those days, Subhash's father was always quick to show his wife her place and objected to her stepping out of the home. He wouldn't even let her meet her women friends. He was a laconic, aloof man. His children—Sunita who was born three years after Subhash and Ashok three years after Sunita—soon began to refer to their father as Dry Hitler. He showed emotion only when he came home after an evening of drinking with his buddies. Those evenings, he would come and wake Subhash up to ask what he was doing. Subhash wanted to retort, 'Sleeping, can't you see?' but chose to stay quiet.

To his relief, Subhash's parents decided to separate when he was ten. But the relief was short-lived. His mother decided that all three children should stay with their father. Subhash loved his mother dearly and was distraught, but she explained to him that this was meant to ensure that his father would always be mindful of his responsibility to give the children a good education. As time rolled by, Subhash found himself filling in for his mother, getting his siblings ready for school, washing their clothes, caring for their meals, and so on.

For a ten-year-old, this was overwhelming. His grades plummeted in school. He sought solace outside the home: with a girl who would flash coy smiles at him; with friends; and in movie theatres. This third business sometimes got him into trouble.

One evening, his father came home and thundered at Subhash, asking if he had taken money from the clinic. The clinic used to have a steel bowl where one paisa coins were kept for the beggars who roamed the area. Subhash admitted he had taken four one-paisa coins to go to a movie with friends. This enraged his father. He took out his cane and gave Subhash ten of the juiciest ones.

Subhash's mother had gone back to Nagpur and become a schoolteacher. She wrote to Subhash every single day. In these letters, some of which ran to six pages or more, she encouraged Subhash to follow his heart and do what he liked.

Subhash liked music, singing and plays. These brought him accolades and popularity in school. But his grades kept slipping. His father told him to give up all the other stuff and focus on studies. 'If you don't,' he said, 'I won't pay your school fees.' It did not help that Subhash's father had brought home a woman who worked at his clinic.

When Subhash could take it no more, he ran away from home. He spent a couple of nights at a friend's house in Shahdara, until the friend's family had to go out of town. Pushed out into the street, Subhash found shelter at another friend's kirana shop, where he worked during the day and slept on a wooden bench at night.

On the fifth day, Subhash's father found him and brought him home. Once they were back, the boy remained defiant. Fourteen years old and already looking after his siblings, he felt bold enough to say: 'I do not like this life. *Mujhe kyon paida kiya* (why did you have to father me)?'

In response, his father slapped him. Several times. Subhash stormed out of the house, seething at the unfairness of it all. And found that sachet of Neela Tota.

Giving into childhood impulse, he woke up the next morning in a hospital bed, with his father sitting at his bedside. The poison had been pumped out of his stomach, leaving him weak and unsteady. Slowly, the events of the previous day came back to him. The slaps, of course, but also something else, which had been at the back of his mind until then. Flashes of his father saying, in between the slapping, that Subhash would never amount to anything.

There, lying in the hospital bed, Subhash made a silent promise to himself: 'Someday, I will become something.'

That day, that hospital bed, and that promise to himself came rushing back to Subhash Ghai two-and-a-half decades later, at a party to celebrate the golden jubilee of *Hero*, the 1983 blockbuster he had directed and produced. *Hero* launched the banner of Mukta Arts, Ghai's production company named after his wife, Rehana (who took on the name 'Mukta' when they got married in 1970).

These days, when films are released simultaneously in hundreds of theatres all over the country, their fate is decided in the first week. Back then, films released across the country gradually, beginning with the larger metros and slowly making their way to the smaller centres. The success of a movie was measured in weeks, not in crores. If it spent enough weeks running in theatres, it was a hit.

Hero was a huge hit: it ran for twenty-five weeks (a silver jubilee) in twenty-four theatres, for fifty weeks (a golden jubilee) in nine, and for seventy-five weeks (a platinum jubilee) in two. It was a milestone for Ghai. He had been a part of the Hindi film industry for nearly a decade, and, finally, *Hero* established him as a filmmaker who knew his craft and understood his audience.

Ghai had delivered hits before—his first two films as director, *Kalicharan* and *Vishwanath*, were both blockbusters. Another of his films, *Karz*, was not an unqualified commercial success, but it was hailed as a landmark film and went on to gain cult status. However, the film industry chose to ascribe the successes of Ghai's films to something or someone other than the director—the hero, the music or the script. They held up Ghai's two flops as director—*Gautam Govinda* and *Krodhi*—to buttress their argument.

With *Hero*, they could find nothing to explain away its success, and, bereft of options, eventually had to give Ghai the credit.

Hero's unqualified success gave Ghai the confidence to throw the biggest party of his life till then, for which he hired Samunder Mahal in Versova. It was the same palace that, in the movie, is shown as the Khandala retreat of Shrikant Mathur, the inspector general of police, played by Shammi Kapoor.

The entire industry turned up at the party. Even people who were seldom seen under the same roof! Prakash Mehra and Manmohan

Desai were not the closest of friends, as they were at the centre of an industry debate about who had played the bigger role in the success of Amitabh Bachchan as the angry young man, but both turned up at the *Hero* party. Unusual for a filmi party, Ghai had also invited the entire unit of *Hero*, including the technicians.

This was the year and the party that first saw the term 'Showman' being uttered in the same breath when one said 'Ghai'. At first, Ghai wondered if journalists using the epithet for him were joking, or worse, mocking him. Reminiscing about those days, he says: 'I used to laugh at it. Sometimes I wondered if they were calling me a show-off.'

He always thought of Raj Kapoor as the Showman. Son of legendary actor Prithviraj Kapoor and a member of the 'first family' of Indian cinema, Raj Kapoor made big, lavish films, and also threw the biggest parties. From the late 1940s, when he directed his first film *Aag* at the age of twenty-one, till his death in 1988, he remained one the most famous film personalities in the country.

Ghai, of course, was from a different universe.

At the time of the golden jubilee party for *Hero*, Ghai's father was in poor health. Doctors suspected cancer. But Ghai wanted his father to be there at the party. He wanted him to know that his son had not wasted his time in Mumbai. He persuaded his father to come, saying he could be comfortable in an adjacent room and watch the party through the window.

Krishan Dayal had come a long way and was, by now, a different person from the brooding father of three young children in Old Delhi. It was a change that had in fact started after Ghai's attempt at suicide. It had made him look at his son in a different, more compassionate, and slightly wary way.

After completing his schooling in Old Delhi and finishing with a percentage languishing in the mid-forties, Ghai had gone on to study commerce at Vaish College in Rohtak, a small town in Haryana a couple of hours from Delhi. Living in the boys' hostel and master of his own time, he flowered as a writer-director of plays and won trophies for his college at the university level.

His father knew nothing about this. So he was downright astonished when he ran into Vaish College's principal at a party and was told that the life had gone out of the college with Ghai's graduation. 'Subhash should go to Mumbai to pursue a career in movies,' the principal said. But Krishan Dayal had already fixed up an internship for his son at an accountancy firm in Delhi.

'When Father told me about the internship, I thought he had pronounced a death sentence on all my dreams,' says Ghai. Fortunately for him, his father took pity on his crestfallen son and asked him what he wanted to do. Ghai told him he wanted to make a career in movies.

'Well, if you want to take up your hobby as your profession, you must first get training,' his father said, and handed him a clipping of an advertisement seeking applications for the Film and Television Institute of India (FTII) in Pune.

Ghai applied, cleared the entrance test, and joined the first acting batch of FTII in 1963.

After *Karz*, Ghai had brought his mother over from Delhi to live with him in Mumbai. After *Vidhaata*, he wanted to bring his ailing father over, so he could give him the best treatment and care. It was going to be a delicate affair, though. His father's second wife would also come along and move in.

Ghai had faith in his mother. She had always told him to do the right thing and follow the right path. One day, he took his mother aside for a quiet word. 'You have taught me so many values,' he said, 'one of which is that forgiveness is the biggest virtue. Can you forgive the other woman and welcome her in this house?'

At first, his mother said nothing. Then, in a voice laced with mixed emotions, she said, 'You are testing me.'

'I am not testing you,' said Ghai, 'I am testing your teachings.'

The next day, he received his father and stepmother at the railway station and brought them home. To his relief and joy, his mother welcomed them—quietly but without malice.

As the *Hero* party gathered steam, Ghai and his family were checking on Krishan Dayal from time to time. Dilip Kumar was by now a father figure to Ghai. They had worked together in *Vidhaata*. Sitting at a table with Raj Kapoor and Ghai, Dilip Kumar sensed that the family members were somewhat distracted.

'Where is your father?' he asked. 'I heard he was not well.'

'He is over there, in that room,' Ghai said, pointing.

'*Othey kyun bithaya?* (Why have you seated him there?)' Dilip Kumar said, switching to Punjabi. '*Raj, chal yaar, Subhash ke father se milte hain.* (Come, Raj, let's meet Subhash's father.)'

The three of them went to the room where Ghai's father was. 'Babuji,' Ghai called out, 'Dilip Sa'ab and Raj Sa'ab want to meet you.'

Krishan Dayal was astounded. The shadow of illness seemed to lift from his face. As Raj Kapoor bent down to touch his feet, Ghai's father began to cry.

'*Dekho tumhara beta kitna honhar hai*,' Dilip Kumar said, '*usko aashirwad do, aur changge ho jao.* (See how talented your son is. Bless him, and get well soon.)'

For a brief moment, Ghai's mind was transported to a hospital bed in Old Delhi some twenty-five years ago, and the solemn promise he had made to himself: 'Someday, I will become something.'

2

Destiny

If things had gone a bit differently, Ghai could have become superstar Rajesh Khanna. Instead, he became writer–director–producer Subhash Ghai, and that was not too bad either. Between 1976 and 1999, he made fifteen films, eleven of which were blockbusters, and a non-hit, *Karz*, which attained cult status. Somewhere in there is a story that proves the old saying that destinies are created and destroyed, every day in the Mumbai film industry.

The best definition of destiny Ghai ever heard was late one night, during a heated debate in a country liquor shop in Bandra. It came from Javed Akhtar—poet, lyricist, and one half of the scriptwriting duo, Salim–Javed, who wrote the scripts of some of the biggest hits of Hindi cinema, such as *Sholay*, *Deewar* and *Don*.

The Mumbai suburb was much less posh in those days. Instead of the fine dining restaurants and bars of today, it was known for its country liquor shops—Pasqual Ka Adda, Aunty Ka Adda, and the like. These were the speakeasies of the day for the film crowd. After a hard day, assistant directors, production managers, technicians, cameramen, makeup men, lighting men and others would throng these joints to let off steam. Naturally, those struggling for a toehold in the industry were irresistibly drawn to these places. These gatherings were especially helpful for Ghai because he was a complete outsider to the industry.

Bandra's liquor shops were full of people who thought themselves true artists. And you were hardly a 'true artist' unless you got into heated existential debates after a round of drinks and joints. Whether you were the type that frequented the Jehangir Art Gallery or Aunty Ka Adda, debate you must. The art gallery type would be richer and more successful, but the Aunty Ka Adda patrons had dreams—and would not be denied their intellectual angst.

One night, as Ghai, Akhtar and a few others sat around the wooden tables, peering through the thick haze of cigarette smoke, and downing fiery orange liquid from steel tumblers, someone wondered aloud, '*Taqdeer kya hoti hai*? (What is destiny?)' In no time, taqdeer, the Urdu word for destiny, became the subject of a full-blown debate. Most people seemed to believe in it. You had to, if you were struggling to build a career in an industry that was known for anarchy and chaos. You needed someone, or something, to blame.

Akhtar was an exception. He did not believe in taqdeer, yet he did not mind arguing in favour of it. His love for a good debate trumped his beliefs.

The argument escalated, drawing others into the discussion. However, it had no impact on the man sitting at the next table, a stranger to this film crowd, who was lost in his own thoughts. A bunch of young men drinking, smoking and talking about movies was not a thing of curiosity in Bandra.

Suddenly, unexpectedly, Akhtar turned to the stranger.

'What's your name?' he asked.

'Magan Lal Dwivedi,' said the stranger.

Akhtar turned back to his own table to settle the debate. 'That man is stuck with that name,' he said. 'He has lived with it all his life and will live with it for the rest of his life. He cannot change it. That, my friends, is what is called taqdeer.'

To a bunch of brains addled with country liquor, cigarette smoke, and dreams of success in the film industry, that settled the argument in favour of destiny being all-powerful.

Incidentally, years later, in *Vidhaata* (1982), Ghai would present the taqdeer/tadbeer (fate/effort) debate all over again in conversations and a hit song between two friends, Gurbaksh (played by Shammi Kapoor) and Shamsher (played by Dilip Kumar). Gurbaksh believes in fate, while Shamsher believes in making his own destiny.

Akhtar, though, had some control over his own destiny, at least in day-to-day matters. Money was a constant worry for all the young guns, but a little less for him. He could have lived a comfortable life, being the son of famous poet and successful lyricist Jan Nisar Akhtar. But he fought with his father, left home and joined the production company of Kamal Amrohi, who was famous for making films like *Mahal*. Amrohi's production manager, Akhtar Farooqui, let him sleep in the costume room.

Ghai was smitten by Farooqui's daughter, Rehana, and harboured dreams of marrying her. They had met in Pune, where Rehana and her mother lived near the FTII campus. Their love blossomed and they moved to Mumbai as Ghai finished his acting course and came to try his luck in the film industry.

One day, Ghai asked Akhtar how he met his expenses.

'How much money do you have on you?' Akhtar asked.

Ghai had all of ₹30 in his pocket.

'Give it to me,' said Akhtar. 'I will turn it into seventy and give you forty tomorrow.'

He was as good as his word.

Ghai later discovered that Akhtar was an ace at card games. Quick of hand and sharp of memory, he seemed to know what cards everyone had been dealt.

Akhtar gave Ghai his first lesson in surviving the Mumbai film industry. 'All these people,' he said, 'are mediocre. You are not. You must pretend to be mediocre to mix with them. But, in your mind, you must always know that you are special.'

As it happened, Ghai very nearly missed these lessons.

Monto, Ghai's friend from FTII, was the one who first took him to those night-time addas in Bandra. Back then, Ghai did not drink. He did not want to, having seen his father come home a different man after a drinking session with friends.

After a few initial visits to the addas in Bandra, Monto stopped asking Ghai to come along. When he hadn't for two months, Ghai asked him what the matter was. Monto said those addas were meant for freewheeling chatter, but no one trusted a non-drinker, certainly not enough to talk freely in his presence.

'You just sit there and stare at the light bulb,' said Monto. 'Everyone thinks you will remember everything the next day. God knows where you might regurgitate it.'

That was hardly a fair accusation, but Monto was adamant. 'This is the way of the industry,' he said. 'You are too simple.'

Ghai decided to get rid of that horrible trait: simplicity. A few days later, a birthday party was planned at one of the addas. The host, in the fervour of the occasion, told Monto to get Ghai along.

Ghai went. And drank.

A peg would cost eight annas, or fifty paise. Ghai finished his first in a few big breathless gulps. It tasted like poison, actually more like a hot dagger piercing through his chest. Someone handed him a plate of salted boiled eggs, which felt like balm for the dagger wound. Soon, the fervour overtook Ghai and he joined the others as they upheld the best traditions of a drunken birthday party, and talked, drank, abused, drank, cursed, drank, sang songs, and drank some more. Until it all went dark for him.

When he regained consciousness, Ghai found himself alone at the adda. The party seemed to have ended a while ago. The shopkeeper said the bill had been paid and suggested that Ghai better head home.

Then it hit Ghai. Go home?

At the time, he was living with his aunt, his father's sister. She was so fond of Ghai that her husband had no option but to tolerate him. Ghai had much respect for their older son, Satish, and much affection for the younger son, Yash. Their house was nearby, in Bandra East, but that night it seemed very far away. Ghai didn't think he was in any state to face them. He stepped out of the liquor shop and on to the Bandra street only to find the city revolving around him—the pavement, the roadside houses, the shops. Everything was a blur.

He sat down on the pavement and wept. When his tears dried up, he crossed the road to a shop that had shut for the night. An empty wooden plank lay in front. He collapsed on it and slept. The early morning sun woke him up. He rummaged through his pockets for some coins. Thankfully, there were enough for him to pay the bus fare.

When he rang the bell of his aunt's house, she opened the door with disapproval in her eyes. 'Where have you been? I was so worried,' she said.

There were no phones in those days, so it was easy to lie. 'I was held up at a friend's place and slept there,' Ghai said. The trusting aunt shooed him into his room with only a mild rebuke.

For the next six days, Subhash did not step out of the house. He read Dale Carnegie's *How to Win Friends and Influence People*, which he had picked up from Satish's shelf. On the seventh day, he was back at the adda.

The appeal of the liquor addas was irreducible. It had very little to do with the liquor or intoxication; it was all about getting a peek into the magical world of movies and basking in a sense of belonging. Those who had already found work in the film industry came to the addas to talk about their triumphs and disasters—there were a few of each every day. Most of them believed that the big directors of the time would be lost without them. In the light of dim 40-watt bulbs, one suspended over each wobbly table, they told newcomers tall tales about making a suggestion that the director accepted, and which changed the course of the film.

Sometimes, bigger names stopped by. One night Om Prakash Mehra, who was an executive from a big studio at the time, came and quickly got drunk. Javed Akhtar was there too. Mehra held the newcomers spellbound with his stories, all of which had him playing larger-than-life roles. When the night was over, Ghai offered to pay the bill.

'I alone will pay this bill,' Mehra thundered. 'Javed, tell Subhash who I am.'

Akhtar made the introduction in the manner of announcing a medieval king's arrival. 'This is the king of kings, the Almighty. Raj Kapoor cannot shoot a scene without him.'

As Mehra paid the bill and got up to leave, the others asked him where he was going.

'Madam is waiting for me,' he said, solemnly.

'Which madam?' his 'courtiers' asked.

'Oh, don't you know?' he said. '*Chalo aaj hum tumhe jashn dikhate hain*. (Come with me, I will show you how to have a good time.)'

He ordered the newcomers into his car and drove them to a kotha to watch a mujra. It was Ghai's first time at a kotha. Sensing his discomfort, Akhtar told him to shut up and try to have a good time. Mehra handed everyone in his entourage wads of ten-rupee notes, which were to be showered on the nautch girls. The youngsters showered some, and pocketed most of the notes themselves.

Mehra dropped everyone back at the adda. As they stepped out of the car, he told Ghai: 'Whenever you need anything, come to me. One day you will be a big actor, Subhash.'

Mehra, for all his knowledge of nautch girls, was not particularly prescient. Ghai's struggle to become a leading man in the movies was going nowhere. Instead of Mehra's prophecy, it was Ghai's cousin Yash's gloomy prediction that was threatening to come true, one that he had made when Ghai had stopped over at his aunt's house on his way to FTII.

It was Ghai's first time in Mumbai and Yash took him sightseeing. In the course of their conversation, Yash said Ghai was making a mistake.

'There is no future in acting. Hordes come to this city and get nowhere. Go back to Delhi.'

That evening, Ghai narrated the conversation to his aunt and told her he was thinking of going back. His aunt was shocked. She was sure he had what it took to be a hero. She found him handsome. Ghai dressed well and spent time grooming himself. He had even adopted a few mannerisms of well-known actors.

'A young man is trying to make something of himself here and this is what you have to say? Give him a chance!' she admonished her son Yash.

At FTII, Ghai was not the most serious student in his acting classes—unlike classmates Govardhan Asrani and Kanwarji Paintal, both better known by their last names. Asrani and Paintal were the best at everything they did, and were serious fellows, a far cry from the screen images they went on to build as comic actors. They were favourites of Professor Roshan Taneja, head of the acting department at FTII, who later went on to set up his own acting school. As time went by, Taneja started to like Ghai, but always doubted his seriousness about being an actor. Ghai finished seventh in a class of seven men and three women.

Ghai's interests were not confined to acting. He attended classes on other aspects of filmmaking as well: direction, editing, cinematography. The teachers did not mind his joining their classes. He quickly made many friends at the institute, helped by his willingness to sing in the canteen, drumming on the table. He could produce interesting sounds from his mouth, like that of a moving train or a gust of wind, and was often sought out by the sound-mixing guys.

The thing Ghai enjoyed most at FTII was interacting with Ritwik Ghatak. Ghatak, who ranks alongside Satyajit Ray and Mrinal Sen among India's most accomplished filmmakers, was the institute's vice-principal. Ghai used to seek him out as much as possible and absorbed everything he said like a sponge.

Ghai rated himself highly—not without reason. In his college in Rohtak, he had been a star. He had singlehandedly resurrected the college's cultural department, writing and directing plays that won inter-university awards, something the college had not dreamed of before him. But, at FTII, students came from all over the country and all of them were stars of their colleges. Ghai could not cope well with not being the brightest of them all.

At the institute, most of his classmates swore by the 'world cinema' of Jean-Luc Godard, the French-Swiss filmmaker, and Federico Fellini, the Italian writer-director. Ghai, on the other hand, worshipped the Indian maestros: Bimal Roy, Raj Kapoor, Mehboob Khan. The Godard and Fellini crowd thought life was art and art was life. Ghai thought movies were for fun and entertainment.

No one at the institute probably expected Ghai to make a mark after he graduated—no one except Ghai himself. A talent hunt in 1965, organized by the United Producers Combine and *Filmfare* magazine, became a godsend for him, the perfect opportunity to prove himself.

The *Filmfare* talent hunt was a big deal; the previous contest, held seven years earlier, had unearthed Dharmendra, who had quickly become a star. United Producers Combine had some of the biggest filmmakers of the time—B.R. Chopra, Bimal Roy, G.P. Sippy, H.S. Rawail, Nasir Hussain, J. Om Prakash, Mohan Saigal, Shakti Samanta, Hemant Kumar and Subodh Mukherji.

Nearly everyone from FTII's acting course applied for the 1965 talent hunt, including those who were yet to graduate. Ghai found himself among the two hundred shortlisted for the final audition. They were put up in Delmar Hotel, in Mumbai's Fort area.

Ghai began to feel that stardom was knocking at his door, and he made it a point to tell Yash so. He started to wear his shirt a little loose at the waist, rolled up the sleeves, and began to go everywhere in sunglasses.

Mohammad Shamim, a journalist with the *Times of India* group which owns *Filmfare*, was put in charge of the contestants. Shamim was known for his film writing as much as for his grip over politics. He told the contestants they had been shortlisted after a week of intense screening of the ten thousand-odd applications that had flooded in.

The auditions began on a Friday and ended the following Monday. Ghai's audition was on the last day. It was in a large hall, with the producers sitting on the far side in a semi-circle. Ghai went in, bowed, and sought their blessings. All two hundred finalists had been given a few common scenes to enact. Ghai knew that the judges had been watching the same scenes being performed over and over. He sensed an opening when one of the judges said, 'Show us something.'

'Sir, you have given me a scene,' he said. 'Should I do that, or...? I have a scene I have written myself ... I could do that.'

B.R. Chopra, known for making powerful thought-provoking movies, was one of the judges. He had also been in Ghai's interview before he was selected for FTII, and recognized him.

'Show us your own scene,' Chopra said.

That was all the encouragement Ghai needed. He had written a courtroom scene in which the judge tells the convict he had decided to send him to the gallows, but will give him two minutes to defend himself. Ghai enacted both the judge as well as the convict's roles. The convict's part was dramatic. At one point, Ghai switched his voice abruptly from a low register to a very high one. The effect was that of a clap of thunder. A couple of the judges looked visibly stunned. When Ghai finished the scene, there was silence. He thought he had messed it up. After a few moments, the judges—all big filmmakers—began to applaud.

Ghai was still emotionally charged when he came out of the audition hall. Someone gave him water to drink. That calmed him down a bit, but what really helped was Shamim's arrival. 'So far, the producers had been moving from candidate to candidate spending just a couple of minutes or so on each. But they spent more than ten minutes discussing your performance. I think your chances are bright,' Shamim said, patting him on the back.

That put the swagger back in Ghai. 'Shamim bhai,' he said, 'I am a born actor.'

That year the contest had five winners: Jatin Khanna, who had done a bit of theatre in college; Dheeraj Kumar, who was still in the first year of acting at FTII; Farida Jalal, a non-FTII applicant; Baby Sarika, who became a child star and then a leading lady in many movies; and Subhash Ghai.

The winners met on Tuesday, the day after Ghai's audition. Shamim had whispered to Ghai that he had been rated number one among the men, Jatin second, and Dheeraj third. So Ghai was puzzled to hear Jatin say he was about to begin shooting for a movie. But he was not too perturbed. 'I was rated the best,' he told himself, 'I, too, will soon be shooting.'

The film industry, though, does not always run on logic. Here, logic is often trumped by taqdeer. And taqdeer had placed itself squarely on Jatin's side by slotting his audition on the first day, Friday.

The next day, Saturday, a crisis meeting had been called at the offices of G.P. Sippy. The producer–director had chosen a new lad to play the lead in his latest project, *Raaz*, a suspense thriller. But Ravindra Dave, the director, said the actor was not able to deliver his lines. Sippy then told him about the young fellow who had auditioned the previous day at the talent hunt and had delivered his lines well. There would be no need to worry much about his acting, which would probably be raw, like all newcomers'. Suspense and horror are genres in which actors can often make do with just two expressions: perplexed and frightened; the situation takes care of the rest. The more important thing was that the sets for *Raaz* were ready and must not go waste. Jatin was summoned on Sunday and made to speak some lines before the camera. He shone in comparison to the actor he was to replace, and was selected to be the hero opposite Babita, who had already established herself as a successful actress. Jatin, of course, would take on the name Rajesh Khanna, and *Raaz* was the beginning of his incredible career.

Ghai could not help wondering if he would be the one shooting for *Raaz* had his audition been on Friday, instead of Monday. It was a thought that would gnaw at him for years.

After *Filmfare* published Jatin's photo to announce that one of the winners of its talent contest had bagged a leading role, Ghai's friends and family began to ask him when he might get a film role, or, at least, a picture in a magazine.

'Having to face family and friends, well-meaning as they are, is a painful ordeal a struggling actor faces, worse than the struggle itself,' says Ghai. 'They expect things to work out immediately. They feel the pressure because they have proudly told other relatives and neighbours that their lad is going to be a hero. Now the relatives and neighbours will keep asking.'

Ghai had no answer for his family and friends. He started doing the rounds of producers, everyone who was part of the United Producers Combine. All of them received him with warmth. It was a rare honour for a struggling actor to be able to meet the likes of B.R. Chopra and Subodh Mukherji. They would offer him tea and words of encouragement.

'Don't worry, you are a good actor, but things take time,' they would say.

When Ghai met Nasir Hussain, the latter said he had thought of a story, which he was going to call *Baharon Ke Sapne* (1967). He had cast Asha Parekh, a regular leading lady in his films, and wanted someone with dramatic acting skills as the hero. The era of colour films had begun a few years earlier, but Hussain wanted to make the film in black and white.

'This will be an artistic black-and-white film, like the ones K.A. Abbas makes,' Hussain said.

Since Ghai's performance at the audition had been impressively dramatic, Hussain told him that he should consider himself in. He told Ghai to come again in a few days, by when the script would be ready. But when Ghai reached Hussain's office on the appointed day, the production manager said Hussain was out of town.

'Sir,' Ghai said, 'he had called me about the new film.'

'Oh, *Baharon Ke Sapne*? We have taken Kaka,' the production manager said, speaking of Rajesh Khanna, who was already being called 'Kaka' affectionately.

Ghai was crestfallen. 'What should I do?' he asked.

'*Miltey raha karo* (keep meeting us),' the production manager said. 'It is important to keep showing up.'

Ghai later found out what had happened. When G.P. Sippy learnt that Nasir Hussain intended to make *Baharon Ke Sapne* with a new hero, he called Hussain and suggested that they pool in their resources. It would be prudent for both to cast the same actor so they could share the cost of promoting a new face. They had nothing against Ghai, just that business logic did not favour him.

Later, when Hussain came back to Mumbai, at a chance meeting with Ghai, he said, 'Yaar, Subhash, one has to do these things in business. But you don't worry, you are a good actor, keep meeting us. By the way, Subodh Mukherji had good things to say about you.'

Taking the cue, Ghai started to make the rounds of Mukherji's house in Bandra. Mukherji was always nice and warm. He had already made a big hit, *Junglee* (1961), and was going to repeat the heroine, Saira Banu, in his new project, *Shagird* (1967). He told Ghai the story of the new film and said he was looking for a new face to cast as the hero.

For the next four months, Ghai met Mukherji at least once a week. Each time, Mukherji greeted him warmly. Finally, with the same warmth, he told Ghai he had signed Joy Mukherji for *Shagird*. He also had a word of advice. 'Subhash, yaar, you are a good actor,' he said, 'but you are thin.'

That may have been true, but Joy was also Subodh Mukherji's nephew, his brother's son. Ghai was back to square one.

Then Monto confronted him. 'You are wasting your time with United Producers,' he said. 'If you want to make it in Mumbai, I will show you the place to be. Come with me.'

And so it was that, late one evening, Ghai found himself at the country liquor addas of Bandra, where he learned the meaning of taqdeer.

3

Becoming a Writer

If destiny had to come in person to transform Subhash Ghai the actor into Subhash Ghai the writer–director, it would have taken the shape of Mohanlal Dave. Dave certainly looked the part. He could easily pass off as Mahatma Gandhi, an aged version of Gandhi that is.

Fittingly, for an embodiment of destiny, Dave had made his name as a writer of mythological films such as *Mahasati Ansuya* (1943). Having begun his career in the 1920s, during the silent era, Dave had also scripted a number of family dramas. He was living a largely retired life when he first met Ghai.

That was the time of Ghai's quest for self-discovery. Although he had determinedly followed the path to becoming an actor, his acting career was going nowhere. The talent hunt failed to launch him into the stratosphere as it did for Rajesh Khanna and as it had for Dharmendra. Ghai did get to act in several films, but they only made him realize how much he actually disliked acting in movies.

The meeting with Dave changed the course of the young man's career by putting him on the road to becoming a film writer.

All of Ghai's films as an actor (between 1967 and 1976) failed to establish him. *Taqdeer*, *Umang*, *Shahar Se Door*, *Grahan*, *Do Bachche*

Dus Haath, *Bharat Ke Shaheed*, *Dhamkee*, *Natak* and *Gumrah* did not exactly send ripples through the industry. The one that did, *Aradhana*, had Ghai in a role so small—he played Flight Lieutenant Prakash, a friend of Suraj (the younger Rajesh Khanna)—that he got no credit for the film's success, though it made Rajesh Khanna India's biggest heartthrob overnight. Nevertheless, Ghai was recognized as a young man who was a good actor and could play the lead or second lead. That was enough for him to acquire the airs of a star. He was in demand, even if his films were not doing well.

Meanwhile, his middling career gave him the modest means—₹700 a month for the duration of the year it would take to film *Umang*—to marry his love, Rehana. The wedding feast could only be called a potluck: every item of food and beverage was brought by some friend or the other. 'The entire expense for our wedding party was ₹1,920,' says Ghai.

No potluck could give Ghai and Rehana a place to stay, though. A friend came to the newlyweds' rescue. He owned a flat in Apsara Apartments, in Bandra's Pali Hill. He was moving to Ahmedabad for business and wanted to rent out his flat to someone he could trust. Ghai got it for ₹400 a month. He and Rehana bought a mattress and rented a cupboard, a table and a few chairs. The furniture was not enough, and most of their décor had to be on the floor. They pretended it was intentional, that they found it artistic to have the settings on the floor. Ghai had learned this from artists in Delhi, who would put a mattress on the floor, a round cushion somewhere, hang a broom from the ceiling, and so on. 'Art is a useful tool to hide poverty and we made full use of it,' says Ghai.

While Ghai was still struggling for roles, many of his FTII mates had become well-known names. Vijay Arora and Navin Nischol were established heroes. Shabana Azmi had done *Ankur*, Shyam Benegal's masterpiece that ignited the parallel cinema movement in Hindi, taking it far beyond the shores of Bengal, where Satyajit Ray, Ritwik Ghatak and Mrinal Sen had been keeping the flame burning. Shatrughan Sinha, though Ghai's junior at the institute, was quickly carving out a special place for himself as the villain audiences clapped for.

Ghai was in awe of Sinha's rapid rise and attributed it to the self-belief the latter projected. As a young man, Sinha used to live in a place called Satguru Lodge, where a cot went for ₹10 a night. Those days, none of them had much money, but Sinha seemed to have even less than Ghai. When they smoked together, they would share a cigarette that Ghai had often paid for. But the lack of money did not dent Sinha's self-confidence.

One day, Bhappi Sonie's production manager came to Satguru Lodge looking for Sinha. Sonie had directed hits such as *Janwar* (1965) and *Brahmachari* (1968), both starring Shammi Kapoor, who had quickly emerged from his brother Raj's shadow with a string of hits. Sonie had seen a movie in which Sinha had just one scene, where he threw a punch and checked his watch—that was all. But it was enough to impress the producer–director. He wanted the young man for a small role in his next film, *Pyar Hi Pyar* (1969), with Dharmendra and Vyjayanthimala in the lead roles.

'Does Shatrughan Sinha live here?' the production manager inquired at the lodge's reception.

'Yes,' said the man at the reception.

'Please tell him Bhappi Sonie Sa'ab wants to meet him.'

The man from the reception found Sinha lounging on his cot. 'The production manager for Bhappi Sonie is here to take you to his office. Sonie Sa'ab wants to meet you,' he said.

Most people in Sinha's place would have rushed to the reception, feeling honoured by this visit. But Sinha asked the receptionist to tell the production manager to wait. He emerged after a good twenty minutes, heard what the production manager had to say, and only said, '*Hum aayenge* (We'll be there).'

'But Sonie Sa'ab wants to see you now. I am here to take you with me,' said the production manager.

'Not now,' said Sinha, 'I have a meeting to go to.'

When Sinha did go to Bhappi Sonie's office, the role was waiting for him. It was a small part, but he clicked with the audiences. They clapped when he came on the screen.

What Ghai gathered from Sinha's rise was that no actor could become a star without 'attitude'. But it was a learning that did Ghai no good. He would end up turning down the story of *Sholay*.

To be fair, it was not that Ramesh Sippy, who directed *Sholay* (1975) for his father's production company, offered Ghai the lead role in the film. The story that eventually became *Sholay* may have been doing the rounds of the industry for some time, or maybe the project that was offered to Ghai was separate from *Sholay* but with a similar storyline. It was narrated to Ghai by Baldev Pushkarna, who later produced *Chacha Bhatija* (1977), directed by Manmohan Desai and with Dharmendra, Hema Malini and Randhir Kapoor in the lead roles.

Manik Prem, who directed *Gumrah* (1963), with Ghai and Reena Roy as the lead pair, was a friend of Pushkarna's. One day, when the shooting for *Gumrah* was in full swing, Pushkarna spoke to Prem. 'Yaar, I have an interesting project about two small-time criminals who are hired by a retired policeman to catch the dreaded dacoit who killed the policeman's family,' said Pushkarna. 'I don't know whom to cast.'

Prem suggested Ghai. 'Take him, and get some other fellow for the second part.'

Ghai heard the story from Pushkarna. To him, it sounded like a B-grade action movie, very similar to a film he had done not too long ago: *Do Bachche Dus Haath*, in which a five-man army goes into the mountains to hunt down a dacoit. He turned it down.

Shatrughan Sinha often claimed that he and Ghai were the two good actors in the industry. When word got around that they were friends, some producers considered Ghai and Sinha for projects that had two strong male characters. Friendship between the lead actors meant hassle-free shoots and would ensure that the film was completed on time. However, when such offers came, Ghai asked to be paid more than Sinha. To no one's surprise, he was promptly cast aside.

No amount of 'attitude' could improve Ghai's situation on the sets. He had been acting since the age of eight in plays at his school and college, many of which he wrote and directed himself. Acting in movies was a different matter, though. He found the scenes absurd; good situations were often marred by mediocre writing. Occasionally, when he asked the director if he could rewrite the scene, he was told, 'You are an actor, better focus on your job.'

Ghai knew he could write scenes. After all, it was how he had impressed the mighty filmmakers during the *Filmfare* talent hunt—by performing a scene he had written himself. But that ability impeded him as an actor.

Ghai ended up a curious creature: a good actor who could not act on the sets. He plodded through scenes without conviction, and that showed in his performance. Young and brimming with ideas, he wondered how he could perform unless he was convinced about what he was doing. He now says about his predicament: 'It was only much later that I fully understood that an actor's job is to make the unreal look real; it does not matter whether he or she is convinced about the scene.'

There were exceptions. He once played a small role in *Dhamkee* (1973), that of a CBI officer who dies right in the beginning of the film. The director, K. Parvez, told him to write the scene himself. The only brief Parvez gave Ghai was: 'You say something to the villain, who is about to kill you.'

Ghai wrote an explosive scene in which he tells the villain: '*Goli chalani hai, goli chalao, bhownko mat. Magar ek baat yaad rakho*, mere *marne se mere desh ki ekta nahi maregi*. (If you have to shoot, shoot, don't bark. But remember, my death will not kill the unity of this country.)'

As the villain pumps a barrage of bullets into Ghai, he collapses and the title of the film flashes on the screen, accompanied by a loud soundtrack. Parvez loved the scene; the theatre audiences applauded.

But such happenings were rare. For instance, Manik Prem, the director of *Gumrah*, was firm; he refused to let Ghai change a single line. Shivam Bedekar, who directed *Bharat Ke Shaheed* (1972), had no time for Ghai's inputs. The film portrayed the stories of more than a hundred freedom fighters. It had a song that was more than fifty minutes long, and played across six or seven different situations, as martyrs were praised and bad people were punished. To Ghai's astonishment, the film did not do all that badly. Patriotic fervour always brought people to theatres.

Shatrughan Sinha had many Bihari friends, all of whom were clever and smart. Two of them, Yogi and Bipin, were the closest to him and would often hang out with Sinha and Ghai. So did Anil Dhawan, who had tasted success as a hero.

It was through Sinha that Ghai first met Amitabh Bachchan as well.

In his spare time, when he was with friends, Ghai would tell stories packed with emotion and drama, employing his considerable mimicry skills to make the stories come alive. Together, they would discuss every new release threadbare. At times, having listened to his analysis of a film, the gang told Ghai that he should write scripts. It was banter, but the thought stayed with him.

At other times, Ghai would seek out fellow students from FTII who had been struggling for years without getting anywhere, and discuss what was holding them back. They obviously had talent, so what was it that was keeping success at bay? He listened as they spoke about the superiority of European cinema over the low-brow output of Mumbai. They wanted to make movies for the intelligentsia but the problem was that no one wanted to finance such movies. Ghai was a Delhi lad who had not been corrupted by intellect. He loved mainstream cinema and its music. He absorbed the stories of Guru Dutt, V. Shantaram, Mehboob Khan and Raj Kapoor from people who were lucky enough to work with them, all the while wondering when it would be his turn.

Ghai deeply admired Guru Dutt's *Kagaz Ke Phool* (1959), the classic tale of a film director who falls from the pinnacle of success and loses everything, dying a lonely and forgotten man in the final scene. But he did not want his career to have the same tragic ending as the film. The thought of turning to writing began to appeal to him more and more.

Among the popular filmmakers of the day, Ghai liked the films of L.V. Prasad. A stalwart from south India, Prasad had given many hits in Hindi as well, such as *Sharada* (1957), *Milan* (1967) and *Khilona* (1970). Those were strong, bold stories. So, Ghai tried and managed to get a meeting with Prasad.

'What are you doing these days?' Prasad asked.

'Not much, sir,' said Ghai.

'Well, if you are not doing much, do something,' Prasad said. 'I am working on a subject that is twenty years old. Go to the writer, work with him, and make it a modern story. If it is good, I'll give you a role in the film.'

That writer of that twenty-year-old story was Mohanlal Dave.

When they met in Dave's Vile Parle bungalow, Ghai told him, 'Sir, Prasad ji told me to work with you on this film called *Parivartan*. He is making it with Sunil Dutt.'

'Beta, I'll pull out the script,' said Dave. 'But I can work with you only on one condition. You will have to come to me at five in the morning. I will work with you till six-thirty or so. After that, I get busy with my day's routine.'

Ghai did not have much choice in the matter. He started waking up at four in the morning to go to Vile Parle. In their sessions, Dave would hold up the script, which was written in Gujarati, and speak while Ghai wrote. In the afternoon, Ghai would go to Prasad's office and hand him what he had written. Prasad would then discuss the draft with his team of writers. Ghai would pull a chair and sit spellbound as he listened to the conversation. Prasad's sense of the scene was astounding. Ghai learned from him how to visualize the audience's reaction. 'There could not have been a better classroom for learning how to write a film,' he says.

The audience, Ghai learned from Prasad, had a collective, not individual, morality. A modern young family might do and say rebellious things in love. They might even drink and smoke on occasion. But, sitting with their family in a theatre to watch a movie, they would be in sync with the collective morality of the rest of the audience.

The writing of *Parivartan* took several months. Ghai loved every day of it, and he learned every day. He started thinking of writing movies the way Prasad would film them. And he came up with a story about a police officer and a criminal who were doppelgängers. The police officer is smart, suave and upright, with a set of principles that no force can bend. The criminal, in prison for murder, is like an untamed animal. By a twist of fate, the criminal ends up taking the police officer's place.

Ghai named his story *Kalicharan*, after the criminal character.

4

Becoming a Director

Yogi, Shatrughan Sinha's friend, instantly loved the story of *Kalicharan* when he heard it. 'Develop it further,' he told Ghai, 'I'll persuade Shatrughan to do it. We will also produce it.'

Ghai fleshed out the story further. One day, Yogi took Ghai to a studio where Sinha was shooting. The three of them met in Sinha's make-up room and Ghai narrated the story, adding that Sinha would play the police officer as well as the criminal.

Sinha had just given a shot that had drawn applause from everyone in the unit. He was visibly ebullient. He heard the narration quietly, which made Ghai think he liked the story. But looks can be deceptive. When Ghai finished, Sinha said it was the worst story he had ever heard. 'Nothing can be worse.'

Ghai came away quietly.

He tried again to get Sinha interested in the project. This time, he narrated it to Pawan Kumar, Sinha's secretary, who dozed off midway through the narration.

During the shooting of *Gumrah*, Ghai became friends with Bharat Bhalla, a comic actor who was also in the film. Bhalla was senior to Ghai by a few years and knew the ways of the industry. He was well-liked by many producers, moved in the right circles, and was invited to the big parties.

Late one evening, when they were chatting after pack-up, Ghai told Bhalla he had written a story, 'Aakhri Daku'. It was about two brothers, one a dacoit and the other a village simpleton. They were separated as children and their paths crossed much later, leading to many dramatic situations. Ghai had written it imagining himself in the role of the simpleton.

'This can be made into a good film,' Bhalla said.

A few days later, he spoke to Ghai. 'I was at Prakash Mehra's place for dinner the other day,' he said. 'I narrated your story to him. He really liked it. The day after the party, he called me to ask whose story it was. He wants to make it. You come with me and narrate your story to him.'

This gave Ghai hope. Prakash Mehra was a successful director and could make Ghai's career. By now Ghai had begun to believe that, if he had to be a good actor, he had to write his roles and films himself. But he had not yet cast himself in the role of a full-time writer. The writing was simply a tool to further his acting career.

They went to meet Mehra and Ghai narrated the story to him. At the end of it, Mehra only said, 'Subhash, good story.'

Next day, Bhalla called Ghai and said, 'Prakash Mehra wants the story.'

'Great,' said Ghai, 'tell him he can have it. I will play one of the two brothers.'

But Mehra would have none of it. He did not want a newcomer. He already had Vinod Khanna and Randhir Kapoor in mind, both established heroes.

Bhalla told Ghai to forget about acting in *Aakhri Daku*. 'Let's become writers,' he suggested. 'We will register our stories. You do the writing, I will negotiate with producers. I will get you good money.'

Although Ghai needed money to keep his kitchen fire burning, the passion for acting still blazed within him. He told Bhalla, 'If I do not get the role of my choice in the kind of film I want in three months, we will turn writers.'

Three months later, Ghai and Bhalla officially become a writer duo by selling *Aakhri Daku* to Prakash Mehra as their first deal. Word quickly got around that a new pair of writers had arrived, just like Salim–Javed, and Prakash Mehra had bought their story.

Writing got Ghai a lot more money than acting ever did. Bhalla had many contacts, and he would frequently unearth demands for Ghai–Bhalla stories. In a year and a half, by the mid-1970s, they had sold half a dozen stories.

Their stories were as good as screenplays, and Ghai narrated them with his usual dramatic flourishes: beginning to end, scene by scene. He would start with the censor certificate flickering on the screen, followed by the name of the film being flashed, and end with the last shot and 'The End' announcing that the show was over. In between, his narration was replete with details, such as the breaking open of doors and the delivery of high-voltage dialogues. Back then, all story sessions took place in the evening, after a drink or two. That was when producers had the time.

One day, Pawan Kumar met Ghai. By now, he was producing films for Shatrughan Sinha's Ramayan Chitra banner. 'You have given so many producers such good stories,' Kumar told Ghai, 'give us one.'

Ghai offered Kumar a story he had just finished—'Khaan Dost'. It was about an incarcerated criminal and his association with the jail's hawaldar. Kumar took it to director Dulal Guha, who had made *Dost* (1974) with Dharmendra, Hema Malini and Shatrughan Sinha in the lead roles. The film had earned Sinha many accolades as an outstanding supporting actor.

One evening, Dulal Guha called Ghai over to his house for a narration of 'Khaan Dost'. When it ended, the director took out a

₹100 note from his pocket and gave it to Ghai. 'This story is now mine,' he said.

That ₹100 was akin to earnest money. That was how producers and directors reserved stories for themselves.

Given Pawan Kumar's involvement, it was clear that Shatrughan Sinha would play one of the two roles, and, considering his image and personality, most likely that of the criminal.

'Who should play the hawaldar?' Guha asked Ghai.

Ghai said it should be none other than Raj Kapoor. He offered to write forty or so scenes, which would be about a dozen pages. Guha could narrate the scenes to Raj Kapoor.

Guha later told Ghai that Raj Kapoor read through the scenes in one go, folded the pages, and said, 'I'm doing this film.' There was no need for a narration. That told Ghai he had done a good job, though he missed out on the chance to meet Kapoor.

That opportunity arose when Shatrughan Sinha took Ghai to the famous Holi bash at R.K. Studio. When Ghai introduced himself, Kapoor patted him on the back and said, 'Good story, Subhash.'

'That was the biggest award I could hope to get,' says Ghai.

Word spread that Raj Kapoor had loved the story of *Khaan Dost*; it reached N.N. Sippy, a well-known producer and distributor, as well. Sippy's most recent film, *Chor Machaye Shor* (1974), starring Shashi Kapoor, was a big hit. It was directed by newcomer Ashok Roy. Naturally, Sippy's confidence was high, because he had given a hit with an unproven director.

Sippy's children were friends with Ghai. They were in the same age group and met at social gatherings. So much so that Ghai used to address Sippy as Daddy, just as Sippy's children did.

One day, Sippy phoned Ghai. 'I have heard about your story, *Khaan Dost*,' he said. 'It seems Raj ji loved it. I also need a good story. I want to make a film soon.'

Ghai did not have any ready stories. Undaunted, he asked Sippy when he could meet him.

'Come tomorrow,' Sippy said.

That was too little time to come up with a new story. So, Ghai fell back on his old favourite. He had recently narrated the story of *Kalicharan* to Sanjeev Kumar, the actor among the stars. Kumar had liked the story and was toying with the idea of producing and acting in it. That strengthened Ghai's belief that it was not such a bad story after all.

When Ghai met Sippy, he said, 'I have a story, but it is an old one. I wrote it when I was starting out as a writer. I must also tell you that it has been rejected by at least two persons.'

Sippy was unruffled. 'What is the name of the story?' he asked.

'*Kalicharan*,' Ghai said.

'Hmm, interesting name,' Sippy said. '*Sunao* (Tell me).'

Ghai narrated the story in his usual dramatic manner. Sippy was delighted.

'How can anyone say it is bad?' he wondered.

'I did not say it was bad,' said Ghai. 'I said it was rejected.'

'Who will direct it?' Sippy asked.

In jest, since he was so close to Sippy and his family, Ghai said, '*Mujhe de dijiye* (Give it to me to direct). I know the story well.'

Sippy was unsure. 'Have you ever been an assistant director?' he asked.

'No,' said Ghai.

'Have you learned film production?'

'No.'

'Have you ever looked through a camera's viewfinder?'

'No.'

'Beta,' Sippy said after a pause, 'a writer is different from a director. They are different breeds. Directing a film means controlling a hundred and fifty people and worrying about not only the script and the shoot but many other things as well.'

Ghai began to fear that in trying to become a director, he might get his story rejected. He sought to lighten the air. 'Daddy, I was joking,' he chuckled.

Sippy bought the story of *Kalicharan*, but Ghai was far from happy. When he wrote and narrated stories, he visualized them in a certain way. Yet, when they were made into films, the directors invariably took them in another direction. There is a difference between writing a story and telling a story; the same story can be made into ten different films. Ghai used to fantasize about making his stories into films.

A couple of days later, Sippy phoned Ghai. 'Yaar, I have two partners. They want to hear the story. I told them it is best to hear it from you. We are coming to Bandra. Can we come to your place?'

'Of course,' Ghai said, 'please come.'

Ghai and Rehana had moved out of Apsara Apartments, where they had a one-bedroom flat, into a two-bedroom unit in the Jeevan Jagriti complex. The rent was ₹1,000 per month, but it was a better place to host story sessions.

Once Sippy and his partners sat down with their drinks, Ghai began narrating the story of *Kalicharan*. 'Not like that,' interrupted Sippy. 'Do it as you narrated it to me, standing up, with all your drama.'

Ghai did as he was told. When he finished, Sippy's partners said, '*Chalegi, chalegi. Hit hai, hit hai.*' (It will work, it will work. It's a hit, it's a hit.)

In the Mumbai film industry's lingo, that was a strong endorsement. A story was seldom called good, or great, or lovely. It was always judged in terms of hit or flop. Nearly every industry person understood the difference between a good story and a hit film, and no one was interested in the former if the latter did not follow.

Sippy and his two partners were soon chatting among themselves about getting a good director onboard to do justice to the story they had just heard. Ghai, excited at the prospect of finally seeing *Kalicharan*—a story he had written from the heart—become a film, was careful not to derail the session and maintained a stoic silence. This time, he made no suggestions, not even in jest, about his being the one to direct it.

Next day, Bhalla told Ghai he had discussed the money part with Sippy and was getting the contract prepared. The day after, Sippy phoned Ghai, 'Beta, we have a party at my home tonight. You must come. Come and meet people.'

Ghai was only too happy to attend. Sippy's home was familiar to him, and he knew the family well. However, that night, when Ghai reached Sippy's house, he was dazzled. The elite of the film industry were present; everywhere he turned, there was a famous face to gawk at.

Sippy saw Ghai and beckoned him over. Introducing him to the person standing by his side, Sippy simply said, 'Meet Subhash, the actor who writes films. He is directing my new film.'

Ghai's heart did a backflip, but he thought what he had heard was a slip of Sippy's tongue. It happened at parties, with spirits running high. But Sippy repeated the same to others while introducing Ghai to them. With each introduction, he became more descriptive, until he was saying, 'Meet Subhash Ghai, a new director. I am introducing him. After Ashok Roy, I am launching another new director.'

Sippy was speaking with the assurance of a man experiencing a high, not from liquor but from success. Ghai, though, was still not convinced. There had to be something amiss. It was too good to be true. He went to the bar and downed a couple of large ones. Sometime later, he caught hold of Sippy and took him aside. 'Daddy, were you joking?' he asked.

Sippy looked puzzled. 'Why do you ask? Didn't we talk about it?' he said. 'My partners loved the way you narrated the story. I have told them you will direct the film and they are fine with it.'

Ghai needed to hear it again. 'Are you sure?' he asked.

'I'm sure. Come tomorrow, we will draw up the director's contract. Make the film just as you narrated the story,' Sippy said. '*Hit hai, hit hai. Picture hit hai.* (It's a hit, it's a hit. The film is a hit.)' With that, he walked away to greet other guests.

Ghai left the party with unsteady steps. He got into his second-hand 1962-model Fiat and went home. Even in that old car, he made it from Altamount Road to Bandra in eleven minutes, his mind racing even faster. When he reached home, he woke up Rehana.

In a sleepy voice, she asked, 'Have you eaten?'

Ghai was in no mood to talk about food. Weighing his words, he said, 'I have got a film to direct.'

'Go to sleep,' said Rehana. 'You have a new story to tell every day.'

5

Kalicharan: Arrival

Next morning, when Ghai woke up, he was still in a daze. He got ready and went over to Sippy's office where he signed the contract.

The only person not quite delighted was Bhalla. His budding career as one half of a writing duo would be nipped if the other half moved into direction. 'Shall we direct it together?' he suggested to Ghai.

This was tricky. Bhalla had helped Ghai during a lean phase and been instrumental in establishing the duo as writers. But there was no way he and Bhalla could have directed it together.

'It would have been a disaster,' says Ghai. 'Directing a film is about one man's visualization.'

In the Mumbai film industry, where people have collaborated to great acclaim as writers and music composers, there have been few successful pairings of directors. Abbas–Mustan, who directed *Aitraaz* (2004) and *36 China Town* (2006) for Ghai's production house, are a notable exception.

Ghai patiently told Bhalla that he could direct *Kalicharan* if he was keen and if Ghai could persuade Sippy to let him direct it, but it would not be prudent for both of them to be at the helm. Then, delicately, he added: 'It is my story, though.'

Bhalla was nothing if not intelligent and pragmatic. He obviously felt bad that their team was breaking up, but accepted it with grace. He managed to get a good price—₹1 lakh—from Sippy for Ghai–Bhalla's last story together.

Sippy paid Ghai another ₹25,000 for direction. All kinds of calculations would have gone into that: it was just one man at work, not two; it was a crucial break for someone keen to turn director; the producer was taking a lot of risk by betting on an unproven person; and so on. All of it was true. It is also true that Ghai would have been happy to direct *Kalicharan* for less, or nothing at all. Here, at long last, was his chance to tell a story close to his heart in his own way and to show all those directors who had scoffed at his suggestions about how to shoot a scene. This was the final step in a prolonged process of discovering who he really was.

'It was my big break, and I was not about to squander it,' says Ghai.

As Ghai started pre-production work for *Kalicharan*, he was nervous and afraid. As Sippy had guessed in their first chat about who would direct the film, Ghai had never even looked through a movie camera's viewfinder. So he focused on what he had done: he recalled how he had narrated *Kalicharan*'s story and scenes to various people and wrote these down. Accepting his deficiencies, he phoned ace cinematographer K.K. Mahajan, who had shot stark and realistic films such as *Bhuvan Shome* (1969) for Mrinal Sen and *Uski Roti* (1970) and *Ashadh Ka Ek Din* (1971) for Mani Kaul.

'Yaar, I am making a movie, but it is a commercial one. Will you do it?' Ghai asked. He was apprehensive about how someone deeply immersed in artistic cinema would react.

Mahajan agreed without a fuss. 'Why not!' he said. 'I should do commercial movies as well.'

Ghai hesitated. 'Yaar, I have never seen through a viewfinder, and I do not know much about lenses,' he confessed. 'But I can envision a scene and narrate it to you visually. I won't be able to tell you the focal length and aperture of the lens to use either, but I can tell you whether we need a close-up, long shot, or mid-range. Please protect me in front of the actors!'

'That'll do,' Mahajan said, 'we will manage.'

On set, they developed a language of their own. Ghai would gesture with his hands to indicate whether he wanted the shot focused on one person or many, or on the landscape, and Mahajan would nod and choose the right lens.

Next, Ghai went to Sippy and said he needed a scriptwriter and a dialogue writer. Sippy was puzzled. 'But you narrated the entire film to us, why do you need these people?' he wondered.

Ghai wanted to make sure that he was not distracted from direction and there were no lapses in translating his cinematic vision to celluloid. He wanted a screenplay writer and a dialogue writer who were more experienced than him, people whose advice he could rely on: Jainendra Jain, who had done the dialogues for *Bobby* (1973), Raj Kapoor's blockbuster about young love, and Ram Kelkar, who had written the screenplays of megahits such as *Be-Imaan* (1972), *Aap Ki Kasam* (1974) and *Sanyasi* (1975).

'Please get me these two, even if you have to deduct their pay from my salary,' Ghai told Sippy. There wasn't much in his director's salary to deduct from, but Sippy agreed to give Ghai the extra hands.

Having got a team in place, Ghai began choosing the cast. He had written the double roles of the police officer Prabhakar Shrivastava and the criminal Kalicharan with Shatrughan Sinha in mind. With that face and mannerisms, Sinha was a natural choice. But he had rejected the story in a manner that did not encourage Ghai to approach him again.

So Ghai played safe and told Sippy: 'Sunil Dutt Sa'ab has heard the story and likes it.'

Dutt, whose production company, Ajanta Arts, was making thought-provoking films such as *Reshma Aur Shera* (1971), was an established leading man and known for playing strong characters who were not always on the right side of the law. He could easily play a police officer and a criminal in the same film.

'He has become a filmmaker himself,' Sippy said. 'He will change your story. What about Rajesh Khanna?'

To Ghai, Khanna was too big a star and too much of a romantic hero to play Kalicharan, a character that was uncouth, illiterate, vulnerable and violent. At best, Khanna could have played Prabhakar, the suave officer, but Ghai was not sure how having two children, as Prabhakar's character did, would go with Khanna's image.

When no obvious choice emerged, Ghai decided to suggest his original pick. 'I wrote the story with Shatrughan Sinha in mind.'

'Shatrughan? He is a hit villain, not a hero,' Sippy said.

'True, but Vinod Khanna was a villain before becoming a hero. And Kalicharan is actually a villain who transforms into a hero.'

Sippy was still not convinced. 'With Shatrughan, we may not get a good price from distributors. Let's think about it.'

According to distributors, the cast was 90 per cent of the film's appeal.

A few days later, Sippy phoned Ghai. 'Subhash, I happened to meet Shatrughan and told him we are making *Kalicharan*.'

Ghai held his breath. Would Sinha's negative feedback to the story jeopardize Ghai's chances of becoming a director? 'What did he say?' he asked.

'He said he had heard the story and loved it. I told him I had picked you to direct the film. He agreed with the choice and said that one day you will be one of the best directors in the world.'

Ghai was not sure he heard it right. 'Is that what Shatrughan said?'

'Yes, yes,' Sippy said, not sure why Ghai sounded doubtful. 'He said you would make a great director and that he has been telling you for years to forget about acting and take up direction.'

Right after Sippy hung up, Ghai called Sinha. 'What did I just hear? Sippy Sa'ab says you loved the story of *Kalicharan* and you think I can become a great director.'

Sinha was unperturbed as usual. 'I just made your life. Superstars are going to work with you. Now write a good script and make it work.'

Ghai was overcome with emotion. 'Thank you, yaar,' he said, 'you saved my career.'

Inspector-General P.N. Khanna, a loud, genial and flamboyant character, dominates large passages of *Kalicharan*. Ghai had written the role with Ashok Kumar in mind. He was one of the early stars of the industry, and perhaps the first to play the anti-hero in *Kismet* (1943), believed to be the first Hindi film to cross ₹1 crore in box office collections. Kumar had moved seamlessly from playing the hero to portraying strong supporting characters. Everyone in the industry affectionately called him 'Dadamoni', Bengali for a dear older brother.

Ghai went to see Kumar's secretary, S.M. Sagar, a venerable old man. Javed Akhtar, who knew Sagar well, had prepared Ghai for the meeting. 'For the first half an hour,' Akhtar had said, 'listen to Sagar Sa'ab's stories and praise them.'

The stories lasted an hour and a half. And then it struck Sagar to ask why Ghai had come. Ghai told him.

'Dadamoni is doing seventeen films,' said Sagar, 'he is busy.'

Akhtar had prepared Ghai for this; according to Sagar, Ashok Kumar was always working on seventeen films—not sixteen, not eighteen.

When Ghai pleaded some more, Sagar said he could not guarantee anything, but would get him a meeting with Dadamoni. Ashok Kumar, upon hearing the story, said that he liked it and that Ghai's lack of experience as director did not deter him.

'I love working with new directors. With them, my films are always hits,' he said. 'I can tell that your film will be a hit. But I cannot do it.'

Dadamoni suffered from asthma and would not be able to shoot in Shimla, which was where many crucial scenes of the film took place. Ghai, unfortunately, could not change the location.

Eventually, of course, IG Khanna was to be played by Premnath.

In the early 1970s, producer–director Sohanlal Kanwar, who had made hits such as *Sanyasi* and *Be-Imaan*, had cast Ghai in the Punjabi film, *Sherni* (1973). The film also had Premnath playing the father of the heroine Radha Saluja.

Premnath had been around in the industry since the late 1940s. He did not taste much success playing lead roles but became a star with films that had him in strong supporting roles or as the villain: *Johny Mera Naam* (1970), *Bobby* (1973), *Dharmatma* (1975), and many others.

During the shooting of *Sherni*, Premnath would drink every night and play the harmonium. Ghai, who had always enjoyed music, joined the sessions and played the tabla. They became friends.

When Ashok Kumar turned down the role of IG Khanna in *Kalicharan*, Ghai thought of Premnath. His powerful screen presence and booming voice would suit the character.

Sippy was taken aback when he heard this. He recounted an incident when the actor was drunk when he reached the set and knocked off his co-star's wig off.

It was an ill-kept secret in the film industry that the luxurious mane of some actors was not natural.

After a few days, Ghai again mentioned Premnath. 'We need a powerful actor to offset Shatrughan's double role,' he said.

Although he was still reluctant, Sippy agreed to let Ghai have his way. 'If you are sure, talk to him, but he will be your responsibility.'

Ghai phoned Premnath. 'Papa ji, I want to meet you.'

'Come, come,' came the bellowing reply on the phone. 'Come in the evening.'

Ghai reached Premnath's home at five in the evening, only to see a hall full of people wearing the white caps worn by Mumbai's dabbawalas. They were singing, dancing and playing music. The gathering could only be described as a mandali.

'Subhash, my boy,' Premnath called out, 'come, come.'

Ghai soon found himself a part of the mandali. For the next few hours, more people came and everyone got drunk. Some left, others arrived. The mandali continued. Ghai was determined not to go back empty-handed. He waited.

At five in the morning, the last man left the mandali. Then Premnath sang only for Ghai. By then, Ghai was ready to throttle himself, but he had to praise Premnath for each song. When the first light of the morning came, it struck Premnath that he and Ghai were the only ones left.

'Did you come for something specific?' he asked.

'Papa ji,' Ghai said, 'I have got a chance to direct a film. I have also written its story and need your feedback.'

Premnath waved to him to go on. Ghai narrated the story of *Kalicharan*, but it was different from the many narrations he had done so far. This time he narrated the story entirely from IG Khanna's perspective.

'Fantastic, fantastic,' Premnath got up and gave Ghai a big, slobbering kiss.

'Papa ji, I want you to play Khanna,' said Ghai. 'Without you, the film cannot be made.'

'Yes, yes, nobody can play the role but Premnath,' said Premnath. 'But, I have a suggestion you must accept. *Kalicharan* is a ridiculous title. You must rename it 'IG Khanna'. It is IG Khanna's story.' With that, he went in.

Ghai was so exhausted that he lay down on the carpet and slept right there. He woke up around 10.30 a.m. Someone gave him tea. He went out and phoned his wife to say he was fine. Then he called Sippy.

'Where have you been?' asked Sippy. 'Your wife called to ask if you were with me. Did you go to meet Premnath?'

'Yes, I did, and I'm still here,' said Ghai. 'I think I have won the game. Now, you must come over. Premnath will probably wake up around noon. Please come and discuss the price.'

'Are you sure he has agreed?' Sippy asked.

'Yes,' said Ghai, 'I am sure.'

Sippy came around noon. Premnath woke up at half past and called Ghai in. 'You are still here?' he admonished him. 'You have such a good story. Why are you wasting time?'

Ghai was relieved that he had not forgotten their conversation about the film. 'Papa ji,' he said, 'my producer is here.'

'Call him in,' said Premnath.

When Sippy joined them, Premnath said to him: 'Subhash has written a good story. I like it. Are you producing it? Produce it well, okay?'

'Papa ji,' Ghai intervened, 'Sippy Sa'ab has come to talk about money.'

'Everybody in the industry knows what I charge,' Premnath said. 'I take overseas.'

'Overseas' was a film distribution territory, a lucrative one. Giving it to Premnath as his fee would mean putting him above what heroes such as Dharmendra, who was a highly bankable star, received.

Sippy hesitated. 'I can't give you overseas. That's too much.'

'Too much?' Premnath said. 'Okay, then give me what you want. What do you want to give me?'

'I will give you ₹8 lakh,' Sippy said.

'Done, done, done,' Premnath said.

Ghai and Sippy left after that. The latter did not look happy. 'Eight lakh is too much,' he said.

'Why did you offer it then?' asked Ghai.

'Yaar,' Sippy said sheepishly. 'I was awestruck.'

Ghai went back to Premnath a few days later. 'My producer is a disciplined man. I want my actors to be disciplined, too. Please promise me you will not come to the sets drunk.'

Premnath promised to be on his best behaviour.

Compared to the effort it took to cast Premnath, getting Ajit to play the role of the villain was a breeze. Ghai had always had Ajit in mind for the role of Deen Dayal, alias Lion, the very respectable pillar of society who also happens to be a crime kingpin. Having seen his performances in *Zanjeer* (1973), Amitabh Bachchan's breakthrough film that made him the Angry Young Man, and *Yaadon Ki Baaraat* (1973), Ghai was certain nobody could match him as the affluent, suave bad man.

The veteran actor needed only one sitting to agree to play Lion. He had only one request. He came from the theatre and had mostly acted in high-voltage films. Ghai's Lion, on the other hand, was someone who spoke in silky tones; shouting was not for him.

'Please make sure I play the role as you've narrated it to me. If I begin to become loud, please stop me,' Ajit said.

'I will,' promised Ghai, 'for loudness, I have got Premnath.'

For the third pivotal supporting character, Ghai got Danny Denzongpa to play Shaaka. Another FTII graduate, Danny had made a mark with films such as *Dhund* (1973), in which he was the villain. Ghai offered him a role that would earn him the public's sympathy and support. The clincher was that his character, a one-legged man, would do action sequences. The uniqueness of this was irresistible to Danny.

Now, like all good Hindi films, *Kalicharan* needed a heroine. Having his plate full with so many other things, Ghai wanted someone who would be easy to work with. He and Reena Roy had become friends during the shooting of *Gumrah*, in which they had played the lead roles. Ghai had also come to know her family well. What was more, *Kalicharan*'s heroine was an outspoken young girl who frequently resorted to using minor expletives; she had to offset the overbearing personality of Kalicharan, the criminal. Roy was perfect for the role and agreed without a fuss. She trusted Ghai.

The first three days of shooting were a breeze. Taking his first measured steps into direction, Ghai kept dialogues and action to a minimum. He began by shooting the scene in which an injured Prabhakar is in hospital, covered in bandages, while IG Khanna paces up and down in the corridor.

This was a pivotal scene for the film's story. Prabhakar, just before he dies, writes 'LION' on a notepad next to his bed, to reveal the identity of the man who caused his death; only the notepad is read upside down after Prabhakar dies, so that 'LION' becomes 'NO17'. A long, fruitless search ensues for someone or something that might be described as no.17. It is only towards the end of the movie that Kalicharan sees a twirling sign at the hotel owned by Deen Dayal (Lion Hotel) and realizes that it is Lion, not no.17, that they should be looking for.

The shot had very few dialogues and Sinha, playing Prabhakar, did not have to emote much because he was covered in bandages. The entire scene was captured without a hassle.

On the fourth day, Premnath was expected at ten in the morning. When he did not show up, Ghai got busy shooting scenes with the other actors. At four in the afternoon, the chorus of a mandali announced Premnath's arrival. The actor, punch drunk, entered singing and dancing. Everyone panicked. Ghai could see Sippy standing in a corner giving him a cold stare. Ghai approached his producer and asked him if they could cancel the rest of the shoot that day. Given the large number of actors involved and the sets erected and schedule planned, each hour of shooting lost was money down the drain. But Sippy trusted Ghai and agreed. Ghai told his assistant director to tell the unit to be ready for pack-up.

Meantime, Premnath approached Ghai and called out: 'Subhash, my boy.' As he prepared to kiss Ghai, the director shouted an emphatic command to the unit: 'Pack up! No more shooting today.'

Premnath was taken aback. 'Why? Let's shoot,' he said.

'Not today,' said Ghai. 'We will shoot tomorrow, when you are on time and not drunk.'

Premnath apologized. 'I forgot,' he said.

That was the last time he came late, or drunk, for the shoot. After that day, he was like a model pupil, following every instruction diligently. He also went on to act in the next four films Ghai directed.

After a few days of shooting, he told Sippy: 'This boy, Subhash, will one day be a big director.'

'Yes, sir, that is why I chose him,' said Sippy.

Sippy was a producer who liked to be involved in the creative process. He liked to think of himself as a filmmaker, not just the man holding the purse strings. When he explained a scene to distributors who visited the sets, he was often heard saying: 'I am taking this shot...'

During the shoot, Sippy used to sit behind Ghai as a scene was filmed. He liked to know what Ghai was doing, what the scene was, where it fit into the story, and so on. Ghai had no problem with that for the most part, but it could be disruptive at times. Once, when they were shooting in Shimla, it was close to sunset and Ghai wanted to finish a scene before the light faded. Some distributors were on the set. Ghai was busy setting up the trolley when Sippy, trying to make an impression on the distributors, asked him, 'Subhash, why are you setting up the trolley?'

This had happened before too, and as Ghai was in a hurry, he merely said, 'Give me a bit of time, the sun is setting. I will explain later.'

'You cannot take a shot unless I tell you to,' Sippy replied.

By now, Ghai had had enough. In a moment of reckless indignation, he snapped: 'In that case, you do it.'

Sippy backed off, but continued to fume. That night, he summoned Ghai to his hotel. His partners were also there, as was Shatrughan Sinha.

Ghai apologized. 'Sorry, I was rude. But you should let me work.'

But Sippy would not be mollified so easily. 'Who is the filmmaker, you or me?' he demanded.

'You are humiliating me in front of so many people,' said Ghai. 'I will quit.'

'Fine, you are out.'

At that Sinha spoke up for Ghai. 'Sippy sa'ab, if he goes, I go,' he said. 'He was only doing his job. Let him work.'

Ghai was contrite. 'Sippy sa'ab, I made a mistake, but please understand my situation. I was doing it for your film.'

Sinha's strong stance and Ghai's continued apology seemed to diffuse the situation.

'I will forever respect Shatrughan for his support to me that day,' says Ghai.

Ghai learned a lot from Sippy about being a producer and how to organize production. No matter where or when they met, he always touched Sippy's feet. 'He was the only one in the industry whose feet I touched,' says Ghai.

During the final mixing of *Kalicharan*, when they were trying to reduce the film's length, a 200-foot scene in which the children are kidnapped became the bone of contention. The scene was close to Ghai's heart, but Sippy wanted to cut it.

One day, Mangesh Desai, a genius at sound mixing, told Ghai that Sippy had had the scene removed. Ghai was in tears. But Desai told him to be pragmatic.

'Subhash, listen to the producer,' he said. 'This cut will have no impact on the film.'

Desai was right. The preview show Sippy organized for his partners and distributors was at Mehboob Theatre. Iqbal, son of legendary producer–director Mehboob Khan, who made *Mother India* (1957), was in the audience. Whenever he was watching a movie, Iqbal liked to keep a box full of paan next to him. When the preview ended, Iqbal spoke to a nervous Ghai. 'I did not eat a single paan when your film was on,' he told Ghai. That was a resounding endorsement about how gripping *Kalicharan* had turned out to be.

When the film released in February 1976, Ghai went to watch the noon show in the Galaxy theatre in Bandra. To his dismay, he saw that people were talking loudly during the film. They seemed to have no emotional involvement at all—they were neither crying nor laughing. Certain that the film would be a flop, Ghai went back home and slept.

When he woke up in the evening, some of his friends had come over. A few said the film was doing well, others said not so much.

Ghai phoned Sippy.

'The picture is doing well, Subhash!' Sippy was ebullient. '*Hit hai, hit hai!*'

The reviews in the next day's newspapers called the film brilliant. It took two or three days for Ghai to believe that he had indeed delivered a hit. He had become a director.

6

Vishwanath: Director's Triumph

If a filmmaker's first film is a trial by fire, the second is perhaps akin to asking someone to take the fire test all over again. The industry loves to see people fail. If that does not happen, they settle for undermining someone's success.

'*Utni nahi chali* (Didn't do all that well),' they'll say. Pressed for evidence, they might add something like: '*Jaunpur mein ruk gayi* (Didn't do well in Jaunpur).' Jaunpur, a small town in Uttar Pradesh, is sufficiently removed from the mainstream and there is unlikely to be any data in the first week to challenge the assertion that a film has not done well there. The country has enough such places to become fodder for the detractors.

Such perverse people do not understand what it takes to make a film. Making a film can take you on a ride of inconceivable joys and unthinkable sorrows. It can stretch friendships, test relationships, and at times, push you to behave in odd ways. Despite all that, the final film may not be what you wanted it to be.

'I experienced all these things during the making of *Vishwanath*, *Gautam Govinda* and *Krodhi*,' says Ghai.

Kalicharan's success gave Ghai the license to experiment. He did not want to repeat anything from his first movie in the second. His next project, *Gautam Govinda*, was to be as different from *Kalicharan* as Jaunpur was from Mumbai. Where *Kalicharan* was a city-based film with the suave Din Dayal 'Lion' as the villain, *Gautam Govinda* was set in a village. Many of the film's characters, including Shatrughan Sinha's Govinda, spoke in a local dialect. The villain, Dharamdutt 'Raja Saheb', played by Premnath, was a feudal lord trapped in the past and in a wheelchair—altogether different from Lion.

However, *Gautam Govinda* ended up becoming Ghai's third film, instead of his second. Pawan Kumar roped him in to do a quickie for Shatrughan Sinha's production house, Ramayan Chitra, which was reeling from the failure of *Khaan Dost*, which had hit the theatres in March 1976 and was rejected by viewers.

'Our film has flopped, but yours [*Kalicharan*] is a hit, although both were your stories,' said Pawan Kumar. 'We need to make a quick movie.'

Ghai's heart was already set on *Gautam Govinda*, but he couldn't turn down a request that was almost a cry for help from Shatrughan Sinha's production house. Sinha and he were close friends and their families were close, too. They had just scored big together with *Kalicharan*. That, as all hits do, had strengthened their friendship.

Pawan Kumar's offer of a partnership and a share in profits clinched the deal. 'We were friends, yes, and I wanted to help. But the idea of being a partner motivated me even more,' says Ghai.

He went to Khandala, stayed in a hotel, and thought of subjects. Two weeks later he was ready with the story of *Vishwanath*—the title character was to be a criminal lawyer who becomes a criminal. The film was about his trials, his transition, and its consequences. Talk about quickies! The producers took the same core cast as *Kalicharan*: Shatrughan Sinha, Reena Roy and Premnath, and added Pran for extra star power.

Pran, the star villain of many blockbusters over the years, had taken to playing strong character roles after his glorious turn in *Upkar*

(1967), Manoj Kumar's ode to Lal Bahadur Shastri's slogan 'Jai Jawan Jai Kisan'. Such was Pran's appeal for audiences that his face dominated the publicity posters of many of his films.

The first time Ghai met Pran was at the latter's house for a narration arranged by Pawan Kumar. In the living room, everywhere Ghai looked, he saw paintings of the characters Pran had played in different films: dozens of them. The actor was known to pay special attention to his get-up and look in every film. When Pran came to the living room and greeted them, Ghai said he was impressed to see all the characters that were on the walls.

'You haven't seen even a fourth of them,' Pran replied.

That told Ghai how much Pran loved his characters, and, in his narration, he focused especially on the characterization of Golu Gawah, the witness-for-rent he wanted the actor to play in *Vishwanath*. Pran agreed.

There was one crucial difference between *Kalicharan* and *Vishwanath*. Ghai had had the time and space to develop the story and script of *Kalicharan*. *Vishwanath*, by contrast, went on the floors within forty-five days of the story being approved by Sinha and Kumar. In fact, *Vishwanath* is one of only four films Ghai started shooting without a script; *Meri Jung*, *Ram Lakhan* and *Yuvvraaj* are the other three.

'I had put in about four years of work into *Kalicharan*. Every line, every scene was at my fingertips. *Vishwanath* had to be done suddenly, quickly, and it had to live up to the expectations raised by *Kalicharan*,' says Ghai.

Ghai still had control over the project. He knew that Sinha's strength was dialogue delivery. The actor could quickly memorize several pages of dialogue and deliver them in a single take, laced with his usual bluster and thunder. Ghai explained to him that the high-octane moments in the film would come from the dialogue rather than physical action. Being an ace lawyer, the hero would be more inclined to use his brain than his muscles.

In the absence of a script, the film had to rely on its characterizations. Ghai and his team spent several days on each character and its build-up. Vishwanath's appearance is preceded by people outside the courthouse placing bets on his victory, like they would at the racecourse. In many scenes, Sinha's voice was given added reverberation—after all, he is described in the beginning of the film as someone to be heard, rather than seen. Every scene exudes the power and influence of the villain, played by Premnath. Ghai beefed up the villainy by roping in Ranjeet to play a feral, animalistic character called Khokha. Every time he is about to do something heinous, Khokha says in a terrifying manner: 'Once in a blue moon, kabhi kabhi.'

Although Khokha appears in the film only three times, that line remains etched in the memory of Hindi film aficionados, as do Shatrughan Sinha's iconic lines: '*Jali ko aag kehte hain, bujhi ko raakh kehte hain. Jis raakh se barood baney, usse Vishwanath kehte hain.* (What burns is fire, what is left are ashes. The ashes that make for an explosion, that is what is called Vishwanath.)'

Sinha, Premnath and Reena Roy played characters starkly different from the ones in *Kalicharan*. In an otherwise grim story, Pran provided comic relief as well as drama.

Vishwanath was a director's film, just as *Kalicharan* was a writer's. The central plot—a criminal lawyer goes on to become a criminal—was quite lean and could not be stretched much. Whatever Ghai knew about filmmaking, whatever he had learned over the years from people like Ritwik Ghatak and Roshan Taneja, and by watching what were called 'treatment' films, he brought it all out to make *Vishwanath* rise above its story and screenplay.

The camera became his friend and confidante. He learned how the trolley, on which the camera is mounted, can move forward, back, parallel to the action or around, to convey emotions such as confusion, nervousness, shock or panic; how the camera can make a character large or small, how it can capture one person's heartbeat or many people's reactions, or bring the scene alive for the audience.

Ghai's mastery over his craft is evident in the film's opening scene itself. More than a minute long, it only shows Ranjeet from behind as he walks through dark corridors and stairwells. Shot with a handheld camera, the scene immediately hooks the audience and compels them to watch.

The build-up of Vishwanath's character is unusually long; the title and credits begin to flash on screen no less than twenty-four minutes after the film has begun.

'Any director could have made *Kalicharan*, so good were its story and screenplay. It was *Vishwanath* that truly made me a director, it was my training ground,' says Ghai.

And yet, the first cut of the film left him worried. When fourteen of *Vishwanath*'s sixteen reels were ready, Ghai watched them at a private screening in a theatre. It is in a theatre that you truly get the audience's perspective, far better than in the editing room. That perspective told Ghai the movie as it currently stood was certain to fail. Ghai believed in telling strong, compelling stories. That *Vishwanath* was not. Not yet.

So, Ghai and his two editors, Waman Bhonsle and Gurudutt Shirali, started to rescript the film in the editing room. Their biggest concern was the second half, which seemed to be falling apart. Some scenes, which should have been in the climax, were coming when a third of the film was still left to go. Together, the three of them revised the entire script, almost recreating the second half. But the film still had defects. Redoing a screenplay in the editing room leaves rough patches, like those left by the darning of cloth. They tried to smoothen these rough patches by adding theme music, which gave a sense of homogeneity. Ghai also needed ten extra days of shooting, to which Pawan Kumar agreed.

'I did this for nearly all my subsequent films,' says Ghai. 'My actors and crew got used to the idea that once the principal photography was done, I would sit and watch the film, and then ask for ten days or more from everyone.'

However, for *Vishwanath*, Ghai could not do everything he wanted; the film had to be readied quickly for release. Although the final product had all of Ghai's style and panache, parts of it remained patchy.

In his early career as a producer, Ghai never pre-sold his films. He did not know how much extra shooting and patching he'd need. Typically, he would raise some money from financiers, take advances from distributors, and let the cameras roll. They—Ghai, the financiers, and distributors—would work out the price once the film was ready. For the seven territories in which India's film distribution was divided, Ghai usually had six distributors. He himself took the seventh territory. They sat with the accountants and took out 20 per cent of the earnings for Ghai as the producer. The rest was divided into seven parts.

To Ghai's surprise, *Vishwanath,* which released in January 1978, earned more at the box office than *Kalicharan*, nearly 20 per cent more, probably because he had made a mass film—for evidence, look no further than the climax—without any thoughts of making it artistic. At that time, stylized acting and dramatic dialogues worked, and *Vishwanath* had these in plenty.

7

Gautam Govinda: The Parting

Before the onset of the multiplex era in the late 1990s and early 2000s, all theatres used to be standalone, often humongous, two-storey structures that could seat more than a thousand people for a single show. The halls were usually divided into Front Stall and Rear Stall or Upper Stall on the ground floor, and Balcony and Dress Circle upstairs. The tickets upstairs were more expensive and drew crowds that wore finer clothes. Those sitting downstairs catcalled, squealed and threw coins on the screen to show their appreciation. Those upstairs clapped and laughed.

Films that catered to the upstairs were called 'balcony movies' or 'class cinema'. These were typically well-made films that did not always make money, but earned effusive praise from critics. 'Mass cinema', meant primarily for the downstairs, was panned by critics but usually made money. Filmmakers used to celebrate if critics ridiculed their films. They saw it as a surefire sign that the film would do well.

Unfortunately, that did not hold true for *Gautam Govinda*. It was panned by the critics and still failed to make money.

Gautam Govinda moved the action away from Mumbai to a lawless fictional village called Dharampur. This village was several kilometres off the nearest paved road and could only be reached by walking for several hours over stony land. The only law in Dharampur was the wish of Dharamdutt 'Raja Saheb', played by Premnath. When Inspector Gautam gets transferred to this village, he discovers that two of his predecessors had been chased away by local goons and the third was killed.

The seeds of the film were sown when producer Shyam Sundar Shivdasani met Ghai. He was friends with Shashi Kapoor, Raj Kapoor's youngest brother and a busy star. Shashi was the hero in *Chor Machaye Shor* (1974) and *Fakira* (1976), hit films N.N. Sippy had produced before *Kalicharan*. Sippy had mentioned to the actor that Ghai, who was directing Sippy's new film, *Kalicharan*, was going to be a great director. When Shivdasani was planning his next project, Shashi Kapoor suggested he approach Ghai.

Shivdasani met Ghai just before *Kalicharan* was released. 'If you want to make a film with me,' he said, 'I can get Shashi Kapoor as the hero.'

Ghai was immediately interested. He thought it would be great to have one more film in hand as a safety net. In case *Kalicharan* flopped, it wouldn't end his career as a director. He was confident that Shatrughan Sinha, who had backed him during the making of *Kalicharan*, would be willing to work with him again. So he suggested a two-hero film to Shivdasani: two brothers separated in childhood and reunited as starkly different adults. Shashi Kapoor would be Inspector Gautam, a city-bred, upright police officer, and Shatrughan Sinha the village goon, Govinda.

When Ghai narrated the story to Shashi Kapoor, he only said, 'All right, we will meet again. I will speak to Shyam.'

Shivdasani later met Ghai and said the actor found the story to be one of the best he had ever heard. Sinha, too, thought it would be a great film and a certain hit. As did everyone else who heard the story. Encouraged by these reactions, Ghai revised his draft with the intent of making a mega film. The frame became bigger, the budget increased, and the characters became larger than life.

That was a mistake.

'One should never try to make a big, monumental film,' says Ghai. 'The right way is to focus on telling a good story in an interesting manner. If the film is meant to become big, it will.'

All those films in which he focused on telling a good story were successful. But success eluded him when his mind was less on the story and more on making a magnum opus. *Gautam Govinda*, *Krodhi*, *Kisna* and *Yuvvraaj* are testimonies to that.

Gautam Govinda should have been made in a year. It took three and a half.

At the outset, Ghai discovered that his two lead actors were as different as chalk and cheese, just like the characters they were playing. Shashi Kapoor was doing several films at the time; the industry grapevine put the number between forty and fifty. He worked four to six shifts each day, of two hours each. To accommodate multiple schedules, he allotted dates in short bursts, say three or four consecutive days of two-hour shifts. He was punctual: he arrived on time and also left on time, regardless of what else might be happening on the set or in the world. Sinha was the exact opposite. For a shoot scheduled to start at nine in the morning, he would turn up on the set at one in the afternoon, or at two, or three.

'As his friend, I knew he meant no harm, that was his nature,' says Ghai.

When ready, Sinha would come bustling to the set, with his usual swagger, and say: 'Don't worry, I'm a one-take artist. I'll complete your scene quickly.' But by that time, Kapoor would be somewhere else, on some other film's set.

If Ghai missed filming a scene involving both actors, the next opportunity would come weeks or maybe months later, when Kapoor gave his next dates (again three or four days of two-hour shifts). Even then the scenes could be filmed only if Sinha was also available on those days, and if he turned up while Kapoor was still around on the sets.

To this heady cocktail of Shashi and Shatrughan, the sensor board added its whimsy. The stupendous success of *Sholay*, packed as it was with thrilling action sequences, influenced most filmmakers of the time. Ghai, too, had packed the script of *Gautam Govinda* with action scenes. However, by the time three or four reels had been shot, the Censor Board clamped down on action and said no fight scene could be longer than 90 feet and no film could have more than three fight scenes. *Gautam Govinda* had many more, and the action scenes were 300 to 500 feet in length.

Ghai had no choice but to redraft the script. He converted the action into dramatic dialogues. Twelve reels were shot with the new script. Ghai was satisfied. There were good movements, emotional relationship, songs, and conflict between the brothers. Everyone said the film was sure to be a hit.

Then the government changed and the Censor Board withdrew its restrictions on action scenes, saying it did not want to curb the industry's freedom of expression. Shivdasani said he liked the original script better and wanted Ghai to restore the action sequences.

Ghai could not resist and started on the third version of the film. He kept the footage he had shot and liked, and he shot new action scenes. He kept extending the climax. The film ended up being disjointed and could not engage the viewers emotionally.

Upon its release in March 1979, *Gautam Govinda* did well for the first three days. However, from Monday, ticket sales began to fall sharply. Ghai sent a team to watch the film in a theatre. They counted thirty-two places where the viewers clapped—something every filmmaker craves. But, after the show, when people emerged from the hall, their immediate reaction was that the climax was too long and boring. Word got around that the film was not all that great.

'The most important part in any film or story is the last part,' says Ghai. 'That is what remains with the viewers and makes up their mind, and that is the feedback they pass around.'

None of this helped Ghai's family life. Once, Rehana, his wife, was upset because there was no money to run the household.

'It is the seventh of the month,' she said. 'You had promised me ₹5,000 on the first, you have not given me any money yet.'

That same day, a producer came to their house with a bag in hand. 'I am coming from the gurudwara. I had gone to offer my prayers,' he said.

Ghai nodded, not quite clear where this was going. The producer handed his bag over to Ghai. It contained ₹1 lakh.

'Keep this money,' he said, 'and do not worry. I want you to make a film for me, but you can make it any time you want, even if it is two or three years later. I will pay you ₹10 lakh then. This is the advance.'

Rehana was somewhere inside the house, but Ghai was sure she had her ears glued to the conversation in the drawing room.

'I cannot take your money now,' Ghai said. 'I will take it when I start your film.'

But the producer left his bag and went away.

Ghai called his brother, Ashok, who had started assisting him on his films. Ashok had studied editing at FTII and was working on *Gautam Govinda*. Ghai gave him the bag the man had left behind, and said, 'Take this to his [the producer's] house. When you ring the bell, most likely his wife will open the door. Give her the bag and say, "Subhash ji has sent this for your husband." Then come away quickly, don't linger.'

Once Ashok left, Ghai got ready and went for his shoot. When he came back home in the evening, Rehana refused to speak to him. She only said in a cold voice, 'Food is on the table.'

'Why are you unhappy?' Ghai asked.

'Reena Roy's mother called me today,' Rehana said. 'She said you sent away a producer to whom she had recommended you. Today, you turned down ₹1 lakh. I have been asking for five thousand to run your house. The household help has not been paid and is threatening to quit. Everyone is right, success has gone to your head.'

'It's okay,' said Ghai, 'I will serve my food myself.'

As he started to eat, Rehana came and sat next to him. 'Everyone says you should cash in now,' she said gently. 'These are your good times.'

'What does that mean? Are you saying that our bad days are round the corner?' Ghai asked. 'Do you want my success to last five years or twenty-five?'

Rehana smiled at that; the answer was obvious.

'Then let me do it my way. I can promise you I will remain a successful director for twenty-five years,' Ghai said. 'I have thought deeply about the success of *Kalicharan*. Did it run because of good luck, its songs, the stars, or because of the director–writer? I think it ran because of the director–writer. The way I made the film, I want to put the same effort in every film.'

Ghai wanted to give everything he had to his films, and he did. But it was not always easy.

Rehana suffered three miscarriages early on in their marriage. While the shooting for *Gautam Govinda* was in full swing, Rehana went into premature labour and gave birth to a boy after only seven months of pregnancy. The baby was placed in an incubator and remained in the hospital. Every day Ghai would finish shooting by six-thirty or so and then go to the hospital to meet his wife and see his son. After about an hour and a half, he would return to the sets to prepare his assistant directors for the next day's shoot. Three weeks later the doctors told the couple that the baby would soon be out of danger and could go home. Ghai and Rehana were overjoyed.

Meanwhile, on the sets, the unit was filming the song '*Tohra bitwa jawan hoi gawa, ma meri shadi karai de*. (Mother, I have come of age and want to be married.)' Sung with gusto by Mohammad Rafi, it was a pulsating song, with rich rural fervour and lots of dancing extras. Sinha was dancing with abandon. The entire set looked like a festive scene.

Jagjit Khurana, a friend of Ghai's from FTII, who later produced *Karz*, had been staying with him. One day, while the shoot was on, he stepped close to Ghai and said in a quiet voice: 'The child is not well.'

Ghai rushed to the hospital. There had been a power cut, as a result of which the incubator had stopped working. After twenty-two days of fighting for his life, the baby had breathed his last. They buried him late that evening.

Shivdasani, the producer, came to the funeral. He said he would cancel the next day's shoot. But Ghai knew he was really asking whether to cancel or not. Ghai did not hold that against the producer. They had only two days left to finish the song before the set would be dismantled. If they could not complete the song in time, the same set would have to erected again in another shooting schedule. Doing so would cost time (coordinating dates of the large number of actors and extras) and money (additional salaries for everyone). Besides, the gap would break the fine rhythm the unit had struck.

At six-thirty the next morning, Ghai was back on the set.

'Filmmaking is like that. It gives you unbelievable joys and unimaginable sorrows,' he says.

Friendships in the film industry tend to be, at their best, mercurial. Each day brings new ways to test and strain relationships.

Gautam Govinda was the last time Shatrughan Sinha and Ghai worked together. While they were shooting for the film, Sinha was seeing Reena Roy. They had been the lead pair in *Kalicharan* and *Vishwanath*. Both films were hits, and the reel pair turned into real-life lovers.

This was par for the course in the industry. When a film did well, its hero and heroine usually felt drawn to each other. If their second film became a hit as well, they were quite likely to become lovers. If they gave a third hit together, they might even begin making wedding plans. It had little to do with chemistry or physics, only with the films' success. As a pair gave hits, everyone started to say they looked good together, that they had good chemistry, that the public liked seeing them together. This constant talk of chemistry provided a fertile ground for relationships to blossom.

'It is pretty much the same now, only a little quicker: just one hit can forge a relationship and just one flop can tear it apart,' says Ghai wryly.

In keeping with the morality of the 1970s, Ghai felt compelled to pick a quarrel with Sinha over his relationship with Roy. He knew Sinha's fiancée, Poonam Chandiramani, a former Miss India, quite well and liked her a lot. (They are still close; Poonam ties Ghai a rakhi every year.) Ghai thought he would be failing in his duties as Poonam's brother and as Sinha's friend if he did not warn him against jettisoning a nice girl. After some time, he raised the issue again, and told Sinha: 'I will be your friend only if you marry Poonam.'

Both Sinha and Reena Roy, who somehow learnt of Ghai's views, got angry and stopped talking to Ghai.

The already strained relationship between Sinha and Ghai received another blow when, after the release of *Vishwanath*, Pawan Kumar claimed there was no partnership agreement with Ghai and that the film was purely a Ramayan Chitra production. Ghai needed to file his taxes—an ordeal in those days, with high rates and complex documentation—and had asked Kumar for the partnership papers.

'You had said we will be equal partners and share profits,' Ghai said.

'Our film went over budget, we have not made much money. There is no question of sharing the profits,' said Kumar. 'Anyway, we did not have a partnership agreement with you. We will pay you as the director.'

There was nothing in writing. In those days, contracts were usually drawn up after a film had been completed. Many films went on the shooting floors with just half the story ready.

Ghai decided to take the matter up with Sinha, but the latter echoed Kumar. 'Yaar, see, Pawan has spoken to me about this. I think he is right.'

Ghai felt let down. 'Fine,' he told Sinha, 'but one thing I must tell you, I will not be able to work with you again.'

Sinha did not seem perturbed. He had many other filmmakers lining up at his door; Ghai would at best make one film in two years.

They did not speak for a year.

The ice broke when one day, out of the blue, Sinha phoned Ghai from London. 'Subhash, I'm coming to Mumbai,' Sinha said. 'And I will marry Poonam.'

Ghai was thrilled. 'The day you marry,' he said, 'I will host the evening reception.'

The party was held at Sea Rock Hotel in Mumbai and was attended by the who's who of the film industry. Ghai put up a banner at the party that said: 'Married Eventually'.

In some ways, life had come full circle for the two friends. Sinha had joined FTII during Ghai's final year. Ghai had acted as Sinha's guide when he finished his studies in Pune and made the inevitable one-way journey to Mumbai. Together, they had struggled as aspiring actors, shared cigarettes, engaged in endless sessions of drinking and chatting, and dreamed of success. Their first film as director and actor brought them closer; their last drove them apart; for a time. And now Poonam had wrought a reconciliation. Their families remain close and meet at all birthdays and every party.

'I have always been Shatrughan's friend and will remain so till the end of my time,' says Ghai. 'But our work ethics are different. I think the key difference is that I have always thought of myself as a student of cinema. Shatrughan, on the other hand, was always a finished product. His ways have worked well for him and mine for me. He remains Shatrughan Sinha, my friend.'

8

Krodhi: The Wrath

The story of *Krodhi*, even more than *Kalicharan*'s, came straight from Ghai's heart. Where *Kalicharan* was a crime drama Ghai wrote using his mind, *Krodhi* originated from the deep recesses of his childhood, from nights spent listening to his mother narrate stories from the epics, the Ramayana and the Mahabharata, and other ancient Indian texts.

Much like a character from the epics, Vikramjit Singh, *Krodhi*'s protagonist, morphs from being the king of the underworld into a saint with magical healing powers. One day, an associate from his days of crime comes to the village where the gangster-turned-saint is living. Now, Vikramjit must weigh his options: kill the associate before his past is revealed or go on the run again.

The final product, though, turned out to be very different from what Ghai had visualized.

When he first came up with the story of the film, Ghai toyed with the idea of speaking to Amitabh Bachchan for the lead role. The two of them had been friends during their days of struggle, and had often hung out together in a group.

But the actor had become too big a star. Although Ghai had begun to be counted among the industry's exciting young directors, he still did not fancy his chances with *the* Amitabh Bachchan.

He did fancy his chances with Dharmendra, who, while never being dubbed the superstar, had remained the steadiest box office draw for years.

Ghai narrated the story to Dharmendra at his home for an hour or so, while the latter sipped his tea. When Ghai finished, Dharmendra didn't say anything immediately. This made Ghai apprehensive. *Krodhi*'s protagonist was a far cry from the strong-man-with-a-heart-of-gold who the actor had played most often.

'This is a good subject. Who is producing it?' Dharmendra finally said.

Ghai had not found a producer yet. He said: 'Sir, I came to you for the narration hoping you will act in it. Anyone can produce it. I can produce it myself.'

Dharmendra said he wanted to produce it.

Ghai was delighted. In one narration, he had got his hero as well as the producer. It always helped when the hero was more invested in the film than just in his role. Having Shatrughan Sinha's Ramayan Chitra as the producer of *Vishwanath* had helped complete it on schedule.

Ghai adapted the lead role slightly to suit Dharmendra, making it a little less serious and less quiet than it would have been had Bachchan played it.

After two weeks, Dharmendra called. 'Yaar, I have two sisters, and they are both married,' he said. 'I have already helped one jija (sister's husband) get into production. With this film, I want to help the other become a producer.'

This was not unusual. Often, when a star produced a film, members of his extended family got involved. Unfortunately, not all relatives could match the star in talent or ability.

Ghai told Dharmendra: 'I do not know your jija, you will have to take the responsibility.'

Dharmendra agreed. 'I will be the real producer, he will only lend his name.' With that, Ranjit Virk and his company, Ranjit Films, came into the picture.

When production started, Ghai realized that Ranjit Virk was an enthusiastic man. *Krodhi*'s canvas was immense, more so than even *Gautam Govinda*'s. Ghai had planned scenes with thousands of people and numerous helicopter shots. The scale excited Virk. He wanted *Krodhi* to be another *Sholay*. To be fair, every producer at that time wanted his film to be another *Sholay*.

Virk started to talk up the film, hoping to get a high price from distributors. One way to do that, he thought, would be to get more stars, although *Krodhi* already had a few.

Shashi Kapoor had agreed to play the cop who chases Vikramjit (or Vicky). Moushumi Chatterjee, who was paired with Kapoor in *Gautam Govinda*, was Vicky's love interest who dies early in the film. Zeenat Aman was the associate who discovers Vicky in his saintly avatar as Swami Shradhanand.

Ghai did not think he could handle more stars. For the remaining roles, he wanted actors from theatre. Virk, though, had other ideas. For the role of the guru who guides Shradhanand, Virk suggested Pran. Ghai was opposed to the idea but had to agree to it when Dharmendra phoned him to say, 'Yaar, Ranjit is right, let's take Pran.'

Virk suggested Premnath for the pivotal role of a dacoit. 'He is your friend. He has worked in all your films,' he told Ghai.

Ghai protested. The role was of a rural dacoit—hardly suited for Premnath's stylized acting and accent.

'He is a friend of yours, come on!' Virk said. With that, another well-known name joined the cast.

Ordinarily, three to four scenes are sufficient for a small role in a film, to give body to the character and move the story along. However, when a star steps into the role, it needs at least seven to eight scenes to let him make his presence felt, validate his standing in the market, and meet the audience's expectation roused by the posters and publicity. Now that Pran and Premnath had joined the cast, Ghai had to rework the screenplay to do justice to their roles.

For the young couple in the film, Ghai wanted absolutely fresh faces. But Virk signed up Sachin and Ranjeeta, the hit pair from *Ankhiyon Ke Jharokhon Se* (1978). 'Let's not pull the picture down,' he told Ghai. 'We will make a big film. You are a big director.'

Virk was a good man, a typical Punjabi—warm, loving, generous, and often over the top. He would tell Ghai: '*Papa ji tussi meri gal maan lo. Kamaal ho jayega. Chhuttiyan ho jayengi sabki.* Sholay *ko mar degi hamari picture. Do sau din nahi utregi*. (My friend, please listen to me. We will do wonders. We will finish everyone off. Our film will outdo *Sholay*; it will run for at least two hundred days.)'

Krodhi had a small character of a courtesan, Phoolwati, for which Ghai had Aruna Irani in mind. She was a popular face, but not a top heroine. She had played Shatrughan Sinha's romantic interest in *Gautam Govinda* and was an accomplished dancer.

But Virk said, '*Maine papa ji naal gal kar li hai. Hema ji ko rakhte hain*. (I have spoken to Dharmendra, let's get Hema Malini to do the role.)'

Hema Malini was a superlative actress who ruled the industry throughout the 1970s. The courtesan's role was too small to do justice to her abilities and star power. But Virk was flying high. He said they would call the role a 'guest appearance'.

Ghai spoke to Dharmendra about it, who said, 'Hema has refused, she thinks it is a lousy role.'

That should have comforted Ghai. Instead, it incensed him. How could a role he had written be dismissed as lousy?

'Sir, this is a great role,' he said. 'Can you arrange for me to meet her?'

Dharmendra did, and Ghai landed up at Hema Malini's house one morning.

'Dharam told me about the role of Phoolwati. It's no good,' she said.

'Have you heard about Vasavadatta?' Ghai asked her.

According to lore, Vasavadatta was a courtesan who lived during the ancient times in Mathura. She fell in love with Upagupta, Lord Buddha's disciple, at first glance. But the monk rejected her overtures. In fact, he refused to even meet her. Much later, when Vasavadatta was suffering, Upagupta came to her and gave her spiritual succour. She embraced Buddhism.

'That is the story of Phoolwati,' Ghai said. 'When a gangster-turned-saint comes to her and helps her, it adds to his glory.'

That set Hema Malini thinking. Then she chuckled, and said, 'You know, Dharam narrated the story badly to me. He only said he is playing a gangster who meets a prostitute. She gets sick, everyone abandons her, then he goes to her.'

Sensing victory, Ghai said, 'Hema ji, would I come to you with a frivolous role?' For good measure, he added that there was also a nice song to be picturized on the character.

Hema Malini agreed to do the film. Ghai wrote more scenes for Phoolwati to suit her stardom.

In those days the principal photography of a film took about ten shooting schedules, each of ten days or so. The first couple of schedules of *Krodhi* went well. Then the cancellations began.

Dharmendra and Hema Malini's love story was an open secret at the time. It had its ups and downs, as every relationship does. During the downs, Dharmendra would sometimes get upset and cancel the shooting. It was, like they say, *ghar ki baat* (a family matter).

However, when a lead actor cancels a shoot, it shakes up the schedule. Fresh dates have to be taken from all the other actors appearing in the scenes. In a film with many top stars, this became a major issue. Dharmendra, Shashi Kapoor, Zeenat Aman—each cancelled their dates a couple of times at least. When they gave new dates, they didn't always match the others'.

With the shooting schedule hurtling from one cancellation to the next, the film took more than three-and-a-half years to complete. The parts shot earlier began to look dated. Some faces changed a bit. Continuity became an issue. And the script lost its homogeneity.

'These days, people fix the release date and stick to it whether the film turns out to be good or bad. This is good for financial discipline. In our time, we wanted to make a good film, no matter what. There were no deadlines,' says Ghai.

The final cut was fifteen minutes short of four hours. Ghai spent two-and-a-half months trying to edit it down to three, to make the length more suitable to theatre schedules. He asked Virk for ten more days of shooting. He intended to shoot a few new scenes to replace some of the original scenes so the film could be compressed and the rough patches smoothed over. But by now, Virk's desire to make another *Sholay* had ebbed somewhat and he wanted to get the film out at the earliest.

When it did release in February 1981, *Krodhi* was sadly not able to set the box office on fire.

With *Kalicharan* and *Vishwanath*, Ghai had taken ownership of the final product. He had a hand in every aspect, right up to the marketing and promotion leading to the release. With *Gautam Govinda*, Shivdasani had taken charge once the film was complete, leaving Ghai out of the marketing and publicity.

When *Gautam Govinda* was released, Ghai's mother wanted to see it. She had taken a liking to its song, '*Ek ritu aaye, ek ritu jaye re*'. Ghai decided to take her to the trial show, which producers usually organized for their friends and distributors. He sent his chief assistant to reserve a seat for his mother.

The chief assistant came back with Shivdasani's message: there was no seat for Ghai's mother at the trial show. He added that when he tried to persuade Shivdasani, saying it was for Ghai's mother after all, the producer said, 'Even if Subhash Ghai comes himself, I cannot show him the film.'

'But Subhash ji is the director,' the chief assistant protested.

'Yes, he is the captain of the ship,' Shivdasani said, 'but I own the ship.'

The bit about 'owning the ship', accurate though it was, haunted Ghai. By now, he understood how deeply the creative aspects of filmmaking were influenced by the producer. He began to wonder if it would be a good idea for him to also 'own the ship', not merely be its captain.

Around that time, Ghai had taken a loan of ₹10,000 loan from a film financier, Ram, for Rehana's medical treatment. He was repaying the loan in monthly instalments. Ram's agent came to Ghai's house on the first of every month at ten in the morning, where he found an envelope waiting for him. The agent used to give Ghai's example in the financier's office as a man who was punctual and reliable.

One day, Ram spoke to Ghai. 'Subhash, why don't you produce a film? I will support you.'

Ghai was wary of lending his name as producer. So, he spoke to his father-in-law, Akhtar Farooqui, who used to be Kamal Amrohi's production manager. Akhtar agreed to set up Mukta Films, after the name given to Rehana when she married Ghai.

They still needed someone to take on the cares of production. Ghai was reluctant to do that himself, lest he get distracted from his primary job of direction. He spoke to Jagjit Khurana, who was staying with him for a while during the making of *Gautam Govinda*. Khurana was a trained cameraman, but was not getting much work, and had decided to return to Jammu, his hometown.

'I don't think I can make it here in the industry,' he told Ghai.

Ghai felt for him and asked him if he could stay for another six months.

'What for?' Khurana asked.

'I might start my own production company,' said Ghai, 'and I would like you to join me.'

'I don't have any money. How will I last six months?'

Ghai asked Khurana how much his monthly expenses were. It turned out to be between ₹1,500 and ₹2,000. Ghai offered to give Khurana ₹2,000 every month while they made the initial preparations for the production company. After that, once they started their first film, Khurana would look after the production and draw a salary.

The stars were aligned. Ghai took the leap, and Mukta Films was launched on 24 October 1978.

Ghai's plunge into production was not driven by business considerations but by his desire to make the kind of film he wanted to make. For that, he needed complete control of every aspect of filmmaking: from the story, cast and schedule all the way to marketing, publicity and distribution.

9
Karz: The Debt

Although Ghai was not a Hollywood aficionado, he did watch the occasional English movie. *The Reincarnation of Peter Proud* (1975) was one such. Peter Proud is a college professor who has vivid dreams of a woman killing a man and is drawn to a place he has never visited. When he finally goes there, he meets the woman from his dreams who turns out to be his wife from his previous life, and falls in love with her daughter, who could be his daughter as well.

Ghai did not relate to much of the film. Everything seemed convoluted to him, especially the part about falling in love with the possible daughter. But the crux of the story stayed with him: a man is reincarnated in another body and meets people he knew in his previous life. Scenes from the film flashed in his mind as if he himself was getting visions from a past life. He caught himself wondering how it would be if he died and came back as another person after twenty-five years—to find his wife working as a housemaid. Shocked to the core by the direction his thoughts were taking, Ghai went to Ooty for a break.

Two weeks later, he came back with the story of *Karz*.

Ghai spent days over the title of his films, choosing one that would capture the story's marrow. It could be the central character's name, if the character towered above everything else. *Kalicharan* was all about, well, Kalicharan. The film belonged to him in every way. *Vishwanath* could have easily been named 'Adaalat', but that would not have been as appropriate as naming the film after the protagonist. Sometimes inspiration for the title came from the theme of the film. *Krodhi* was about the hero's defining characteristic, anger, and how he dealt with it.

The same went for the names of characters. Ghai made films for a wide audience hailing not only from the metros and cities, but also from the villages of India. So his heroines were Ganga, Radha and so on, and his heroes were Ram, Lakhan, Vishwanath, Govinda, etc. Ghai used to come up with eight to ten names for each character, and strike them off one by one while thinking of their characteristics, until he was left with the most appropriate name.

Choosing the title of a film is a skill Ghai says he learned from L.V. Prasad. 'He taught me that a title should be simple, full of meaning, and acceptable to families. He once told me a film's title should be such that a son or a daughter would not hesitate to say it to their father when stepping out for a show. It should not be, say, "Nangi Jawani", or some such,' he says.

Universal acceptance and appeal was critical. With the rise of multiplexes and small auditoriums, it is now possible to make a film for a specific segment of the audience, like a *Pink*, or a *Dear Zindagi*, or a *Piku*. Back in the 1970s and 1980s, single-screen cinemas used to sometimes accommodate a thousand people; films had to have something for everyone.

'The cinema we used to make was different. It drew entire families to the theatre. Our target age group was six to sixty,' Ghai reminisces. His film would be the complete Indian thali.

Karz, given the dominant role of music in its narrative, could easily have been called '*Saaz Ki Awaaz*' (The Sound of the Guitar). But *Karz* was more than just a musical. It was a story about unfinished business from a past life, a debt that had to be repaid. After Ravi Verma is murdered by his new bride, his mother says: 'Ravi had promised me that he will come home. He has to keep his promise. He has to repay the debt of his mother's milk.'

So *Karz* (The Debt) it was.

Ghai had watched *Peter Proud* only once. He did not want to make the same film. He took its core—the concept of rebirth and reincarnation—and wove his own plot, subplots and atmosphere around it.

As the director, he thought of himself as the film's auteur, who needed specialists for different functions, especially co-writers. 'Film writing is a specialized function. The scenes and dialogues have their own grammar, and must be economical. The reactions must be spot on,' he says.

One of the first people he spoke to about working on the film was Sachin Bhowmick. An industry veteran, Bhowmick had already written the screenplays for more than twenty films, including *Jaanwar* (1965), *Aradhana* (1969), *Khel Khel Mein* (1975), *Hum Kisise Kum Naheen* (1977) and *Gol Maal* (1979). Ghai found Bhowmick to be a joy to work with. They would go on to collaborate on six more films: *Karma*, *Saudagar*, *Taal*, *Kisna*, *Yuvvraaj* and *Black & White*.

For the dialogues, Ghai roped in Rahi Masoom Raza, the Urdu poet who later wrote the script and dialogues of the television serial, *Mahabharat*. Raza's writing was eloquent and poetic. Ghai wanted the dialogues to be simple, so he wrote many of the dialogues himself, but kept Raza's name as the dialogue writer in the credits. When Raza saw the film, he told journalists: 'Subhash has made a good film. The dialogues, good or bad, are his.'

Music is an integral part of any Hindi film—at least it was back then. Laxmikant–Pyarelal (L–P) had scored the music for *Gautam Govinda* and *Krodhi*, and the songs had been bigger hits than the films. Ghai was quite in love with their Indian sounds and notes. L–P liked Ghai because he treated them as integral to the filmmaking process. He would begin by narrating the story to them, just as he did for the actors, and had done for the producers of his previous films. Together they would look for song and music situations. Anand Bakshi, who wrote the lyrics for eleven of Ghai's hit films, joined for many of those sessions. The four of them used to chat all the time. If a song had twenty-five steps, Ghai would be involved in each, including when the flute would play and when the brass or drums kicked in.

Ghai wanted *Karz* to have an Indian soul, with family, prayers, gods and the victory of good over evil. But he also wanted it to be a modern film. Its protagonist, Monty, was a pop star, and the music had to reflect that. Some of Ghai's friends suggested he ask R.D. Burman to be the music director. Burman had brought new sounds and beats to Hindi film songs and created a new genre of music which was a mix of rock, jazz, electronic pop, folk and classical.

Once while having dinner with Pyarelal at his home, Ghai mentioned he was considering taking R.D. Burman for his next film. When the composer asked what he was making, Ghai told him the story of *Karz*. Pyarelal said it was imperative to get the right composer; however, he and Laxmikant would be up for the challenge.

Ghai met Laxmikant and told him about this conversation with Pyarelal. Where L–P's music was dominated by the sounds of the dholak, tabla, flute and sitar, Ghai wanted the guitar, drums and violin to take centre stage in *Karz*. The music had to be really new to Indian ears, on the lines of Western pop.

L–P loved the story of *Karz* and found several song situations in it. The first song situation they worked on was the scene where the hero sees the heroine at a party and falls in love. The song, which Anand Bakshi wrote and Mohd. Rafi sang, was '*Dard-e-dil, dard-e-jigar*'.

The first time Ghai heard the song as Laxmikant had composed it, he thought it was a ghazal. Ghai wondered how this could be the kind of song a pop star would sing. Pyarelal, a genius at orchestration, told him not to worry, and asked him to come to the recording studio the next afternoon. Recording had started at nine in the morning. When Ghai heard the song as orchestrated, it blew his mind. It sounded every bit as modern as he could have hoped; and it was perfect for the scene.

The film's soundtrack was a hit and the songs are still popular with Hindi film and music buffs. Many of the songs of *Karz* went on to become film titles in later years—a testament to their sustained popularity.

'*Om shanti om*', in particular, is a cult favourite. Ghai was certain that Kishore Kumar alone could do justice to it and infuse it with the energy it needed. But Kishore was proving hard to get. So Laxmikant, for the moment, recorded the song in his own voice.

Laxmikant, ace composer that he was, was also an outstanding vocalist, better than some of the known singers of his time. His voice touched hearts. When the song was played for guests at a dinner at Laxmikant's house, everyone said he had sung it brilliantly, which he indeed had. After a few days, Laxmikant told Ghai that he wanted to retain his own vocals for the song. He would record it afresh for a final take and there would be no need to chase after Kishore Kumar for dates.

Ghai was not so sure, but did not know how to handle the situation. Laxmikant was a stalwart of the industry and someone Ghai held in high regard. So, he went to the other half of the composer duo, Pyarelal, and told him about his dilemma. Pyarelal agreed that it was Kishore who had the right vocals for the song and said he would speak to Laxmikant about it.

Now, Ghai had to somehow get Kishore Kumar's dates to record the song. He went to the singer's house uninvited and told the person at the gate to inform Kishore Kumar he was there. Kishore was about to leave for a recording and asked Ghai to accompany him in his car. Ghai played the song in the car and requested the singer to record it the next day. Fortunately for him, Kishore agreed.

Kishore Kumar created magic with the song. Laxmikant had also sung it well, but the great singers—Kishore, Rafi, Mukesh—had voices that could hold a theatre packed with a thousand people spellbound.

'Not every good singer can be a good playback singer. For instance, few ghazal singers, although great in their own way, have been successful at playback singing,' says Ghai.

However, Laxmikant was not quite pleased with Ghai's insistence on having Kishore Kumar record the song, and they did not speak much for a year. At stage shows, Laxmikant would sing '*Om shanti om*' himself and closed the performances with it.

For the background score in *Karz*, Ghai wanted a theme that would play several times through the film. Of the options that L–P came up with, Ghai chose the one that was not the composers' first choice. But Ghai defended his decision saying there was a haunting quality to the tune which made it perfect for the film. In many ways, the pinnacle of *Karz*'s music is not any one song but the instrumental piece Monty plays on his guitar when he goes to meet Kamini in her palace. Gorakh Sharma, Pyarelal's brother, wielded the guitar for it.

Karz's opening song, '*Paisa ye paisa*', which introduces Monty the pop star, was the last to be filmed. Shooting these 'modern' pop songs was also a challenge for the self-confessed 'Hindi-medium' type from Delhi. Ghai did not know much about Western music or videos, but he was a fast learner.

During a vacation in London, he asked his host to get him a dozen videos of songs by American and British pop and rock stars. Disco was in fashion then. From those videos, Ghai understood what it took to make a music video the Western way.

Back in India, he told his cinematographer, Kamalakar Rao, to adorn the song with screams and cheering from the audience and use fast cuts and psychedelic lights. It was shot in Bhai Das Hall, in

Mumbai's Vile Parle. In the song, there is a place where a heavy voice says 'Paisaaa' in a loud and heavy voice. Ghai had told his unit to get a fat man to say it. He visualized it as a man sleeping in the auditorium who wakes up to the chant of 'Paisa'. When Ghai set up the cameras for the shot and asked for the fat man, his unit looked at him and said, 'Who better than you?' They had already planned this.

'That started the trend of my making fleeting appearances in my movies, usually in a song. My unit thought it brought good luck,' says Ghai.

Once Ghai had a grip over the story and music, he began looking around for actors.

The hero's first appearance on screen was as Ravi Verma. It was a small part—he is killed eight minutes into the film and makes only brief appearances later. In that short time, the actor had to endear himself to the viewers and make them feel bad about the injustice done to him so they would care about his vengeance. Raj Kiran, with his easy charm and winning smile, fit the bill.

For the hero's reincarnation, Monty, Sachin Bhowmick suggested Rishi Kapoor, who had played the singing-dancing hero in *Hum Kisise Kum Naheen*. Rishi Kapoor's many hits were interspersed with less memorable films. That held him back from becoming a star in the league of Dharmendra, Vinod Khanna and Rajesh Khanna.

That Rishi Kapoor was not the biggest star of the day worked in Ghai's favour. His own reputation as a hitmaker had taken a knock. Although he had established himself as a good director, he had not been able to replicate the highs of *Kalicharan* and *Vishwanath*. *Gautam Govinda* had run, but its budget had ballooned because of delays. The film's price to the distributors was high and it did not make much profit for them. *Krodhi* was progressing at a snail's pace and ended up releasing after *Karz*.

Fortunately, Rishi Kapoor liked the story and wanted to do the film.

For the heroine, Ghai wanted a new face. He had heard about Tina Munim, who was working with Dev Anand in *Des Pardes* (1978). This was one of Ghai's early attempts to work with absolute newcomers. Now that he had reached a position of relative success, he wanted to extend the ladder to others who needed it.

When Ghai first met Tina Munim, he found her to be a charming, uninhibited person, shorn of unnecessary formalities. She was not only friendly but also treated everyone around her as a friend and equal. Ghai wrote the heroine's character in the same mould as Munim's real-life personality. While shooting, he would tell her to simply be herself.

For the role of the villain, the one all the other villains deferred to in the film—Ghai uses the term 'chairman villain'—he went back to Premnath.

'I'm doing a new film,' he told Premnath. 'There is not much of a role in it for you, but you are doing it.'

'Really, not much of a role and I'm doing it?' Premnath asked sardonically.

'I will not pay you much either but I can promise you people will remember you for this film.'

'And what is this non-role you are making me do for not much money?'

'You play a man who cannot speak,' said Ghai.

'But I'm known for my dialogue delivery!' protested Premnath.

'True, but I want you to play a character no one has seen you do yet.'

'But how do I communicate?' Premnath asked.

'You communicate by knocking your fingers on the glass tumbler in your hand,' Ghai explained. 'I'll give you a sidekick who'll interpret your knocking for the others.'

Premnath loved the idea. The iconic Sir Judah was born.

As Bhowmick and Ghai progressed on the screenplay, the character of Kamini, the chief antagonist, shaped up as the most influential of all. Many in the industry who heard the story advised Ghai to cast Bindu, an established actress who was known for playing the vamp with aplomb. She was popular and, undoubtedly, capable.

Kamini, though, is more than a vamp. *Karz* is as much about her as it is about Ravi Verma and Monty. Hindi cinema had not seen a female character like her before—negative but unapologetic, without a sob story to justify her actions.

In one of her very first scenes in the film, Kamini witnesses a murder and does not flinch. Her brother describes her as a woman who loves many men. She wears a modern dress and smokes. She speaks directly to Sir Judah and agrees to a plan in which she marries Ravi and, within three days of the wedding, kills him. Later in the film, she emerges as the Rani Sahiba, a mature and attractive woman living in a magnificent old palace. Her accent and her frequent use of English in her speech suggest she is someone who considers herself a notch or two above the rest. There is a certain class, a certain sophistication to Kamini.

The more Ghai thought about Kamini, the more convinced he was that no one other than Simi Garewal could do justice to the role. An army child, she had spent her formative years in London. She had been acting since the early 1960s and played small roles in hit films: the schoolteacher whom the young Raj Kapoor, played by Rishi Kapoor, lusts after in *Mera Naam Joker* (1970), Amitabh Bachchan's love interest in *Namak Haraam* (1973), Vinod Khanna's in *Haath Ki Safai* (1973), and some others. She had created ripples with her role in *Siddhartha* (1972), based on Hermann Hesse's famous novel, but the film had gone unnoticed in India. Her talent was largely untapped, and her list of forgettable films was getting longer.

One day, Ghai went to a party hosted by Sohanlal Kanwar, whose film *Natak* he had acted in. Kanwar knew Simi Garewal. Ghai told him about *Karz* and Kamini's role in it and asked him what he thought of casting Garewal in the role.

'She is a great actress. You take her,' Kanwar replied.

Ghai took Garewal's phone number from Kanwar and set up an appointment with her. When they met, he narrated the story of *Karz* to her from the perspective of Kamini. He presented Kamini as a woman driven by ambition, one who carries the film's narrative forward, and makes things happen. Garewal liked the story but turned it down because she thought Ghai was offering her a vamp's role with a lot of spit and polish.

'I am a heroine,' she said. 'I will either play the female lead, or a role parallel to the lead.'

When Garewal remained adamant in her refusal, Ghai spoke to Rishi Kapoor. Apart from *Mera Naam Joker*, he and Garewal had also acted together in *Kabhi Kabhie* (1976). Ghai asked Kapoor if he could persuade her to play Kamini. That was not a wise move. Kapoor, with his effusive charm, seems to have told Garewal it was a good role and she should do it, but that it was indeed the role of a vamp.

Ghai started to make frequent visits to Garewal's apartment. He would arrive in the evening and nonchalantly stay till dinner. Most of the time, he would just beat about the bush before, eventually, steering the conversation to *Karz* and how good Kamini's role was. For those few minutes of Kamini-centric conversation, he would spend nearly three hours talking shop and trying to be funny. He would even tolerate the many cats in the house sniffing at his feet, even though he disliked cats.

'I had become obsessed with the idea of getting Simi ji to play Kamini,' says Ghai.

On one such visit to Garewal's house, her sister was also there. Ghai narrated the story of *Karz* to her and tried to convince her that it was the right role for the actress. He offered to pay any price they quoted. The sister said Simi would take the role, but on one condition. 'Will you give her the script beforehand?' she asked.

Ghai readily agreed. He could always change things during the shooting and justify them later as 'treatment' and the 'director's vision'.

He was confident Garewal would love the film and her role once she saw the final cut.

When shooting started, Garewal was passionate about the part. She had immense grace, maturity and sophistication—qualities that were necessary to play Kamini.

'While Simi ji was on the set,' Ghai recalls, 'the unit tended to speak more in English and less in the informal Punjabi-laden lingo we usually employed.'

Garewal was also sensitive. She could lose her temper if something went wrong. So could Ghai, and that was a volatile mixture. As the shooting rolled on, Ghai felt she was not putting her heart into the role, her acting did not have conviction.

'Subhash, I know I have accepted this role,' Simi said when he spoke to her. 'But the more we shoot, the more it appears to be the role of a vamp.'

Ghai reiterated that Kamini was a pivotal character: she was a shrewd antagonist with dignity and a regal presence. She was not going to do lowbrow songs. But Garewal was still uncomfortable. As a result, Ghai was having problems capturing shots. That filled him with despair. To him, the final shot mattered more than anything else, and he had to get it right no matter what it took: money, prayer or deceit.

Once, they were shooting late into the night. It was the last day of the set, which was to be dismantled the next morning. The unit was rushing to finish the scenes. One of the last scenes to be shot required Garewal to shout at her dead husband's mother and sister, asking why they were trying to kill her, and then tell them to get out of the house. This was one of Kamini's deceits. The mother and sister were innocent, and she, with her brother's help, was trying to get rid of them.

Anticipating trouble, Ghai had told his chief assistant to keep the dialogues of that scene for the last and tell Garewal she would get her lines on the set. The scene and accompanying dialogue were essential to the story. They showed the audience the depth of Kamini's treachery.

When Garewal came on the set, Ghai was talking to Durga Khote, a senior actress who had famously played Prince Salim's mother, Jodha Bai, in *Mughal-e-Azam* (1960). She was Ravi Verma's mother in *Karz*. After explaining the scene to Durga Khote, Ghai went to Garewal. She had received her lines and looked as if there was something building up inside her.

'I want to ask you something,' she began. 'You told me this was not the role of a vamp. But look at the lines you have given me and look at the whole scene. I am shouting at my dead husband's mother and sister, and my brother is abusing them and dragging them out of the house.'

'This is an important point in the story,' Ghai began patiently. 'I have told you about it. You throw them out after being provoked by your brother, and when your husband's reincarnation comes, he finds them working as maids in others' houses. That has a big impact on him and will affect the audience similarly. If you do not throw them out, the story will not move ahead.'

'Sorry,' Garewal said, 'I will not do this.'

Ghai's options were clear: give in or fight it out. He chose to fight. He could not let the story down.

Turning away from Garewal, he told the unit: 'Lights out!' Then he walked up to her and spoke with as much control over his voice as he could muster. 'Simi ji,' he said, 'you are getting ahead of the scene. Let's stay in the scene. This is what the story demands.'

She was quiet for a few minutes, deep in thought. Then she said, 'Okay, but you must change the lines.'

Ghai said he would change the lines, but their meaning would not change. This was the point in the story where Kamini's character had to look bad. Garewal was given new lines, and the cameras began to roll again. However, she was delivering her lines too softly, without the force needed to stir the audience's emotions. There was no anger in her voice, no venom, no fire. Ghai told her she had to shout, but she refused.

Ghai's patience ran out. Turning to his unit, he shouted: 'Pack up, I am shelving the film.'

It was midnight and there were over a hundred people on the set, but you could hear a pin drop. Ghai turned to Garewal, and said, 'Simi ji, there is a car waiting for you outside. The film is shelved. I will burn the negatives. I will not make this film if you are not going to put your heart into the role.'

'Seventy-five per cent of the film was complete. But, at that moment, I really was ready to shelve it,' says Ghai. 'I used to have fun on the sets, played pranks and cracked jokes. But I could also get angry. When I blew my top, I could blow the roof away.'

The unit called for a tea break and some of its members came to pacify Ghai. His chief assistant walked up to him and said, 'Sir, Durga Khote ji is calling you.'

Both Garewal and Durga Khote were in the former's make-up room. When Ghai entered, Durga Khote said in a gentle but firm voice, 'Subhash, calm down. You should not be shouting so much.' At that moment, she looked every bit like one of her on-screen characters admonishing her errant son.

'Durga ji, I'm sure you understand this,' Ghai said. 'This is an important scene. If I cannot get it the way the story needs it, what am I to do?'

He had barely finished speaking when Garewal screamed at him, 'But you were shouting so much … you threatened to shelve the film.' With that, she began to sob.

'What could I do?' Ghai said. 'You refused to listen to me.'

Durga Khote stepped in. 'Simi, I can tell you that Subhash is making a great film and you have a wonderful role in it,' she said. 'You will get a lot of appreciation and credit. Take my word for it.'

Grewal was still hesitant to deliver her lines as per the directions.

Ghai offered a compromise. 'It is close to midnight,' he said. 'We will not have this set for long. If Simi ji agrees, she should go ahead and deliver the lines the way I want them. Later, if she does not like the scene, I will cut it during the editing and reshoot it.'

'That is fair,' Durga Khote said. 'Subhash is the director, and he is a good one.'

Garewal got her make-up done, came back to the set, and delivered the lines exactly as Ghai wanted. Only, instead of telling the mother and sister to get out of the house, she said, '*Aap log ye kyon nahi kehte ki main aatm hatya kar loon? Mere khaane mein zeher daalkar meri jaan lena chahti ho tum? Meri jaan ke peechhe kyun pade ho tum log?* (Why don't you say that I should kill myself? You want to kill me by poisoning my food? Why do you want me dead?)' It was left to Kamini's brother to abuse Ravi Verma's mother and sister and throw them out.

When the first cut of *Karz* was ready, a special screening was organized for Garewal's family and friends—nearly forty of them—in a theatre. Ghai told his assistants to be ready to face trouble, that the actress would ask for reshoots and cuts.

The next day, when the unit was reshooting some parts, Garewal came to the set and asked to speak to Ghai.

'We saw the film,' she said. 'Since morning, I have been getting flowers and messages of congratulations. Sorry, I could not understand that you would present my role so well. Everyone said I was the highlight of the film.'

'Don't worry,' Ghai said. 'I have faced worse. I have worked with Shatrughan Sinha,' he laughed.

Simi Garewal won the Filmfare Best Supporting Actress award for *Karz*.

Rishi Kapoor was easy to work with. Charming and endearing, he was one of the best actors in the industry at the time, alongside Dilip Kumar, Amitabh Bachchan and Sanjeev Kumar. He was instinctive and reacted well to situations. Half his acting was done by his face, which was full of emotion.

On the actor's first day of shooting for *Karz*, Ghai decided to film the song '*Dard-e-dil, dard-e-jigar*'. He went to Kapoor's make-up room and played the song for him.

'Theek hai. Fine,' the actor said, slightly patronizingly.

'When songs became popular, the stars owned them, as if they had composed them and sung them as well. While shooting the song, though, they were often doubtful. They hardly ever called a song great during filming,' says Ghai.

When Kapoor arrived on the set to shoot the song, Ghai set up the camera and trolley.

'Where is the dance director?' asked Kapoor.

For every song, even sad ones, there had to be a dance director, who would tell the actor the movement, where to look, and how and where to walk.

'We don't need a dance director for this song,' Ghai said. 'You are singing and playing the violin, and the girl is watching you.'

Kapoor was doubtful. 'Yaar,' he said, 'do you have a sense of music and rhythm?'

He knew Ghai as someone who made crime dramas like *Kalicharan* and *Vishwanath*. How was he going to make a musical?

'Why don't we give it a shot?' Ghai suggested. 'Let's see how it goes.'

Probably because it was the first day of shooting, and he did not want to start on the wrong foot, Kapoor agreed to follow Ghai's instructions. The song would go on to become a rage across the country. Kapoor and Ghai became buddies, and remained friends till Kapoor's death in 2020.

'Rishi was a director's actor, and child-like. He would see something and immediately call it "fantastic". If someone pointed out that the thing was not so good, he would immediately change his opinion and call it "bloody shit". He could swing from one view to the next in less than sixty seconds. We both often laughed about this,' says Ghai.

Karz released on 27 June 1980. Although critics praised it, doubts lingered over its commercial success. It was not a flop, but nor was it a hit. Its box office collections were affected by *Qurbani* which had released just the previous week and became a blockbuster.

Karz failed to click with the masses. Some said it was doing well in the big cities, but in the smaller ones, people were getting confused. Apparently, they wanted to know why Rishi Kapoor was seeking vengeance when Raj Kiran was the one Simi Garewal had killed. Fed on a steady diet of double roles, viewers could not understand why the hero looked different when he came back for his second life.

A friend said, 'Subhash, you made this film ten years ahead of time. This film will get its due later.'

'What is the point?' said Ghai, dejected.

But the friend was right. *Karz* became the premier film of Mukta Arts, which Mukta Films morphed into with *Hero*. It was remade into Tamil as *Enakkul Oruvan* (1984), in Telugu as *Aatma Balam* (1985), and in Kannada as *Yuga Purusha* (1989). The Hindi remake came much later, in 2008.

This came about when Himesh Reshammiya, the music director for *36 China Town* (2006), a Mukta Arts production, approached Ghai. He wanted to remake *Karz* and play the hero in the remake.

Reshammiya brought in Bhushan Kumar of Super Cassettes as the producer, and Satish Kaushik as the director. They called the film *Karzzzz*.

Mukta Arts made more money by selling the rights for the Hindi remake than it had on the original. However, Ghai never saw the remake. 'I took the money and got out of their way,' he says.

There had already been an 'unofficial' remake in 2007: *Om Shanti Om*, which had more or less the same storyline as *Karz* (with a male rather than a female villain), and a climax inspired by *Madhumati* (1958). *Om Shanti Om* started with the iconic song from *Karz* being filmed with Rishi Kapoor on set, with Shah Rukh Khan's character

Om, a junior artist, in the audience. A young Ghai can be seen cheering on from beside the camera as the song is picturized.

Shah Rukh Khan told Ghai, with a touch of pride, 'Subhash ji, you will be glad that your *Karz* is being remade by us.'

Ghai chuckles. 'They were making a remake without buying the rights and meant it to be an honour to me. Not just that, Shah Rukh wanted me to make an appearance in the film.'

Shah Rukh Khan had, not too long ago, turned down a film Ghai had offered to him. Regardless, Ghai did make an appearance in *Om Shanti Om*, alongside Rishi Kapoor; they presented the Filmfare Best Actor award to Om Kapoor, Shah Rukh's second character in the film.

'Shah Rukh has so much charm he can get away with murder,' laughed Ghai.

10

Vidhaata: The Maker

After the success of *Kalicharan* and *Vishwanath*, several major stars reached out to Ghai. 'If you have a good script, come to me, we will work together,' they all said.

When Ghai tried to approach them after *Karz* and *Krodhi*, however, he discovered that they had become rather particular about personal hygiene. When he called them on the phone, many of them were reported to be in the bathroom. When he called back, after the approximate time a person is expected to take in the bathroom, they had already got dressed and left home.

Ghai would chuckle and ask sometimes if they left through the bathroom window.

He was not angry; he knew things would change. He had confidence in his abilities.

Distributor and financier Gulshan Rai was a stalwart among producers, with certified blockbusters like *Johny Mera Naam* (1970), *Deewar* (1975) and *Trishul* (1978) in his portfolio. In later years, he would go on to produce *Tridev* (1989) and *Mohra* (1994). Rai and Ghai met through Pawan Kumar. At the meeting in Rai's office, the producer said he liked Ghai's work and wanted him to direct a film for his banner. Ghai, who was still working on *Karz*, said he would start a new film only after this one was done. That was fine with Rai. 'Take your time,' he said, 'but consider yourself signed.'

When Ghai, staggering from his third consecutive fumble—*Krodhi* came after *Gautam Govinda* and *Karz*—failed to get Gulshan Rai on the phone, he landed up at the producer's office.

Rai received Ghai warmly but minced no words. 'Yaar, I know you are a good director,' he said, 'but you have been declared a flop. I make films with stars. If you can get stars to act with you, come to me.'

It was not going to be easy. The industry had, more or less, written Ghai off. The stars were not keen to talk to him. And Rai wouldn't work with newcomers.

'I need big stars,' he said.

'Who do you want?' Ghai asked.

'Amitabh Bachchan.'

Ghai had shied away from approaching Bachchan for *Krodhi*. But he thought he was in with a chance now. Rai's *Deewar* and *Trishul*, both directed by Yash Chopra, had Bachchan as the hero. The bond of two blockbusters between the producer and the hero should be strong enough to lead to a third film together, even if someone else was going to be in the director's chair.

Ghai landed up at Mohan Studio, where Bachchan was shooting. He was cordial. 'I have heard good things about *Karz*,' he said.

'It did not do well,' Ghai said.

'I heard that too.'

'Gulshan Rai has signed me up for a film. Will you work in it?'

'Subhash,' Bachchan said, 'I can work with you, but not with Gulshan ji.'

Ghai was startled. Bachchan explained that Gulshan ji said things about him in the media, something about his stars not being aligned well.

Ghai came away disappointed, but also armed with a tool to get even with Gulshan Rai.

'Amitabh is ready to work with me, but not with you,' he told Rai, 'because you made loose statements about him to the press.'

Rai confessed, 'Yaar, I know, I tell journalists all sorts of things.'

That evening, wondering whether his career had reached a dead end, Ghai asked himself what he was good at. The answer was: telling stories. Next day, he got up at five in the morning and started to write. After a few days of this daybreak writing, he completed a story. Then he called Rai and asked to see him again.

'If you do not like my idea, I won't bother you again,' Ghai said.

Rai was a generous and genial man. 'Sure, come over,' he said.

'Not your office,' said Ghai. 'I want to see you at your home and have a meal with you.' He was betting on the warmth that Rai's home always had in plenty.

When Ghai reached Rai's house for dinner, the producer took out a bottle. They drank some of the contents, which fuelled the conversation. Rai complained that the industry was in a bad shape, finances were drying up, and the censor board was playing spoilsport.

'You are such a big producer, you have given so many hits,' Ghai said. 'I don't think your films were hits because of the stars, it was because of the subjects you chose, the stories.'

Rai liked what he heard. 'Yes, people appreciate my story sense,' he said. 'I have counselled so many distributors and producers and they have all benefited from my advice.'

'In that case,' Ghai said, 'shouldn't we focus on the story?'

'Of course,' said Rai, 'the story is king.'

Ghai knew that was not entirely true, but decided to seize his chance. He narrated the story of *Vidhaata*—about the relationship between a man and his grandson whom he has raised since infancy. The grandfather, Shamsher Singh, forced by circumstances, is sucked into a world of crime which brings him into inevitable conflict with his upright and principled young grandson, Kunal.

Ghai-watchers can spot where the title came from. In *Karz*, Monty's mentor, G.G. Oberoi, played by Pinchoo Kapoor, is fond of saying, 'I am the maker.' Ghai translated this into 'Vidhaata'.

By this point, the dessert had arrived, but it lay untouched on the table.

Ghai's next gambit was crucial.

'Now, let me put together a star cast for you,' he said. His story was part of a clever ploy: it did not require a big hero, only a formidable old actor and a bright newcomer. 'The grandfather, Shamsher Singh, will be played by a big star who is now in his second innings. He does not do many films nowadays. Dilip Kumar. For the grandson, I want to get Sanjay Dutt. His father, Sunil Dutt, is making a film to launch him.'

Ghai had met Sanjay Dutt through Tina Munim. The young man was handsome and possessed a fair bit of acting potential.

Throughout the conversation, whenever Rai looked uncertain, Ghai reminded him that he was a big producer who valued the story more than anything else.

Eventually, Rai said, 'This is a great idea, we will make this film.'

They dug into the dessert.

The next day, Ghai phoned Rai to ask if he had indeed meant what he had said the night before. Rai confirmed his commitment. 'I told my wife about your story, she loves it,' he said. Many producers liked discussing projects with their wives. Perhaps it was a sound mechanism to test how families might react to a film.

With a force like Gulshan Rai backing him, Ghai went about his business. The first task was to approach Dilip Kumar and get him to agree.

Dilip Kumar was a legend. As a young boy in Old Delhi, Ghai would save every penny he could to buy tickets to Dilip Kumar's films. He was also a formidable personality. Suave and cultured, he spoke both English and Urdu with a felicity few in the industry could match. Although Ghai had been in the industry for several years now, he had never met the legendary actor and was in awe of him. But his career was at stake.

Ghai learned that Dilip Kumar was visiting Bangalore, where he was staying with R.N. Mandre, a big distributor, whose family continues to be prominent in the Kannada film industry. He begged Mandre for an audience with the actor.

'Come home,' Mandre told Ghai. 'I have told Dilip Sa'ab you are a good young director with an interesting subject. He will meet you.'

Ghai flew down to Bangalore and arrived at Mandre's home a bundle of nerves. The three of them talked of this and that, without touching upon the reason for Ghai's visit. Eventually, Ghai broached the subject and narrated his story.

'This is an interesting story,' Dilip Kumar said. 'Give it time, and work on it more. It has potential. Come back to me later.'

When Ghai was leaving, Mandre came to see him off at the door. 'He has shown interest, I think he will do the film,' said the distributor.

Back in Mumbai, Ghai got down to developing the story and characters further. The film could not just be about the old man and his grandson. He introduced another character, the old man's friend, Gurbaksh Singh, played by Shammi Kapoor, another leading hero who had turned to playing strong characters.

Shammi Kapoor heard the story and readily agreed to do the film. He was forthright about his reasons. 'I can see you have a good command over the screenplay. I will do it because of that, and because I'll get to work with Dilip Kumar.'

For the heroine, Ghai signed Padmini Kolhapure. She had played the female lead with aplomb in Raj Kapoor's *Prem Rog* (1982) and was perfect as the young, innocent girl with whom the grandson falls in love.

The chief anatagonist in *Vidhaata* was played by Amrish Puri. Ghai had first met him on the sets of *Vishwanath* when he came to meet his brother Madan Puri. When Ghai first saw Amrish, he thought of a ferocious face like a bulldog: big eyes, wide face, and a gruff growl for a voice. He exuded a certain force. So, when Ghai needed an actor to play a mafia don in *Krodhi* who could rival Dharmendra, he asked Madan Puri if his brother would be willing.

Madan was sceptical. 'He only works in art films and theatre, he detests commercial films,' he said. However, when Ghai met Amrish Puri and told him about the character, the latter immediately agreed to do the film.

'It was perhaps Amrish ji's first commercial outing. He had a small role [in *Krodhi*], but it left an impact,' says Ghai.

As Ghai developed the screenplay of *Vidhaata* further, a pivotal character emerged: Abu Baba, the Good Samaritan, who helps raise the grandson and infuses him with principles of honour and morality.

Ghai wanted Amjad Khan for the role of Abu Baba. The character was a principled man who was also physically strong and capable of action. Starting with *Sholay*, Khan had made a name for himself as a villain and then moved into more positive roles. In *Qurbani*, his Inspector Khan had been the scene stealer.

Ghai went to meet Khan at his residence. After greeting the visitor, Khan sat down on the carpet in his vast living room. Intimidated by his aura, Ghai, too, plonked down on the carpet, about six feet away from the actor. Khan was courteous and offered Ghai tea, but did not ask him to sit any closer. Ghai felt awkward, hesitant and small—like a subject in the presence of his king.

Eventually, Ghai took a deep breath and began to narrate the story of *Vidhaata* and the character of Abu Baba. He began with the scene where Abu Baba meets Shamsher Singh and tells him why he stopped being a flower seller.

It was the story of a young man who used to regularly buy flowers from Abu Baba. They used to talk. The young man bought flowers from Abu Baba for his wedding, and again when his son was born. One day, the young man came crying and asked to buy just one flower—his son had died. That broke Abu Baba's heart. He thought his flowers had cheated him, and he shut his shop.

It was a dramatic scene. When Ghai finished narrating it, Khan raised a regal hand and said, 'I do not need to hear any more. I will do the film.'

'That was extremely nice of him, but he was nice in the way kings granted favours to their subjects. But that did not concern me. I had worked with Shatrughan Sinha and Premnath; I could work with anybody,' says Ghai.

He sent Khan a cheque for ₹25,000 as the signing amount. He phoned Gulshan Rai to say Amjad Khan had agreed to join the cast that already had Dilip Kumar, Shammi Kapoor and Sanjay Dutt.

Rai was ecstatic. '*Package ban gaya* (The package is complete),' he said. That was when Ghai learned that a film's cast could also be seen as a 'package'.

The screenplay was now packed with dramatic scenes, many of them confrontations. Ghai roped in Kadar Khan to write the dialogues.

A month before shooting was to start, Ghai prepared Amjad Khan's look for Abu Baba. He got an artist to make a sketch and sent it through his chief assistant director, Kuku Khanna, to Amjad. Next, Ghai wanted Amjad to meet the wig maker, and sent his chief assistant to get a day and time from him.

Khanna came back in tears. He said he had just been shouted at by Khan.

It so happened that when Kuku Khanna went to meet Khan at Filmistaan studio, he was watching cricket on television with other actors in his make-up room. He told Khanna to wait. Khanna waited for an hour or so, then knocked on Khan's door again. The match was in full swing, and Khanna was asked to wait for some more time.

When Khanna knocked a third time, Khan lost his temper. He said something like, 'What kind of a man are you? Don't you sense the mood of the artiste?'

A teary-eyed Khanna said to Ghai, 'Sir, I do not want to work on this film. If I do it, I will not interact with Amjad Khan.'

Ghai pacified him, but felt horrible. This was no way to talk to anyone. He phoned Gulshan Rai and asked him whether the 'package' would be dented much without Amjad Khan.

'I think the film will get delayed if Amjad is in it,' Ghai added.

'If you do not want him, don't take him,' Rai said.

Ghai wrote a letter to Khan. 'Dear Amjad, I respect you a lot,' he wrote. 'You are a big star and a powerful actor. But somehow, I feel we should not work together on this film. I look forward to working with you on my next.' He sent the letter with a bouquet of flowers.

Amjad Khan did not speak to Ghai for two years after that.

'That was a stand I had to take. No one can say who was to blame. Amjad might have felt I should have shown more patience and spoken to him before taking this decision. Instead, I trusted my assistant director. In my view, Amjad had insulted not just the assistant director but also the director. If the director does not command respect, the project is doomed,' says Ghai.

Ghai went to Sanjeev Kumar and narrated the story and Abu Baba's role to him. He told him that Amjad Khan had been signed for the role, but was no longer doing it.

Ghai had reworked the character to suit Sanjeev Kumar's personality and image. When Khan was playing the role, Ghai had made it sensitive because his personality emanated force, but for Sanjeev Kumar, he had to put more action in the back story because the actor's personality was already soft and sensitive. In this new back story, Abu Baba was a policeman who had ended up killing a criminal and been dismissed from the force.

Now a milder, more social person, Abu Baba first appears on screen when Shamsher Singh is on the run from the police, and his grandson, Kunal, an infant, gets thrown out of the moving car. Abu Baba catches the infant. Shamsher Singh and Abu Baba get talking, and the former persuades Abu Baba to work for him and care for the child.

At the centre of Ghai's narration to Sanjeev Kumar was a scene of confrontation between Abu Baba and Shamsher Singh. The two quarrel over who has more rights on Kunal, and whether Abu Baba has a say in the young man's life. At the end of the scene, Abu Baba delivers powerful lines, saying that Shamsher Singh has become a rich man but not a big man, and, before he can dismiss Abu Baba from his service, Abu Baba dismisses him as his master.

'I will do the film,' said Sanjeev Kumar. 'I understand it's a small role. But I will do it for that one scene of confrontation. And I will charge my full rate.'

Initially, Ghai was uncertain about Sanjeev Kumar's approach to acting. For the all-important confrontation with Dilip Kumar, he had been asking for his lines, but Ghai could only give them at midnight. The shoot was the next morning. On the set, with the cameras about to roll, the actor looked distracted. He looked for his pack of cigarettes, asked for something to be brought from his car, bantered with his make-up man about strands of his fake beard—he did not seem focused.

However, the moment Ghai said 'Action', Sanjeev Kumar magically transformed into Abu Baba. Pouring out all his sorrow, disillusionment and pain before the cameras, he moved even the hardened unit members to tears. The shot was okayed in one take.

That was when Ghai realized that the actor had worked on the scene all night and was so well prepared and so confident of his abilities that he seemed unconcerned and unfocused on the set—until the cameras came to life.

Sanjeev Kumar is still remembered for playing Abu Baba. His confrontation scene with Dilip Kumar is film folklore. Of course, the legendary actor earned much fame and acclaim for his roles in *Sholay*, *Trishul*, *Aandhi* and many other films, but Abu Baba stands out because it was a small role that made a big impact.

And to think that he was not even Ghai's first choice for the role!

During the first three days of shooting with Shammi Kapoor, the actor had to be on the set without having much to do: just one or two shots a day, with a line here and a line there.

Miffed, he summoned Ghai one evening.

'Do I have any good scenes with any good lines?' he thundered. He had had a drink or two. 'I do not care about Dilip Kumar, I am a big star myself. You call me, shoot a small scene, and send me back. What is happening?'

His wife, standing behind where he sat, gestured to Ghai to let the storm pass. Ghai kept quiet. When Kapoor paused, Ghai said, 'Sir, it's not like that, I really respect you.'

'No, yaar, you will reduce me to a sidekick,' Kapoor said. 'Are you trying to prove that I do not matter next to Dilip Kumar?' What had probably added to his ire was that he and Dilip Kumar were not the best of friends in those days.

'I made a mistake,' reflects Ghai. 'I should have shot at least one long scene with Shammi ji on the very first day.'

It's what he did for the remainder of the shoot. He started filming long scenes with plenty of lines for Kapoor. He also featured the actor in a couple of songs, including the saucy and controversial '*Saat saheliyan khadi khadi*', about seven women singing of the kind of nights they have with their husbands. Very soon tempers cooled and good humour was restored on the sets.

Shammi Kapoor won the Filmfare Best Supporting Actor award for his performance in *Vidhaata*.

There could not have been any acting awards for Sanjay Dutt for playing Kunal, Shamsher Singh's grandson. He was too raw back then. He caused the unit some inconvenience as well. When they were shooting in Agra, he used to go to Delhi nearly every day to meet his friends, which made it difficult for him to wake up on time for the next morning's shoot.

Dutt, who was born to star parents, perhaps did not think of film stardom as a big deal. He came across as someone who did not care much about being an actor. Maybe he was nudged into the profession by his father. Ghai was careful not to expose the young man's limitations before formidable actors such as Dilip Kumar, Shammi Kapoor and Sanjeev Kumar, but he could succeed only to a certain extent.

Dutt needed to emote uninhibitedly in many scenes in the film. One of these was when Abu Baba dies. Kunal had never seen his parents. His grandfather was always busy looking after his business affairs. Abu Baba was the one true parent he had known; and now he was dead.

Ghai needed Dutt to howl like a wounded wild animal. Just before the scene was to be shot, Ghai took the young man aside and spoke to him in a soft whisper. 'Abu Baba is the one who brought you up. He was your mother as well as father,' he said. 'I remember when Nargis ji died. I was at the funeral. I remember how you cried. We will shoot this scene only once. Just do what comes naturally to you.'

Then, Ghai quickly turned to the unit and said, 'Start sound. Camera. Action.'

It was well known that Sanjay loved his mother, Nargis, dearly and her death had thrown his life in disarray. Once the cameras started, he moved totally into the character of someone who had lost a parent and gave one of the finest shots of his career.

When Ghai first told his friends he was directing Dilip Kumar, their reaction was more concern than joy. They thought his days as director were over, that Dilip Kumar would take matters into his own hands, change the script, direct the film and turn it into something completely different from how Ghai had visualized it.

Naturally, then, when Dilip Kumar suggested they go to Khandala, near Mumbai, to discuss the script and scenes, Ghai was worried. They spent three days there, chatting about inconsequential things for the most part. But for a couple of hours each day, they discussed the script.

As Ghai narrated the scenes, Dilip Kumar suggested things to add, what more he could do, and so on. He said that Sanjeev Kumar's and Shammi Kapoor's characters had immense dramatic possibilities and ought to be given more prominence, at times by subduing his own part.

It was the first time Ghai was seeing an actor asking for more play to characters other than his own. This gave him hope and courage. As he and Dilip Kumar sipped on their tea one evening, Ghai began nervously: 'Sir, I want to say something. You are too big a person for me. I have been your fan since I was running around in shorts. I am intimidated by you. People say you direct the director. Let us be clear. Who will direct this film, you or me?'

Dilip Kumar stopped sipping his tea, pointed a finger at Ghai, and said, 'You.'

'Are you sure?' Ghai asked.

'Yes, you will direct this film,' Dilip Kumar said, and chuckled. 'I enjoy this reputation I have. But I know you are in control of the script. I have worked with directors who were not, so I had to contribute.'

He was true to his word. Ghai directed him like any other actor.

Once, while shooting in Goa, the sun was about to set and Ghai needed more shots with Dilip Kumar in that location and in that light. Naturally, he became brisk, telling the actor to look this way and that, and speak a line here and a line there while the cameras rolled.

Dilip Kumar did as he was told but was not happy about it. 'I do not work like this. You have to give me time. Do not tell me where to look and when to smile,' he said.

Ghai promptly apologized, saying he had done it only because the light was fading rapidly.

Later, at dinner, Madan Puri, who had worked with Ghai earlier, told Dilip Kumar, 'I have worked with Subhash. Leave these things to him. When you see the film, you will realize how well he uses these shots.'

Dilip Kumar calmed down. He must have liked working with Ghai on *Vidhaata*. A few years later he agreed to do *Karma* with Ghai. They would also work together again on *Saudagar*.

Working with Dilip Kumar was a career-defining, life-changing experience for Ghai. He was not merely an actor, but also had a keen understanding of the story and characterization, and he understood the environment of the industry.

'He taught me how to live and breathe films,' says Ghai.

Once, when Ghai and his unit were shooting in a remote area in Goa, Dilip Kumar flew in from Mumbai to join the unit. The production manager reached the airport late. Dilip Kumar took a taxi and reached the shooting venue all by himself.

Ghai was embarrassed and apologetic. But Dilip Kumar told him, 'These are production hazards. Such things happen. Do not worry about me, you focus on the shot.'

Ghai was amazed. 'Even small-time actors threw tantrums. But here was Dilip Kumar, the legend, being a part of the unit in glitches as much as in glory.'

On the last day of an outdoor schedule, Ghai was shooting a confrontation between Shamsher Singh and his grandson, in which Kunal leaves his grandfather and his home. Dilip Kumar had to deliver two pages of dialogue. Actors usually gave two to four takes, six at the most; Dilip Kumar gave thirty-two. Ghai finally okayed it on the thirty-second take.

After Ghai called for pack-up, Dilip Kumar summoned him to his room. 'I have never asked for anything from you, until now,' he told Ghai. 'Can we do one more take?'

Ghai had worked with actors who did not want to give more than two takes, even if they had not been very good, because they had to be elsewhere. They would leave things to be fixed during editing. Once more, he found himself in awe of Dilip Kumar's dedication and passion.

Even though the unit members were leaving for Mumbai early the next morning, Ghai got his production manager to arrange an hour's shoot with a skeletal crew. The cameras were mounted once again, the lights were set up, the cables were plugged in. Dilip Kumar gave a brilliant shot this time, far better than the thirty-two takes he had done the previous evening. It was perfect.

During editing, Dilip Kumar's scenes used to present the biggest, happiest, most delicious headaches for Ghai, as he pulled his hair out while having to choose the best take out of many fantastic ones.

Once Ghai gave him the final scene, complete with dialogues, Dilip Kumar would go over the scene several times—not just his own lines, but also those spoken by other characters, so he could work on his reaction. Then he would write the whole scene on paper in his own handwriting, in Urdu.

When the time came to shoot, he would be outstanding in every take, but different in each. If a scene had five takes, Dilip Kumar would deliver his lines in five different ways, changing the tone and emphasis and sometimes also a word here and there.

'Dilip Sa'ab never compromised on the quality of his work. He was extremely concerned that he must give 100 per cent in every scene,' says Ghai.

Vidhaata was released in December 1982 and became a huge hit. Its success was the push Ghai needed. He bought his first house, in Cliff Tower, Bandra, where he and Rehana still live with their younger daughter, Muskaan.

Once the film was declared a hit, people started to pop out of their bathrooms to speak to him and urge him to 'forget our problems'. But Ghai was now in two minds. Was he again going to leave the fate of his films in the hands of stars? He watched animation films and marvelled at how they could entertain viewers without having any actors. They confirmed his view that a film was the director's medium, and what mattered the most was content: story, screenplay, dialogues and characterization. How else could animation make you laugh, cry and clap?

Ghai was not able to speak to Dilip Kumar until three days after *Vidhaata*'s release.

'*Mubarak ho*,' said Ghai when they finally connected, 'your film is a hit. Gulshan Rai is delighted.'

'Yes, I heard,' Dilip Kumar said. 'Let us thank God that we avoided a flop. We did the best we could. Think of it this way: the film might have failed, but it has passed. Now, make sure the next one is better.'

Ghai's next film was *Hero*.

11

Hero: A Musical Odyssey

When Ghai was making *Vidhaata*, he also looked after the finances and other aspects of production.

'I am not a production guy,' Rai had said. He attached his accountant and cheque book to Ghai and left the rest to him. All he wanted was for Ghai to make a good film on time and within budget and give him an amount equal to the profit of one of the seven distribution territories. If Ghai could do that, Rai said he would support Ghai in starting his own production house.

This Ghai did. Mukta Films, which had produced *Karz*, was a sort of partnership between Ghai, his father-in-law Akhtar Farooqui, and Jagjit Khurana, his friend from FTII, with the latter two getting credited as producers. Ghai was credited only as the director for *Karz*.

For his next production, *Hero*, Ghai formed Mukta Arts as a private limited company, for more transparency. He named his wife Mukta and his father K.D. Ghai as the executive producers, and finally dropped his qualms and agreed to be named the producer. *Hero* became the first film to say 'Written, Produced and Directed by Subhash Ghai' in the opening credits.

Hero brought Ghai back together with Laxmikant–Pyarelal (Kalyanji–Anandji had scored the music for *Vidhaata*). And it became the first Ghai film to have all its songs choreographed by Saroj Khan, who had done one song for *Vidhaata*.

For Mukta Arts' first outing, Ghai decided to make a musical. He wrote a story and named it 'Sangeet'. It was about a destitute musician who goes door to door, repairing musical instruments. He falls in love, but sacrifices his love for his sister, who is about to get married.

Ek Duuje Ke Liye (1981), produced by L.V. Prasad and directed by K. Balachander, was about to release. Gulshan Rai, who was one of its distributors, told Ghai about the immensely talented lead pair, Kamal Haasan and Rati Agnihotri, and organized a trial show of the film for him.

Ghai loved the film, and, unlike Rai, thought it was a certain hit. Rai was less sure of its prospects. The people he had spoken to expected the film to flop because of its sad ending.

Ghai was struck by the performance of Kamal Haasan, who, until then, was only known as a South Indian star based in Chennai. He decided to cast him as the destitute musician in 'Sangeet' and approached him. Haasan had seen *Karz* and readily agreed to work with Ghai. 'In the south, we have a lot of respect for directors such as you,' he said.

Rati Agnihotri, while lovely and talented, did not suit the idea of the heroine Ghai had in mind. He signed Jaya Prada, who had delivered a big musical hit with *Sargam* (1979) and established herself as a dancing star with acting skills to boot.

Now that he had signed the lead pair, Ghai spent the next four months working on the story of 'Sangeet'. He and Kamal Haasan would meet whenever the actor happened to be in Mumbai, usually at Ghai's home. Kamal Haasan was full of story ideas himself and, during these meetings, they would end up discussing many stories, not just that of 'Sangeet'. They agreed to start shooting in three months.

Meanwhile, *Ek Duuje Ke Liye* released and became a blockbuster, propelling the lead pair to nationwide fame and acclaim. On Kamal Haasan's next visit to Mumbai, when Ghai went to meet him in his hotel, he found a gaggle of producers in the lobby, waiting for their turn to meet the new sensation. Ghai gathered from the conversations around him that they were willing to offer Kamal Haasan five to six times what he was planning to pay him for 'Sangeet'. When he finally met Kamal Haasan, he found the actor to be in an ebullient mood. He had already signed a few Hindi films and his schedule was getting packed.

'He was flying high,' says Ghai. 'It was like a Hindi film star had hit the big time in Hollywood. His photos were everywhere, with predictions of a bright future.'

Kamal Haasan suggested that they should look to start shooting for 'Sangeet' after six months or so. Balachander, who had directed *Ek Duuje Ke Liye*, was making another film and it would be a priority for Kamal Haasan because Balachander was like a mentor to him.

Ghai agreed and came away. However, the starting date for 'Sangeet' kept shifting. There was always some other project that took precedence. Losing patience, Ghai spoke to Kamal Haasan's secretary and asked him what the problem was. The secretary explained that Kamal Haasan had signed too many films and suggested that Ghai should start his film after six months.

Ghai penned a letter to Kamal Haasan to say he was shelving 'Sangeet'. 'It will be better for the two of us to work together when we have more time,' he wrote.

He had written 'Sangeet' visualizing Kamal Haasan as the lead actor and could not imagine anyone else playing it.

'This happened to me at times. I would write a character with a particular actor in mind and wouldn't be able to think of anyone else,' says Ghai. It did not come easily to him to drop an actor and replace them with someone else. When he did, he rewrote the character.

'I had written the character of Vikrant Kapoor in *Taal* with Govinda in mind. When I had to replace him with Anil, I reshaped the character. Anil did not have a musical body, so I changed Vikrant from a dancer to a music conductor,' says Ghai.

Once 'Sangeet' was shelved, Ghai began working out the details of his next project. This one was about two young men, both musicians, who become jealous of each other and become rivals.

R.D. Burman, with whom Ghai had planned to collaborate on 'Sangeet', told Ghai about Kumar Gaurav, a young actor with potential. His father, Rajendra Kumar, who was known as Jubilee Kumar after giving a string of hits in the 1960s, was launching Kumar Gaurav in a home production called *Love Story* (1981). Burman had scored the music for the film, which was ready for release.

Ghai told Burman that he had a subject that needed two heroes. He could ask Sanjay Dutt if Burman could get Kumar Gaurav. Burman arranged a meeting between Ghai and Kumar Gaurav. By the time they met, *Love Story* had released, created a mass frenzy, and made Kumar Gaurav the new sensation.

'He had the glow of a new star, lustre in his hair, a shine on his face, a certain style to his movements and the way he sat. It was like his body had got choreographed. I liked him,' says Ghai.

Ghai told him the story of the two musicians. Kumar Gaurav liked it. Still recovering from his experience with Kamal Haasan, Ghai thought it best to make matters clear. 'I know your first film is a hit,' he said, 'but you have worked in only one film so far. Sanju [Sanjay Dutt] has done two films, one of them with me. I am signing both of you thinking of you as newcomers. I do not plan to work with stars.'

Kumar Gaurav said he was keen to work with Ghai.

The next day, Rajendra Kumar phoned to say he was glad Ghai had met Kumar Gaurav and wanted to work with him. 'Why don't you come over and meet me?' he suggested. When Ghai went to Rajendra Kumar's office, the latter was full of praise for him. 'You are a good director, I have seen your films. You should get an even better writer. Do not hesitate to spend on the project.'

'It was an odd thing for him to say, but I was used to hearing odd things from people. I took it in my stride, and dismissed it with "*Haan ji, haan ji* (Okay, okay)",' says Ghai.

A few weeks later, Rajendra Kumar's secretary came to meet Ghai in Hotel Sun & Sand, where Ghai had taken up a room to work on the subject. After pleasantries, the secretary asked how long it would take to start the film. Ghai said it would take six months or so to finish writing and shooting would begin after that. The secretary said Kumar Gaurav's market rate was ₹12 lakh, but as he admired Ghai as a director, he would charge him a couple of lakhs less.

This took Ghai by surprise; ₹10 lakh was the market rate of established stars such as Dharmendra and Jeetendra.

Ghai phoned Burman and said he did not want to make the film. 'I smell trouble, I will not be able to make a good film,' he said. 'I have escaped the web of stars with difficulty and do not want to get caught in it again.'

A surprised Burman said he would talk to Kumar Gaurav. But Ghai did not hear back from him on the subject. That was the end of that project.

Ghai was not angry with either Kamal Haasan or Kumar Gaurav. Both were in demand and were making what they believed were the right decisions for their careers. His reason for shelving the two projects was simple: he did not want his lead actor to be distracted by producers offering astronomical prices. If that were to happen, the schedule of his film would suffer, and he would not be able to make the kind of film he wanted to make.

Other stars wanted to act with Ghai, including those who had abandoned him earlier. 'Let me know when you have a good script,' they would say, or, 'When are you narrating a good script to me?'

'Stars know when to be sweet to you. I was used to it by now,' says Ghai.

Ghai turned his feelings of anger and frustration towards a new project: *Hero*. The story was about a criminal who kidnaps the daughter of a police officer. He can wield weapons as deftly as the flute and is aptly named Jaikishen. The young lady, Radha, calls him Kishen, one of Lord Krishna's names. Kishen falls in love with Radha, who helps him give up his life of crime. Then, when Radha gets into trouble with other gangsters, Kishen rescues her.

Once Ghai conceptualized the flute as part of the story, he knew he wanted none other than L–P to compose the music. Their music was rooted in Indian sounds and instruments, and they often worked with Hari Prasad Chaurasia, the world's best flautist.

Ghai and L–P had quarrelled after *Karz*, paving the way for Kalyanji–Anandji to do the music for *Vidhaata*. Kalyanji–Anandji had also bailed Ghai out by scoring the background music of *Krodhi*, which released soon after *Karz*, though L–P had composed its songs. But Ghai knew the foundation of his relationship with L–P was strong, rooted as it was in mutual respect and fondness. Someone just had to break the ice.

That 'someone' was Dilip Malavankar, a close friend of Ghai's and Pyarelal's wife's sister's husband. Ghai narrated the story of *Hero* to him, and asked who, in his opinion, should be the music director. Malavankar was no fool. He immediately knew what Ghai wanted him to do. He said only L–P could do justice to this story, and promised to arrange matters so Ghai could discuss the project with them.

When Ghai finally met L–P, the ice simply melted away. Ghai felt he was back on home turf, discussing the story, song situations and music with L–P and Anand Bakshi.

'I always liked discussing my films with them,' says Ghai. 'They were not just song and music stalwarts, they had a deep understanding of Hindi cinema and the Indian ethos.'

L–P were also happy with this reunion. It was a sort of lean period for them as several of the hit albums of the early 1980s—nearly all the hit films of Jeetendra–Sridevi—were composed by Bappi Lahiri.

Together, the four of them—Ghai, Bakshi and L–P—set out to make the 'musical love story of a criminal'.

The guitar theme in *Karz* had not been Pyarelal's first choice. He and Ghai had debated it endlessly before going with Ghai's pick. However, when it came to choosing the flute theme in *Hero*, Ghai loved the very first tune Pyarelal hummed for him. Once developed and refined, it was left to Hari Prasad Chaurasia to do justice to the melody. Flautist and composer worked on the tune for hours, then they called Ghai in.

Chaurasia opened a box that had fifty or sixty flutes of varying thickness and length. He wanted Ghai to choose one. A clueless Ghai left the choice to Chaurasia, who told him to come back after a couple of hours or so.

Ghai wondered why Chaurasia needed so much time; the tune had already been finalized and only had to be rendered on the flute. When he came back and Chaurasia played the tune for him, it blew his mind. The melody was so perfect it gave him goosebumps. He had not heard anything like it before. He quickly reopened the script to make room for the tune in as many places as possible, apart from the songs.

Ghai, L–P and Bakshi used to classify songs as those that were music-led and lyrics-led. For instance, the song '*Pyar karne wale kabhi darte nahi*' was lyrics-led. This is the first time Radha, performing on stage, openly declares her love for Jaikishen while her father watches in the audience. Ghai told Bakshi it was a situation similar to the one in *Mughal-e-Azam*, when Anarkali sings '*Jab pyaar kiya to darna kya*' while Akbar watches.

As usual, Ghai wanted the film's songs to take the narrative forward. He disliked how movie songs usually stalled the story and gave the viewers a chance to take a smoking or loo break. He wanted his audience to stay riveted when the songs came on screen. This approach helped him deal with the parts where Radha becomes friendly with Jaikishen's entire gang.

Initially, Ghai had written this part as a sequence of scenes in which they do things together—cooking, eating, cleaning, playing games—in and around the cottage where the gang is keeping Radha hostage after convincing her that she is, in fact, in protective custody. When the sequence turned out to be too long, Ghai turned it into a montage song showing snapshots of the developing friendships as the group moves from place to place while being chased by the police. The result was the extremely popular 'Ding dong, O baby sing a song', where Ghai makes his customary appearance, this time as a disgruntled fellow whose car has broken down.

Just like the song '*Ek haseena thi*' had dominated the climax of *Karz* and '*Pyaar ka imtehaan*' was the centrepiece of *Vidhaata*'s climax, Ghai once again chose to have the final scenes in *Hero* dominated by a song. There were the fights, of course, but the song '*Mohabbat ye mohabbat*' was the highlight. For this, Anand Bakshi came up with eight words to describe love—qayamat, nazakat, shararat, shiqayat, sharafat, adawat, inayat and ibadat—all of them containing the same number of syllables.

Saroj Khan had choreographed '*Pyaar ka imtehaan*' for *Vidhaata*. She had been recommended by Aruna Irani. When Ghai first met Saroj Khan, he saw a small and simple young girl. He told her that the song was going to be a challenge because it was a vigorous number filmed on Sarika, who, though a fine actress, was not the nimblest of dancers. Saroj Khan did such a good job that Ghai asked her to choreograph all the songs of *Hero*, and of many of his future movies as well.

'My heroines were all beautiful and good dancers. However, none of them could really match Saroj. When Saroj danced, the entire unit watched only her,' says Ghai.

The protagonist of *Hero* was a goon and a criminal. So, he had to look like one. Since Ghai had decided not to work with established stars, he auditioned several young and aspiring actors but was not too impressed with any of them.

One day, Ashok Khanna, brother of Kuku Khanna, Ghai's chief assistant director, told him about a friend who had just started modelling. He gave Ghai a magazine in which the young man had appeared in an advertisement for a brand of cigarettes. He had a soft, smooth and chiselled face. Ghai told Khanna to bring him over for a meeting.

The model, Jackie Shroff, came to meet Ghai at his home the following Sunday, in the evening. Shroff turned out to be tall and lean, perfect for modelling. But he was nervous. His hands trembled slightly when he shook hands with Ghai.

Ghai asked him what he thought of acting. Shroff spoke in the language of Mumbai's streets: '*Sir, apun kiya nahi kabhi* (I have never acted).'

What about dancing, asked Ghai.

'*Sir, abhi dance kaise karega* (How can I dance now)?'

Had he done any plays, asked Ghai.

'*Koi chance nahi, sir. Apun udhar ek chawl mein rehta hai. Ek motorbike hai apne paas.* (None. I live in a community housing colony. I have a motorcycle.)'

When Shroff was talking, he looked interesting, very watchable. Many shades of emotions crisscrossed his face and his honesty was touching. Ghai asked him if he could do a small scene. He only had to read some lines in front of a camera.

'Sir, I am not an actor. You give me this scene and give me a couple of days. I will memorize this and come back.'

Ghai told him to forget about the scene and any performance. 'Let's just talk,' he told Shroff, and, unbeknownst to the young man, reached out behind his sofa and flicked on the switch of a hidden video recorder.

They talked about Shroff's chawl and his family, how they lived in a small place that was pretty much just a room and a bathroom. He talked about his brother, who had drowned in the sea while trying to save a girl. Shroff narrated the story with pain and a deep sense of loss.

Ghai asked questions that would make his expression change.

'Do you flirt with girls?' he asked.

Shroff blushed and said, 'I have a girlfriend.'

'Will she beat you up if you flirted with other girls?' Ghai asked.

Shroff chuckled.

The evening ended with Ghai asking Shroff to come to the Mukta Arts office the next day.

After Shroff left, Ghai picked up the magazine with the cigarette advertisement. He took a pencil and got to work on the smooth, chiselled face, covering parts of it with a wispy moustache and a scraggly beard. He made the eyebrows thicker and added a few lines here and there. Slowly, a face emerged that was just as handsome as the original but had more character—it was the face of a man who had struggled through life.

Around eight in the evening, Ghai called Ram Kelkar, his screenplay writer, and Kuku Khanna over to his house. He played the video recording for them on his television. They were accustomed to seeing actors perform scenes for their auditions and wondered why Ghai was showing them a man having a general conversation. They were nonplussed when Ghai told them the fellow on the screen was perfect to play Jaikishen. 'He is not an actor,' Ghai told them. 'But, when he talks, his entire face speaks.' They would have to train him, but that was up to the writers and the director.

Although they were uncertain, Kelkar and Khanna agreed to see how it went.

Shroff came to the Mukta Arts office at noon the next day. Ghai told him the story of *Hero* and offered him the lead role.

Shroff could not believe what he was hearing. 'Are you sure, sir?' he asked.

'Yes, I have thought about it,' said Ghai.

Shroff nodded and said, 'Fine, if you are sure.'

He got up and said goodbye. At the door, he hesitated and came back to Ghai's desk. 'There is something I have not told you,' he said. 'Dev Anand Sa'ab is making a film, *Swami Dada*. I play Shakti Kapoor's sidekick in it. It is a really small role.'

Ghai asked him if he had shot any scenes for it. He had, just one scene. Ghai told him not to worry. 'I'll speak to Dev Sa'ab and see if he can delete this one scene,' he said. 'If he cannot, we will still manage.'

'It is my duty to tell you, sir,' Shroff said. Once again, his honesty and truthfulness shone through.

During his search for someone to play the unbesmirched Radha, Ghai heard some good things about a new girl who was playing the heroine in *Painter Babu* (1983), the film Manoj Kumar was making to launch his brother, Rajiv Goswami, as a hero. Ghai phoned Manoj Kumar and asked to see a few reels of the film, which was still in the making.

Ghai was quite shocked by what he saw. Meenakshi Seshadri, the heroine, was wearing a tiny, bright red two-piece dress and dancing in the snow. Her moves were neither refined nor subtle. She was a far cry from *Hero*'s Radha, who was a demure girl and the darling of her large, traditional family. Ghai decided to continue his search for the right girl.

A few days later, Seshadri called the Mukta Arts office. She had heard about Ghai seeing a few reels of *Painter Babu* and wanted to meet him. Ghai did not want to turn her away and agreed to a meeting.

In person, Seshadri looked nothing like the girl in *Painter Babu*'s footage. She came with her mother and was dressed in a simple salwar-kameez with a chunni. Her hair was done in a simple manner with no frills. The picture she presented was so serene and radiant that Ghai was taken aback. He could only say, 'Well, you look different.'

'You saw me in the get-up I was given,' said Seshadri. 'I was merely doing what I was told to do. It is my first film.'

Ghai cast her without hesitation.

Painter Babu released, and flopped. The film did not fetch Seshadri many positive reviews, and people wondered why Ghai was working with her.

'Wait and watch,' Ghai told them. 'You might be surprised.'

In his new look with a beard and moustache, Shroff looked perfect for the part. When Ghai began shooting with him, they shot only action scenes and parts of a song in the first four to five days. Fight scenes do not require much acting and would have helped Shroff get used to facing the camera. He did not have to act much in the song, either—only lip sync and some body movements, no real dance steps for him.

One of the first scenes to be shot was when Billa, a goon played by Manik Irani, comes to disrupt the wedding of a Bengali school teacher. Jaikishen (Shroff) who runs a vehicle repair workshop and is also the local strongman, has made a promise to the teacher that there will be no disruption. He ties a string across the gate and challenges Billa to cross it. Then he beats Billa to a pulp.

Shroff looked stiff doing the action scene. He became self-conscious and tense the moment he saw the camera, and it showed on his face. But Ghai was not worried. He had the storyboard clear in his mind.

He would simply take small shots and string them together at the editing table to create homogenous scenes.

On the eighth or ninth day of shooting, cinematographer Kamalakar Rao and Kuku Khanna spoke to Ghai. It was a good story and a prestigious project, they said, which had to be saved from its hero. Ghai agreed that Shroff was raw and the rest of the crew had to work twice as hard to cover for his lack of finesse as an actor, but there was no way he was going to change the hero. That would have signalled to the financiers and distributors that Ghai had lost confidence in his project. Besides, he was determined to stand by the commitment he had made to Shroff; chucking him out of the film would have been the end of his career.

It was also a matter of ego: Ghai was out to prove that he could make a hit film with absolute newcomers who were not the finest of actors.

Soon, Saroj Khan was echoing Rao's and Khanna's sentiments. While they were filming the title song '*Tu mera jaanu hai*', Saroj complained to Ghai. 'Who have you got to play the hero? If you get such heroes, how can we go on?'

Ghai tried to make the best of Shroff's awkwardness by turning it into cuteness. He micro-directed every scene and every moment Shroff appeared before the camera. While shooting the title song, in which Shroff was to hold a garland of leaves, Ghai told him: 'Hold this garland like this, now look through it … now do cartwheels … fall...'

He also taught Shroff, who did not have a deep sense of music, to hold the flute the right way and sway his head to a count.

To be fair to Ghai's team members—Rao, Khanna, Khan—they were not the only ones sceptical about Shroff. Producer Gulshan Rai was as well.

Hero's mahurat (ceremonial inaugural shot) was a grand affair. Before then, mahurats used to be on the shooting floor: a guest would give the clap, the hero or heroine (typically the hero) would come and speak a few lines before the camera, sweets would be distributed, and that was that. For *Hero*'s mahurat a special stage was created. The ceremony began with the unveiling of the Mukta Arts logo—arc lights with headphones—to the chant of the Gayatri mantra.

'I had worked hard on the logo and wanted it to be one that'll last a lifetime. Light and sound will always be around, that's why the arc light and headphones,' says Ghai.

Once the logo had been unveiled, Shroff and Seshadri were presented on stage as a song played in the background.

Gulshan Rai, encouraged by *Vidhaata*'s success, was financing *Hero* and also distributing it in the large territories of Mumbai and overseas. After the ceremony ended, he spoke to Ghai.

'Yaar, I do not like your hero. He is so stiff, he looks like any other handsome model in the market.'

Ghai was not perturbed. 'I'll manage,' he told Rai, 'my character is like that. As you know, I managed to get good work out of Sanjay Dutt.'

'Yaar, please do not feel bad about this,' said Rai. 'I'll finance your film, but I do not want to distribute it.'

This was a setback. When word spread that Gulshan Rai had pulled out of distribution, other distributors became jittery. Although this created financial troubles for Ghai, he went ahead as planned.

By the time the film was completed, the Mumbai territory, critical to a film's success because it is so large, had still not been sold. A month before *Hero*'s release, N.N. Sippy, who had produced *Kalicharan*, phoned Ghai. He had heard that Rai had quit the territory and wanted to see if the film was worth distributing. Ghai showed him four songs. Since he had built a reputation for filming songs that were crucial to the narrative, distributors had started judging his films by their songs.

Sippy liked the songs and signed up to distribute the film.

It was a decision he would come to regret in the first week after *Hero*'s release.

December 1983 was dominated by Amitabh Bachchan's *Coolie*, which broke the box office from day one. Thousands thronged the cinema halls to watch their favourite star in action after his near-fatal accident on the sets.

A week later, *Hero* came and went virtually unnoticed in its first week of release. By the second week, it looked to be a flop. Words of consolation poured in for Ghai.

'Please do not feel bad, but your music was terrible,' said a distributor.

'Your hero is stiff,' said another.

'Why did you have to take *Painter Babu*'s heroine?' wondered a third.

Ghai was used to eating paan when he felt stressed. By the second week of *Hero*'s release, he was emptying dibba after dibba of paan in his office.

In the third week, he told his administration manager to remove the film's posters from the office walls. But, the manager said, the film had risen a bit that week.

'What could have happened?' Ghai asked.

'*Coolie* has settled,' he was told. 'Now people are coming to watch *Hero*.'

Collections indeed rose in the third week, and again in the fourth. The fifth week onwards, theatres were putting up 'House Full' boards. The film went on to complete a golden jubilee run in twelve centres and a silver jubilee in twenty-four centres. When it was declared an unqualified blockbuster in the Mumbai territory, Gulshan Rai's son, Rajiv, asked his father how he could leave such a film and how could he not like Shroff.

When *Hero* completed its silver jubilee, the income tax department raided Mukta Arts on suspicions that the company had underreported its income. The truth was that despite the popularity of the film, Mukta Arts did not make much money from it because of rampant video piracy. Small video parlours would screen the film on television sets without paying any fee to the production company. To make matters murkier, distributors dealt mostly in cash, and not all accounting was transparent.

The tax people did not get anything from Mukta Arts' office, but the raid taught Ghai a lot. He vowed never to work in cash—a vow that was not easy to keep back then. For his subsequent films, he told his actors he would not work with them if they wanted cash. He hired chartered accountants and lawyers to make sure that the company's accounts were impeccably transparent.

'I wanted no trouble from the tax department. I wanted to focus on making good films. As a creative man, I wanted no distractions,' says Ghai. 'The tax raid made me a better producer.'

Buoyed by the success of *Hero*, which had absolute newcomers in the lead roles, Ghai made other significant changes to his way of filmmaking. '*Hero* earned me respect and goodwill and gave me the confidence as well as the elbow room to grow as I wanted to,' says Ghai.

In his own way, he curbed the star culture in his projects. He started working with only the stars he liked. He chose actors who were disciplined, respected his script, did not interfere with the creative aspects, and agreed to the price Ghai offered invariably less than their market rate.

Ghai would open these negotiations by narrating the story and their role, and by asking the actors if they would give the dates he needed. Then he quoted the price he would pay.

Initially, there would be hesitation. '*Nahi, sir, aisa kya hai, sir* (Why, sir, what is the problem)?' Ghai told them the money he was shaving off their remuneration would go into making the film better, not making Mukta Arts richer. Eventually, the stars understood that if Ghai's film did well, their market rate for other producers would rise. That they agreed to the lower price gave Ghai the confidence that they were really keen to do his film.

Mukta Arts always paid its technicians, usually underpaid across the industry, more than the market rate. If a film was a hit, the technicians' salaries went up by 20 per cent. If it was lukewarm, salaries would still rise by 10 per cent. In addition, there were three bonuses in a year. Mukta Arts' costume designer, dress suppliers, lighting people, accountants and other staff never quit.

'I built Mukta Arts with certain principles,' says Ghai. 'If I stand on a stage and say that my success is the team's success, I have to truly share this success with the team. *Hamare desh mein kai log kaafi baatein karte hain, lekin jeb se kuchh nahi nikalte* (Many people talk a lot, but do not put their money where their mouths are),' says Ghai.

The mahurat of *Hero* and the party to celebrate its success were only the first of the big events organized by Ghai and Mukta Arts. Like the big Holi celebration at R.K. Studio, Ghai started hosting Holi parties at his bungalow in Madh Island, which was attended by the who's who of the industry as well as the lesser-known folks such as technicians.

Soon enough, a film magazine wrote that Ghai had become the new showman. Not that Raj Kapoor was in decline; he was making *Ram Teri Ganga Maili* (1985), which had a wide canvas and a profound message. But he had slowed down somewhat with age, as everyone does. His asthma had become acute, curbing his participation in events, parties and Holi bashes.

Ghai stopped his big parties after *Pardes* (1997), when he started receiving ominous phone calls from Dubai. That was around the time Gulshan Kumar had been killed in a mafia hit job, sending shivers down the industry's spine. The nature of the Holi parties were such that everyone was invited and anyone could come, making security the first concern.

12

Meri Jung: The Battle

After *Hero*'s golden jubilee celebration, Ghai's father warned him that he would be watched closely henceforth—people would be waiting for him to stumble.

Dilip Kumar, who had come to treat Ghai like a younger brother, had similar advice to give. 'Subhash,' he said, 'you have to tread carefully now. You will be on trial with every film you make.' He also told him never to move away from his roots, which lay in family values, which were important even in a crime thriller.

Such affection and thoughtfulness from one of the industry's stalwarts gave Ghai, a rank outsider who had no connection with the film world when he came in, immense comfort and a sense of belonging.

'Dilip Sa'ab was one of the most knowledgeable and learned persons I have met, and the most articulate,' says Ghai.

For his next project, he had taken a fancy to a story about three criminals sentenced to death. They were talented in their own ways, but now their lives were about to go to waste. How could their skills be utilized? They could be turned into fearless soldiers if someone, a father figure perhaps, convinced them that they would be spared if they promised to devote their life to the country. The person who would go to them with that proposal—a jailer—would have an intriguing backstory of his own. He was out to seek vengeance for his family and his jail's inmates, who were killed when terrorists attacked the prison.

This was the idea that became *Karma* (1986). Its original plot construction was just about the jailer and the three criminals. But, heeding Dilip Kumar's advice, Ghai created a family story around the jailer, played by Dilip Kumar himself.

Ghai did not want a big star cast, but, as he worked on the script, it kept expanding, pulling in more and more people. It ended up having quite a collection of strong actors and star power—Dilip Kumar, Jackie Shroff, Anil Kapoor, Naseeruddin Shah, Sridevi, Poonam Dhillon, Anupam Kher and others.

In April 1984, a few months after *Hero*'s release, Ghai was approached by N.N. Sippy. The producer, who had launched Ghai's career as a director with *Kalicharan*, was in a difficult situation. His two most recent films, *Phir Wohi Raat* (1980) and *Ghazab* (1982), had flopped. An income tax demand was looming and had to be paid in a few months.

'You are a hitmaker, Subhash. Can you make a film for my banner?' Sippy asked.

Ghai respected Sippy like a family elder. He asked for a week's time to come up with a story that could be made quickly, in time for Sippy to pay the tax demand.

Ghai met Javed Akhtar, his friend from their days of struggle. Akhtar had now separated from his scriptwriting partner, Salim Khan, and gone solo. On his own, Akhtar had had mixed success with *Betaab* (1983, Sunny Deol's launch vehicle) and *Mashaal* (1984, with Dilip Kumar). While splitting, Salim and Akhtar had divided their bank of stories between themselves. Among the stories Akhtar took was a courtroom drama, the story of a rivalry between two formidable lawyers, one of them young and upright, the other older, crooked and cunning. Originally, it was supposed to be directed by Ramesh Sippy of *Sholay* fame, with Amitabh Bachchan and Amjad Khan as the leads. There was much anticipation about this project because it would have been the first time Bachchan played a lawyer. However, the project fell through when Bachchan walked out to focus on his political career.

The first scene Akhtar narrated to Ghai was the one in which Arun Verma, the upright lawyer, drinks poison in the courtroom to prove his client's innocence. The scene was at the core of the character's development and left Ghai in no doubt that this was a story worthy of becoming a dramatic movie. It was anyway difficult not to like a story told by Akhtar, so good was he at narration. Being a courtroom drama, the film could be made quickly since the same set—that of a courtroom—could be used to shoot large passages of the film and with largely the same set of people: lawyers, cops, court staff. It did not have much spread in terms of locations.

Akhtar, in his usual upbeat manner, said it was a superhit story. Ghai told Sippy about the plot and he, too, liked it. However, when Ghai went back to Akhtar and asked for the script, he got a two-page writeup that contained the story, but there was no screenplay. As it turned out, the script did not exist. Akhtar knew the story well and had narrated it in a gripping manner that sounded just like a script, filled with all the drama a film needed. But Ghai wasn't worried; both he and Akhtar were writers and would manage between them. Akhtar was known to be a spontaneous writer and could write quickly anywhere. Word in the industry was that he had written a few scenes of *Sholay* on the bonnet of his car even as the scene he was writing was being readied to be shot.

Akhtar recommended taking Anil Kapoor to play the hero, Arun Verma. Incidentally, when Bachchan was to play the hero, Kapoor was being considered to play the villain's son, the role that eventually went to Javed Jaffrey. Anil Kapoor was a young, up-and-coming actor who was serious about his craft. Ghai remembered giving him a test when he was a student at Roshan Taneja's acting school and rating him highly.

Sippy thought it would have been better to take Jackie Shroff, since he was already a hit hero, and Meenakshi Seshadri could play the heroine. Repeating a hit romantic pair was believed to increase the chances of a film's success. And both would have been happy to work with Ghai again.

Ghai had other ideas. Shroff, he explained to Sippy, had immense charm and vulnerability—two things that had worked wonders for *Hero*—but he wasn't an accomplished actor yet. Anil was a trained actor and would do well in the dramatic courtroom scenes as well as in the deeply emotional scenes with the mother. He was hungry for success, and his face had gravitas that would look good on a lawyer. Sippy agreed to go with Ghai's choice.

When Anil Kapoor came to the Mukta Arts office, he looked extremely thin and seemed very young, like someone in his late teens. Ghai told him to stop shaving and come back after a week. Four days later, he came back with an unshaved look. 'Look, sir, I have a stubble now,' he said and pointed to parts of his face where facial hair had grown. Ghai chuckled appreciatively, more for the actor's keenness to work than for his stubble.

That keenness remained intact not only through the making of *Meri Jung* (1985) but also all the other films Kapoor did with Ghai. While *Meri Jung* was being filmed, he used to visit Ghai's house every second or third day, without an agenda, leaving only after Ghai had told him a scene or two. He would tell Ghai about the other films he was working on, their directors, and their style of functioning. That spurred Ghai to explain the significance and meaning of the scenes he was working on.

'Those were our little workshops. Anil was passionate about acting as much as I was passionate about filmmaking,' says Ghai.

Meenakshi Seshadri came in to play the heroine, to exhibit more of her dancing skills and add her recently acquired star power to the film.

Amrish Puri was the unanimous choice for G.D. Thakral, the crooked lawyer-villain: tall, roaring and snarling, he was quite the lion beside Anil Kapoor. This was apt, because the film was all about how the young lad, a mouse before a lion, evolves into a lion himself.

Nutan, a leading lady of the 1960s who had graduated to playing character roles, was playing Dilip Kumar's wife in *Karma*. She stepped in to play Anil Kapoor's mother in *Meri Jung*. Girish Karnad, a doyen of theatre and art films, played the father.

Ghai and Akhtar discussed the script, scene by scene. The character of Vikram 'Vicky' Thakral, the villain's son, turned out to be another bone of contention between the writer and the director. Ghai wanted to make him a carefree character and gave him the round spectacles that John Lennon used to wear. It created a significant impact when viewers saw the same carefree young man commit murder. Ghai signed Javed Jaffrey for the part. In those days, Jaffrey used to take part in dance competitions, so it was a no-brainer to make Vicky a dancer to capture his popularity among girls.

Akhtar scoffed again, as he saw this as another attempt to add music to the dramatic screenplay, but gave in. The song '*Bol baby bol*' became an instant hit. It may have been the first instance of a Hindi film song having English rap, which was performed by Jaffrey himself.

'L–P, Javed and I had no idea what Jaffrey was saying in his rap parts, but we felt that whatever it was, it was working,' says Ghai.

Meanwhile, Ghai received the rushes of the one schedule he had shot for *Karma*. He postponed the rest of the shooting by six months and asked everyone working on the film for new dates.

The key to *Meri Jung* would be its dialogues, which nobody could write better than Akhtar. However, Ghai told Akhtar, the screenplay had become dialogue-heavy and needed more music.

Akhtar sat down and said, 'I know, Subhash, that you love music in your films, but this is a genre that does not and should not allow for much music.'

He was not wrong. As far back as 1960, B.R. Chopra, known for making thought-provoking films with strong messages, had made a film called *Kanoon*, with Ashok Kumar and Rajendra Kumar in the lead roles. As the name suggests, it was a courtroom drama that—astonishing for a film in that era—had no songs.

'You will have to change your mindset and make the film as I have written it,' said Akhtar.

Ghai had great respect for Akhtar and his work, but he asked for a chance to modify the script. He added an element to the young lawyer's backstory. He made the lawyer's father, who gets wrongly convicted, a pianist, and his mother a singer. Then he wrote a line: '*Zindagi har kadam ek nayi jung hai* (At every step, life is a new battle)'. Akhtar, who was in his early phase as a lyricist, wrote the next line, '*Jeet jayenge hum, tu agar sang hai* (We will win as long as we are together)'. This would be the young lawyer's family song, which he, his parents and his sister sang together.

Ghai took the two lines to Anand Bakshi who readily wrote the antaras for the song. Next, Ghai took the lyrics to Laxmikant–Pyarelal and told them the story and the situation. He also told them that he was adding music to the script against Akhtar's wishes.

With a team like Ghai, L–P and Bakshi, there was bound to be more than one song. The title track and its piano strains feature in the film on several occasions, providing a running thread, much like the theme music had done for *Karz* and *Hero*. It even plays in the background, with a faster tempo, during the fight scenes of the climax, punctuated by sounds of punches, kicks and crashes.

Ghai took the embellished screenplay to Akhtar. When the scriptwriter began reading it, he was sitting on a sofa. When he finished reading it, he lay down on the sofa with visible vexation. 'This film will not work, no way,' he said dejectedly. 'You have spoiled its narrative.'

Akhtar was indeed unhappy, but the two of them were used to having differences within a creative team. Since they were friends, their conflict remained muted. Other creative teams, while debating a scene, had been known to throw plates at one another and sometimes break the table they were working on. The general belief in the industry was that the more the fights, the better the screenplay.

Ghai stood his ground. 'As the director, I can visualize it clearly,' he said. 'Your story and characters are present in all their glory; I have diluted nothing.'

Akhtar agreed reluctantly and said he would keep sending the dialogues as the shooting progressed, and would leave the rest to Ghai.

As work on the film progressed, Sippy told Ghai that he would have to take care of production as well. By this time, Sippy was a different person from the one who had produced *Kalicharan*. Back then, he liked to be on the set all the time and get involved in every aspect of filming, asking Ghai to explain what he was shooting and why he was shooting it that way. Now he appointed his son, Pravesh, as the associate producer, but mainly to help and assist Ghai.

Ghai did not mind; he believed that a director should be responsible for aspects of production as well. When Sippy phoned him after a shooting schedule, Ghai would respond to his greeting with the list of solutions he had found to various problems.

'I knew he would have heard from other people of the unit about issues that crop up while shooting any film. I also knew that was the reason he was calling me. I was ready with the answers,' says Ghai.

A day came when Sippy got upset with him. 'Can I at least ask how you are before you start talking about work?' he protested.

Meri Jung was made in nine months. When the film was ready, the first trial show Ghai arranged was for Javed Akhtar. The scriptwriter watched it with a few of his friends at a theatre in Bandra, not far from Ghai's house. After the show, he came straight to Ghai's house and hugged him.

'Yaar, Subhash, only you could have done this,' he said. 'The way you wove music into the script and the way it elevated the emotions, no one else could have done it.'

'The generosity of his praise brought tears to my eyes,' says Ghai. He was expecting a rebuke.

Film lovers still remember the piano strains when Arun Verma goes to meet his mother in a mental asylum. The music plays as she walks in from the other end of a long corridor, her mind frozen in a moment fifteen years ago. She cannot recognize her children, who have grown up now; she thinks they are still young and waiting for her at home. Not many eyes in the theatre remained dry at the end of that scene.

Much of the credit for how the music in the film elevated emotions should go to Anand Bakshi, says Ghai. An unassuming man, Bakshi could write lyrics to suit a situation like no other. His words were spot on. For instance, the point where Nutan's character gets her memory back, the words are: '*Main hoon ek tasveer, tu mera roop rang hai* (I am a picture, you are my shape and colour)'. The lyrics conveyed that the mother had recognized her children in a way several paragraphs of dialogue could not have.

Released in October 1985, *Meri Jung* went on to complete a silver jubilee. Sippy got the money he needed, Ghai the money he expected, and Anil Kapoor graduated from being an up-and-coming actor to a performer with maturity who could do complex, dramatic roles.

13

Karma: The Extravaganza

Karma was a product of its time. In the 1980s, terrorism was the big threat facing India. Prime Minister Indira Gandhi, who had carried out Operation Blue Star in Punjab, was assassinated by her own bodyguards, sending the nation into paroxysms of fear and worry. Less than forty years after independence, the nation was faced with grim realities and disturbing questions.

The film industry was going through its own existential crisis. Many were pronouncing the death of 'cinema', the big-screen extravaganza that filmmakers such as Ghai embodied. Those were the days when unauthorized VHS tapes of films were freely available at the local video store even in small towns, and pirated prints of new movies would reach those shops on the day of the release itself. A walk down any lane could easily find you as many video rental shops as paan shops, probably more.

As more and more households came to own a VCR—or its poor cousin, the VCP (video cassette player)—the VHS rental business expanded rapidly. For those who did not own a television set or a VCR/VCP, there were video parlours. These were small halls that seated twenty or twenty-five people and screened the latest movies on a television screen using a VHS tape. These charged an admission fee of ₹2 or less, compared to ₹8-12 charged by the big theatres for a good seat. The makers of these video cassettes—the video pirates—and the owners of the rental shops and video parlours paid no fees to the film production company, so the prices within the VHS trade were profitable at penny levels.

It did not help that many cinema theatres of the time had become inhospitable, especially for women and families. Visits to theatres were often painful affairs marked by torn seats, bad sound and projection systems, and made worse by dirty toilets in a constant state of disrepair. There would be paan stains everywhere, especially in the stairwells. Families, while planning an evening out, stopped including movie shows as a thing to do. It was better to watch a film in the comforts of one's home, for a pittance.

It was in this near-dismal state of affairs that Ghai made *Karma.* He addressed the subject of terrorism through the film's storyline and countered it with patriotism. Along with it, he fought his own battle, the one against video pirates, with the twin swords of technology and creativity.

The plot of the film—criminals turn soldiers—was not astonishingly new. Ghai was influenced by V. Shantaram's black-and-white classic *Do Ankhen Barah Haath* (1957), about a progressive jailer who gets permission from his superiors to take six hardened criminals serving life sentences to an agricultural farm in a bid to rehabilitate the farm and reform the criminals. The 1970s saw two hit films which adopted variations of the same plot: *Mera Gaon Mera Desh* (1971), in which Dharmendra is a reformed thief who fights a dacoit played by Vinod Khanna; and *Sholay*, where Amitabh Bachchan and Dharmendra, playing small-time crooks, fight the infamous dacoit Gabbar Singh, portrayed by Amjad Khan. In both films, the criminals become heroes for the villagers who were being terrorized by the dacoits.

In *Karma*, Ghai modified the plot and raised the stakes. Instead of small-time criminals, the heroes are three men facing the death penalty for murder. The small village being looted by dacoits gets replaced by the nation—India is under attack from a terrorist organization called Black Star, headed by Doctor Michael Dang. *Sholay*'s Thakur Baldev Singh was reimagined as Rana Vishwa Pratap Singh, the jailer, played by Dilip Kumar. He visits the three convicts and says he can save them from the gallows if they are ready to die for the country, and takes them on a mission against Black Star.

When it came to casting Rana Vishwa Pratap Singh, Ghai could not imagine anyone other than Dilip Kumar. This would be their second outing together, after *Vidhaata*. The actor had not seemed suitable for any of the characters in *Hero* and *Meri Jung*, but for *Karma*, he was a shoo-in; no one else could have been as authoritative playing the seasoned, reformist jailer stricken with grief or sounded as credible while talking about patriotism and sacrificing one's life for the country.

Dilip Kumar liked the story. But he cautioned Ghai, 'See to it that it does not end up becoming merely an action film. It will be great if you can say something more in it.'

'How much will you charge?' asked Ghai, who liked to get the money question out of the way during his very first discussion with actors.

'Subhash,' said Dilip Kumar, 'must you be such a mercenary all the time? Let's focus on making a good film.'

'But my company needs to know how much we have to pay you,' said Ghai.

Dilip Kumar smiled and said, '*Baniya hai tu, baniya* (You are a merchant at heart).'

'Filmmaking is also about commerce,' Ghai responded.

'How much did you pay me for *Vidhaata*?'

Ghai told him.

'You will raise it a little, won't you?' asked Dilip Kumar.

'A little, yes,' said Ghai, without actually mentioning a figure.

'Okay, send me your note and I'll sign it.'

Actors who had worked with Ghai knew that he liked to put the terms of engagement on a 'note', a simple one-page document that mentioned the money, the starting date of shooting, the character the actor would play, and the number of days he or she needed to shoot. It was a non-legal document, signed by both Ghai and the actor, and treated as sacrosanct.

'Dilip Sa'ab never sent anyone to talk to me on his behalf,' says Ghai. 'He only wanted me to make a good film. That is how the stars of the time were. These days, scripts are selected and approved by agents and managers.'

Back in the day, Ghai did not give a written script to anyone; he would only narrate it.

'If I gave the script in writing, I wouldn't be able to make changes,' he says, referring to the many issues of actors, locations and money that cropped up during production and had to be negotiated one way or another. 'Filmmaking is about improvisation. Actors, characters, music and lyrics evolve.'

As usual, Ghai and his favoured co-writer, Sachin Bhowmick, spent hours and days and weeks discussing each character. They gave distinct identities to the three prisoners facing the death penalty: one was from Uttar Pradesh, another a Maharashtrian, and the third a Hyderabadi. One was intense, another a romantic, and the third a joker. Ghai and Bhowmick wrote their back stories and why they were sentenced to death down to the last detail, even though those stories were unlikely to—and ultimately did not—make it into the film. Even minor characters who had barely half a dozen lines got in-depth biographies.

The character of the prisoner Dharma, played by Dara Singh, has a brief but crucial story about how he, in a fit of rage, murdered the policeman who detained him and broke the bottles of blood he was taking for his sick brother. This incident was at the heart of Vishwa Pratap Singh's premise that some people are forced into crime by circumstances. They should be treated with compassion, and differently from the likes of Doctor Dang, who create the circumstances that force people into crime.

The most elaborate story, of course, is the jailer's. He has two grown-up sons, and a third who is much younger than his siblings, born when the jailer was not very young. The jailer treats the prison inmates like family. Many of the prisoners are killed, along with everyone in the jailer's family other than his wife and youngest son, in a terrorist attack. It is these deaths that the jailer is out to avenge.

His wife, Rukmini, played by Nutan, is a loving, kind-hearted woman who tends to sick prisoners and writes patriotic songs. In fact, *Karma*'s patriotism, the reason why it is telecast on television at least twice a year—on Independence Day and Republic Day—flows from Rukmini. When the writers were discussing Rukmini's character, the things she would do as the jailer's wife in a small town and the kind of songs she would write, Ghai blurted out: '*Dil diya hai jaan bhi denge, ae watan tere liye* (I've given you my heart, O my country, I'll give my life for you as well).'

Bhowmick liked the line; it promised to be just the kind of song a nation under attack from terrorists would sing.

Ghai took the line to Laxmikant and Pyarelal, only to find them occupied with other producers. He told them the one line. Laxmikant wrote it down in his notebook.

'Can we work on this the day after tomorrow?' he asked.

Ghai was fine with that. He came out of L–P's music sitting room and, in the waiting area, met a producer he happened to know. They spoke for a few minutes and Ghai excused himself to visit the loo. When he came out, Laxmikant's assistant was waiting to take him back into the music sitting room.

Once Ghai sat down, a bit mystified, Laxmikant opened his harmonium. 'Now, listen,' he said and started playing the now famous tune of '*Dil diya hai jaan bhi denge*'. He played the entire tune.

Ghai was ecstatic. 'Now we don't need to meet the day after tomorrow,' he told Laxmikant. 'We can hand it over to Bakshi ji.'

Anand Bakshi, the lyricist, did the rest.

'That was the magic that Laxmikant ji could create in minutes,' says Ghai.

The role of Rukmini was one that Nutan accepted readily. Playing her second innings in the movies, like Dilip Kumar, she had wowed awards juries with her performances in *Main Tulsi Tere Aangan Ki* (1978) and *Meri Jung*. As one of the leading ladies from the 1950s and '60s, she was known as much for her acting abilities as her beauty and grace. Interestingly, despite the fact that her career had run parallel to that of Dilip Kumar, the reigning king among actors back then, *Karma* was the first time these two doyens of Hindi cinema acted together in a film.

With Dilip Kumar and Nutan on board, Ghai needed three male actors to play the condemned men. By now, he had developed close bonds with both Jackie Shroff and Anil Kapoor. They agreed to take up two of the three roles. Ghai changed Shroff's flute from *Hero* to a banjo and cast him as the Maharashtrian Baiju. He decided to utilize Kapoor's versatility by giving him, after the intense role in *Meri Jung*, the UP-ite joker-criminal Johnny's role in *Karma*.

Ghai wanted the third actor to be different from them and thought of Naseeruddin Shah, who, having earned acclaim all over the world for his work in art films, had started to dabble in mainstream cinema. He would be good for the Hyderabadi character of Khairu, Ghai thought.

'The best thing about making *Karma* was that no actor asked me a second question. They heard the story and their remuneration and agreed,' says Ghai, then quickly corrects himself. 'Except Naseer.'

Naseeruddin Shah, Ghai's junior from FTII, readily agreed to work in *Karma*, but was affronted by the note Ghai sent him the day after their meeting. The note offered to pay Shah the same amount as Shroff and Kapoor. Ghai thought he was being fair: the two actors were more established as box office draws, though Shah easily outscored them in histrionics. It was a fine balance. But Shah was outraged at being equated with Shroff and Kapoor. He believed he was an actor of a certain pedigree who deserved more—10 to 15 per cent more.

Ghai thought Shah's arrogance would suit his character in *Karma*, and agreed to pay him the price he wanted.

'He is a class act and a wonderful person,' Ghai says of Shah. 'But during *Karma*, he probably used to wonder what we were up to, singing songs and doing other stuff that had no place in the cinema of Shyam Benegal.'

While Ghai, Jackie Shroff, Anil Kapoor and some of the other actors and unit members had fun on the sets—usual for a Ghai film—Naseeruddin Shah remained aloof. The unit understood his need to have his own space. But there were some tense moments arising out of Shah's equation with Dilip Kumar. Probably both thought the other a bit overrated.

To utilize the duo's formidable acting abilities, Ghai had included a high-voltage confrontation in the film. The audience was bound to expect a few scenes to see how the two stalwarts measured up against each other. Perhaps the actors were also worried about the same thing. The scene proved tricky to shoot. Whenever Ghai planned it, he could not get both Dilip Kumar and Shah on the same day. Eventually, it was shot on two separate days: the first time with only Dilip Kumar and the second time with just Shah. There is only one frame during that confrontation in which the two appear on screen together. Ghai had to make special requests to both actors to stay on the set together for at least an hour.

If it was Shah's arrogance that worked for him, it was Anupam Kher's coolness and undeniable charm that made his Doctor Dang, the dreaded terrorist, one of Hindi cinema's most memorable bad guys.

In his search for the right actor to play Doctor Dang, Ghai first thought of Amrish Puri, who had played the villain in *Meri Jung* and *Hero*. But in their discussions, Bhowmick and he toyed with the idea of getting someone new, who was not already associated with a certain character in the minds of the audiences. After all, pitting a newcomer against the formidable personalities of Dharmendra, Amitabh Bachchan and Sanjeev Kumar had worked in *Sholay*.

While Ghai was still in the middle of his search, Sanjeev Kumar happened to tell him about *Saaransh* (1984), a film by Mahesh Bhatt he had seen recently. Kumar was supposed to do the film but could not, and it had gone to a newcomer, who according to him had done a wonderful job.

A few days later, as Ghai emerged form Hotel Sea Rock at two in the morning after attending a party, someone called out to him. When he turned in the direction of the voice, he noticed a man coming toward him with quick and small steps. The man had feline grace. When he came closer, Ghai saw he had an extremely fair complexion, bright eyes and an almost feminine charm.

'Sir, I want to work with you,' the man said. 'My name is Anupam Kher, I have done *Saaransh*.'

Ghai looked at him for a long moment and asked him to come to his office the next day around noon. When Kher came, Ghai gave him tea, and narrated the story of *Karma*. He finished by saying he wanted Kher to play Doctor Dang, the chief antagonist to Dilip Kumar.

Kher was stunned; Ghai had neither seen *Saaransh* nor given him a screen test.

'You look the part,' Ghai explained. 'And I know you are a trained actor. I have no doubt you will do well in this role.'

Doctor Dang was not the usual Hindi film villain who snarled, sneered and shouted. He was a sophisticated, English-speaking man who had travelled the world and appreciated the finer things in life. When he first arrives as a prisoner at Vishwa Pratap Singh's jail, Dang tells the jailer how much he liked his book on reforming convicts. He then asks for a writing desk in his prison cell, with a telephone and flowers. 'You see, I'm very fond of flowers,' he says.

Dang's nonchalance, the smallness of his frame and his dangerous charm made his cruelty and crimes all the more chilling. 'I chose Anupam just because of that coolness I saw on his face,' says Ghai. 'He did not look cruel, but what he did was extremely cruel.'

At this point, Ghai realized he had created an all-male ensemble cast with only Nutan for a strong female presence. His team suggested bringing in Sridevi, who had become a big star in Mumbai and would be a good foil to the powerful male characters. But there was no role meaty enough for her.

Ghai met Sridevi and told her about *Karma* and its star cast. He explained that it was an action film driven by vendetta and women had only a small part to play in this story. Her role would not be pivotal. When she asked to hear the story, Ghai narrated it and also described a few scenes which would involve her, including the one in which she makes her entry, shooting at a couple of bears that are actually Jackie Shroff and Anil Kapoor in disguise, trying to escape from the jailer and his mission.

Sridevi agreed to do the film, saying she wanted to work with Ghai, but insisted on charging her market rate. Ghai had not worked with her before and they did not have a relationship. He agreed to pay her full price, making her the second-highest paid person in the cast after Dilip Kumar.

Like Naseeruddin Shah, Sridevi kept to herself on the sets and came across as an introvert. But once the camera began to roll, she was electric: bold and captivating, giving just the right expressions at the right moment, not even a fraction of a second out of place.

'She was magic,' says Ghai.

When everything seemed to have fallen in place, Gulshan Rai dropped a bomb.

'There is no point making this film,' Rai, whose stature as a producer and distributor had grown over the years, told Ghai. *Karma*, he said, had become an expensive project and judging by the way video piracy was eroding the business of films, there was no way he would be able to recover such a large cost. Even *Hero*, which had clocked jubilees in so many centres, had not made too big a profit.

'Sir, I am making a big motion picture, not a small film,' said Ghai.

'You are living in a dream world, Subhash,' Rai said. 'Where is your audience? Even if you call it a motion picture, it will be seen more in video parlours than in theatres.'

Ghai came away, disturbed by the idea of his magnum opus being seen mostly on small screens at homes or at unlicensed screenings in video parlours. He needed an audience, but how was he going to find them?

'I was upset only for two days,' he reminisces. 'It was as if a divine force had taken hold of my senses.'

He promised himself that he would bring the audiences back to theatres. What was the magic of cinema? he asked himself. The answer was big screens, big visuals and big sound. He decided to recapture the magic of *The Ten Commandments* (1956) and *Ben-Hur* (1959)—Hollywood's epic dramas known for their large canvases, sweeping scapes and larger-than-life characters. Most of the scenes in *Karma* are either wide-angle long shots or tight close-ups capturing dramatic dialogues. There are scenes in which the camera simply lingers on the sloping mountains and undulating meadows where Rana Vishwa Pratap Singh has camped with his three-man army.

Kamalakar Rao, the cinematographer, proved to be an able ally once again. Although computer technology was nascent and computer-generated imagery (CGI) non-existent at the time, Rao managed to translate Ghai's vision on to the screen. He used to take separate shots, roll the film backward and forward, and mix it all up to create special effects.

Sound was as important as the visuals, and Ghai chose to give *Karma* six tracks of it. When Rana slaps Doctor Dang, the sound moves up in notches as all six tracks open up one by one. That sound—the famous '*thappad ki goonj*' (the echo of the slap)—shook the walls and roofs of theatres. It took time and effort. Ghai did the sound mixing at Prasad Lab in Chennai, taking thirty days to do what other films accomplished in a fortnight. The sound in every scene had to crackle, every footstep needed to be heard. For the '*thappad ki goonj*' scene alone, he spent thirteen hours mixing the sound.

The result he was hoping for was a film that had to be seen—and heard—in theatres. You simply wouldn't get the same experience on a small screen and with tiny speakers.

The real battle turned out to be in the theatres. Forget six tracks, sound systems in theatres could barely do justice to one at the time. Ghai's team drew up a list of the top ninety theatres in the country. He personally wrote letters to the owners of each, telling them about his new film that had six-track Dolby sound, and requesting them to upgrade their audio systems. Mukta Arts would help with the upgrade logistics and also bear the cost. Less than half the theatre owners replied. The others probably thought Ghai was either joking or had gone mad. But they would soon have Ghai visiting them in person to discuss the upgrades.

When Ghai visited the Odeon theatre in New Delhi's Connaught Place, the owner told him the glory days of cinema were over. If a film ran for a week, that was a big deal. The owner took him to his office balcony, which overlooked the theatre's car park. There was only one car parked there. 'That one,' he told Ghai, 'is mine.'

When Ghai insisted that audiences would flock to his theatre if he made changes, the Odeon owner gave in. It was Ghai's money after all, and he had the right to waste it.

Ghai also went to the Metro theatre in Mumbai and got it renovated, improving the interiors, the toilets and, of course, the sound system. Eventually, twenty-odd theatres were upgraded, all paid for by Mukta Arts.

Karma released ten days before Independence Day, 1986, and ran to packed theatres all over the country in the first week, even in non-Hindi speaking areas. During the second week, when it was still drawing nearly full houses, Ghai went to the Odeon in New Delhi again. The owner was beside himself with surprise and delight.

'This is a miracle,' he said, as he took Ghai again to his office balcony. The theatre's car park was now full.

Interestingly, people who saw *Karma* on a television screen, panned it. But those who saw it in theatres felt it was a completely different film from what the small-screen viewers were describing; a different experience altogether. That distinction becomes clear—actually, one should say loud and clear—in the first two-and-a-half minutes of the film.

When *Karma* begins, the picture occupies a small, cropped screen, like an inset, less than half the size of the full screen. The Mukta Arts logo appears to the chant of the Gayatri mantra. Dilip Kumar, the jailer, swears his inmates to an oath, and then they shout: 'Karma.' With that, the film's title comes on screen, and the small screen expands to its full size, with loud claps of thunder. The six audio tracks open up one by one, enveloping the entire theatre as the sound rises to a crescendo.

For viewers whose eyes had adjusted to the cropped screen, this sudden expansion was like an explosion. It was one of Ghai's cleverer tricks, his way of telling the audience that, for the first two-and-a-half minutes, they had been watching a video parlour film; they could now sit back and enjoy the visual extravaganza of the big screen.

While *Karma* lured families back into movie theatres, it also brought into business those who sold tickets in black. Mutterings of '*dus ka tees*' and '*barah ka chalees*' (a ₹10 ticket for ₹30, a ₹12 ticket for ₹40) rent the air again. The film became one of Mukta Arts' biggest hits, celebrating golden jubilees in more than a dozen centres and clocking diamond jubilees in some others. By fighting video piracy, *Karma* became a much bigger money spinner for Mukta Arts than *Hero*, even though the latter had a longer run in theatres. The profits were higher also because of the increased transparency in accounts. Ghai saw to it that every actor and every technician was paid their entire fee in cheques.

'Many things happened during the making of *Karma* that changed my destiny—as a person, as a filmmaker, as a technician, as a businessman, and as a producer,' says Ghai.

Something significant happened immediately afterwards, too, which forced Ghai to break his vow of not working with big stars.

14

Devaa: The Magnum Opus that Was Not to Be

'It is easy to misunderstand Amitabh Bachchan, perhaps because it is difficult to get to know the real him. I have been lucky enough to have a few glimpses of the real him,' says Ghai.

Actually, Ghai has seen more than a few glimpses of the real Bachchan—they had hung out together in their early days in the industry; but he has not been able to make a film with him. He came agonizingly close, though.

Ghai first met Bachchan when Shatrughan Sinha introduced them when both were struggling to make a mark as actors. Ghai already knew Bachchan from the movies he had done by then: *Saat Hindustani* (1969), *Anand* (1971) and others. Sinha and Bachchan were not only friends but also had the same secretary at one time. Ghai often met Bachchan as part of a larger group.

At Ghai's wedding, on 24 October 1970, Bachchan arrived at the venue, but refused to step out of the car. It turned out he had ordered a new suit for the occasion but it had not been delivered in time. And he wouldn't attend the wedding wearing anything else. A sophisticated man from a cultured family, Bachchan wanted things a certain way, and refused to lower his standards.

He had an extremely funny side to him as well. 'He laughed like a child, so much that he would roll off the bed laughing and continue to laugh sprawled on the floor,' says Ghai. 'And he could also be serious and intense, almost pensive.' Ghai used to describe Bachchan as 'Devdas, son of Kishore Kumar', because he had both an intense person and a madcap persona lurking inside him.

As their careers took off on different trajectories, Ghai got to see even less of Bachchan's funny side. With *Kalicharan*, Ghai was drawn into his own matrix of filmmaking, production and managing stars and units. Bachchan, beginning with *Zanjeer*, rose to unprecedented heights of stardom and was busy making several films a year.

'When I think of how light-hearted and fun he used to be, I wonder if his stardom became a burden for him,' says Ghai. 'When you are one of the most recognized faces in a large and populous country, you can hardly be yourself.'

Their paths would cross again, and Ghai's resolve not to work with big stars, made after the debacle of *Krodhi*, would vanish into thin air. The prospect of working with Amitabh Bachchan could weaken the strongest of resolutions.

Soon after *Karma* released, Ghai met Manmohan Desai at a party. Desai had directed many hits with Bachchan: *Amar Akbar Anthony* (1977), *Parvarish* (1977), *Suhaag* (1979), *Naseeb* (1981), *Desh Premee* (1982), *Coolie* (1983) and *Mard* (1985). He was a warm person and generous with his praise. He took Ghai aside for a word.

'Subhash, you must make a movie with Amitabh,' he said. 'He is a disciplined actor, just like you are a disciplined director.'

Ghai was in two minds. Following the success of *Vidhaata*, *Hero*, *Meri Jung* and *Karma,* his standing in the industry had become preeminent and his confidence was at an all-time high. He had seen other producers and directors work with big stars, and did not like what he saw. Intentionally or not, a big star could influence the director, any director, and the entire making of a film.

However, it had been some time since the *Krodhi* debacle, and Ghai's wounds had nearly healed. Besides, Bachchan was not just any star, he was *the* star. He had been the number one actor in the industry for more than a decade. In fact, some said that he was numbers one through ten; the next biggest star would be counted only in the eleventh place. Added to that was the actor's enormous success in playing roles with shades of grey, the colour of several of Ghai's protagonists.

Shatrughan Sinha was a convicted criminal in *Kalicharan*; a criminal lawyer who took to a life of crime in *Vishwanath*; a village goon in *Gautam Govinda*. In *Krodhi*, Dharmendra was a criminal who became a saint. Rishi Kapoor, in *Karz*, was all positive, but the film's most memorable character, Kamini, played by Simi Garewal, was all negative. Dilip Kumar was a criminal in *Vidhaata*. Jackie Shroff was a goon in *Hero*, and in *Karma*, he, Anil Kapoor and Naseeruddin Shah were convicted felons. This was not strictly by design. It just so happened that Ghai was drawn to stories with unconventional heroes, who were not just chocolate boys. The more he thought about it, the more the idea of doing a film with Bachchan appealed to him.

'He was the finest actor in the industry after Dilip Sa'ab. As a director, you always want to work with the best actors. I had already made two films with Dilip Sa'ab, but I had yet to make one with Amitabh. Then, of course, we had known each other for a long time, although we were not really close friends,' says Ghai.

A few days after his chat with Desai, Ghai happened to see a film with Bachchan in it. He loved it. Next day, he sent a handwritten note—his favourite tool of communication—to Bachchan, complimenting him on his performance. In response, Bachchan phoned Ghai and said he was touched by the note. Seamlessly, the conversation turned towards the possibility of making a film together.

Ghai was delighted, and could not stop telling Rehana about it. A few days later, he packed up and went to Bangalore and checked into the Best Western hotel. He was there for nearly a month, all by himself, writing. For the first time since *Kalicharan*, Ghai was writing a story with the lead actor in mind. Usually, he wrote the story and then thought of the actors. This time, though, he wanted to write the most powerful character Amitabh had ever played, different from anything else he had done.

Ghai returned from Bangalore with 'Devaa', the story of a dreaded dacoit's redemption. The dacoit is more than forty years old, dedicated to his brother and sister who live and study in Mumbai. Devaa pays for their education and upkeep. One day, in the forest, he meets a girl and falls in love with her—it is the first time he has fallen in love—and is inspired to mend his ways. He comes to Mumbai to stay with his siblings, but they are scared of the law and society, and refuse to take him in. Nevertheless, Devaa finds his own place in the city. Eventually, he begins helping the police catch other dacoits, and realizes that the nation is more important than family.

Ghai ran the story past Sachin Bhowmick, who loved it. Confident, Ghai told Bachchan he was ready with a subject. The actor was glad, but not keen to discuss the details of the script. He only wanted the broad storyline. 'Subhash,' he said, 'I'm sure you will take care of things.'

Ghai told him the subject in ten lines. Bachchan liked it very much.

That was the easy part.

It was important for Ghai to get the issues of money and dates out of the way. With these ticklish matters behind him, he found it easier to focus on the job at hand and forge rewarding relationships with his actors and technicians. His unit was like a large family.

'I am a chap who gets attached to people. I would share my stories and scenes with one and all, sing my film's songs with them, and have parties with them. If you do not enjoy making a film, it will not be a good one,' says Ghai. 'When I got my actors' and unit's affection, it gave me the confidence that I was a good man.'

Ghai knew that working with Bachchan would be different. To the latter, acting was serious business, and he went about it like a professional. He always came to the sets on time and maintained an impeccable work ethic. He also needed his own space. And that was fine, Ghai told himself, he did not need to be a part of everyone's family.

But he did need the note he got his actors to sign, describing the project, the actor's role, broad dates, and the money. So, Ghai asked Bachchan how much money he expected for *Devaa*.

'Subhash, I have known you for so long,' Bachchan said. 'We are friends. Let's not fret over money.' He asked Ghai how many days he would need. Ghai said about a hundred. Bachchan said he would tell his secretary, Sheetal Jain.

This was a different approach from that of Dilip Kumar and the others Ghai was used to working with. Normally, he discussed the important things directly with the actors. For instance, Anil Kapoor's affairs were managed by his brother Boney, but Ghai and Anil discussed the terms of their engagement directly, without Boney.

Sheetal Jain was a fine gentleman—cultured and well-mannered, like everyone else in Bachchan's office. Mukta Arts was different, as befits the office of a Punjabi: boisterous and full of banter; half the people in the office, if you did not know them well, might have seemed impertinent.

When Ghai met Jain for Bachchan's dates, the secretary said, 'I believe you need a hundred days from Amitabh. Take seventy for now, we will figure out the other thirty later.'

Ghai agreed. During the first schedule, he filmed a wonderful song scored by Laxmikant–Pyarelel. He sent the rough cut to Bachchan, who liked it.

The matter of money had still not been resolved, so Ghai asked Jain about it. Only when Bachchan's fee, one of the largest components of the film's cost, was fixed, could the rest of the budget be finalized. A sharp focus on the budget was imperative to make the price remunerative for distributors. By now, Ghai had come to understand that it was not just the actors' performances or the music or the story that made a film a hit or a flop, it was also its price to distributors.

But Jain did not come back with a number, and Bachchan continued to be dismissive of the money question. '*Chhod na, yaar* (Forget it, dude),' he would say in jest, '*do rupaye de dena* (pay anything you wish).'

Although that was extremely nice of Bachchan, Ghai was getting anxious because his note, spelling out the terms, was still unsigned. When he pursued the matter some more, Bachchan called him over to his office. Ghai went, explained his financial position and discussed the budget.

Since Bachchan had been so generous as to leave the money matter to him, he had taken the liberty to quote a figure in his note, along with a description of the film, Bachchan's role, and the number of days of shooting. Always gracious to a fault, Bachchan signed it, and Ghai gave him a cheque for the signing amount.

'Are you happy now? Is it okay for you?' Bachchan said, with a tinge of admonition in his voice.

'I felt ashamed. I thought I was being a kameena (rascal) who was hung up about the money and the dates, and wanted to put everything in writing,' Ghai says. 'Why could I not be more large-hearted and trusting?'

Laden with Bachchan's munificence, Ghai felt more motivated than ever to make *Devaa* a magnum opus worthy of the megastar. Not only was he working with the biggest star in the industry and one of its finest actors, but also a superb human being. What could possibly go wrong?

Bachchan and Ghai's collaboration made news and set the film industry abuzz. Distributors lined up outside Mukta Arts to say: '*Price aapki, film hamari* (Name your price, give us the film).' With everything going for him, Ghai felt he owed it to the industry to deliver a spectacular film. He went to Bangalore again and spent another twenty days polishing the script further. He made it tighter, punchier, and gave it a bigger canvas.

Perhaps the buzz was too much.

Soon after his return to Mumbai, amidst pre-production work for the next shooting schedule, he received a phone call from Bachchan, requesting a meeting. When Ghai arrived at the actor's house, he found half a dozen other producers already present. They were Bachchan's regulars. The atmosphere was sombre, as if everyone was slightly weighed down by an unseen cloud hanging over their heads.

'Yaar, they are not happy,' said Bachchan.

Ghai realized that several people in the industry were unhappy about the terms on which Bachchan was working with Ghai. For Ghai, it was like being in a courtroom scene where he was being cross-examined.

After a day or two, he visited Bachchan again at his home. 'I can see you are in a dharam sankat (grave dilemma). I don't want to see you so conflicted because of me,' he said. 'Perhaps we should not make this film.'

'Please do not say that,' said Bachchan. 'Let's think of a way out.'

Ghai went back and discussed the issue with his friends and confidantes. He thought of his negotiations with Dilip Kumar, which usually lasted a mere few seconds, with Dilip Kumar saying, '*Chal theek hai* (fine), let's make a good film.' And that would be that.

Nevertheless, Ghai shook off the negative thoughts and told himself to get on with the job of making a good film. *Devaa*, after all, was his dream project. It certainly was given the mahurat that the coming together of the biggest star and the biggest director deserved. It was held at the Leela Kempinski and drew the biggest names from the film

(From left) Prem Chopra, Randhir Kapoor, Jitendra, Ghai, Rishi Kapoor and Shatrughan Sinha at an event.

A still from *Kalicharan*, Subhash Ghai's directorial debut. He went on to cast Shatrughan Sinha (left) in *Vishwanath* and *Gautam Govinda* too.

(Right) Laxmikant-Pyarelal, the famous music director duo, gave music for most of Ghai's films.

Official poster of *Kalicharan*.

Official poster of *Gautam Govinda*.

Official poster of *Krodhi*, the first film where Laxmikant-Pyarelal collaborated with Ghai.

Ghai with Tina Munim and Rishi Kapoor on the sets of *Karz*.

Donning his dancing shoes during a party with the cast and crew of *Karz*.

With friends and cast of the film during the mahurat of *Vidhaata* in 1981.

The logo for Mukta Arts Pvt. Ltd, the production house started by Ghai in 1982.

Dilip Kumar with Ghai on the sets of *Karma*. He went on to do more films with the director and form a life-long friendship.

Ghai with Rajinikanth at an event.

With Amitabh Bachchan on the sets of 'Devaa'. The film was never completed.

Ghai shared a very close and special bond with Yash Chopra.

Meri Jung established Anil Kapoor as a rising star in the industry.

(From left) Ghai, Jackie Shroff, Dimple Kapadia and Anil Kapoor during the shoot of *Ram Lakhan*.

Anil Kapoor as Lakhan.

Ghai with the cast of *Ram Lakhan*.

Vivek Mushran and Manisha Koirala with Ghai on the sets of *Saudagar*.

Ghai with Dilip Kumar and Raaj Kumar, the two leads of the film.

Ghai on the sets of *Saudagar*.

Sanjay Dutt during the filming of the title song of *Khal Nayak*. This film created the cult of the anti-hero in Hindi films.

(From left) Sanjay Dutt, Ghai and Jackie Shroff during the filming of *Khal Nayak*.

Saroj Khan (middle) choreographing the famous song 'Choli ke peeche kya hai' with Madhuri Dixit (far left) and Ghai (far right).

A still from *Pardes*, with Shah Rukh Khan and Mahima Chaudhry. This was Mahima's debut film.

Ghai shot parts of the film at Fatehpur Sikri, Uttar Pradesh. The crowd that gathered to watch the shooting were used in some of the shots in the film.

(From left) Shah Rukh Khan, Ghai and Amrish Puri during a shoot abroad for *Pardes*.

Behind the camera on location for *Taal*.

Ghai with A.R. Rahman and Aishwarya Rai during a promotional event for *Taal*.

Official poster of *Yaadein*.

Hrithik Roshan and Kareena Kapoor with Ghai during the promotion of *Yaadein*.

On the sets of *Yuvvraaj* with Anil Kapoor and Salman Khan.

Official poster of *Kisna*.

Official poster of *Black & White*, which Ghai directed after a long break.

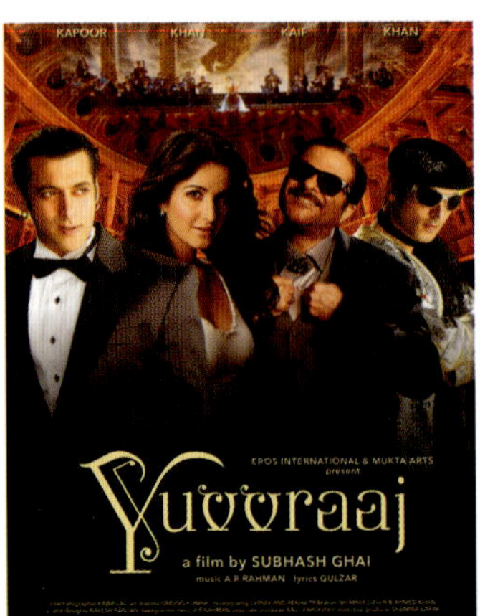

Official poster of *Yuvvraaj*.

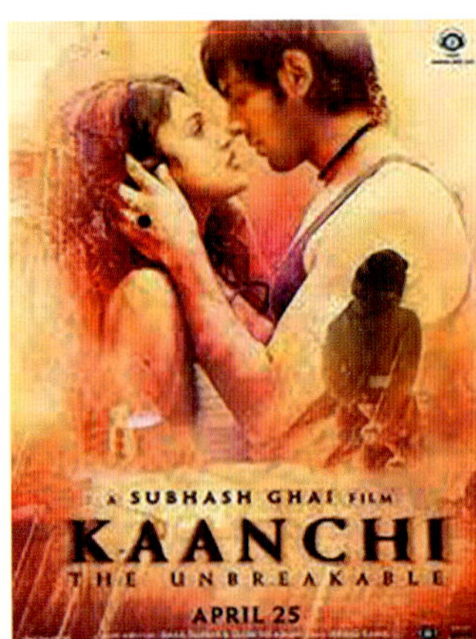

Official poster for *Kaanchi*, which was released in 2014.

Ghai is famous for making short cameos in his films. (Left) His cameo in *Karz*.

His cameo appearance in *Hero*.

Usually, he would appear during a song, as seen here in *Karma*.

Singing a few lines in *Ram Lakhan*.

Hats-off in his blockbuster hit, *Khal Nayak*.

Ghai with his wife, Mukta Ghai.

Ghai with his elder daughter, Meghna Ghai Puri, and her husband, Rahul Puri. Meghna is the president and Rahul is the director at Whistling Woods International.

With his younger daughter, Muskaan.

Ghai and Meghna at the Whistling Woods International campus.

Gulzar at Whistling Woods International, with Ghai and Meghna.

Kamal Haasan at a ceremony at Whistling Woods.

Meghna and Ghai have worked hard to make Whistling Woods International the best film institute in India.

Looking to the horizon from Whistling Woods.

Working to create and improve the art of film-making in India.

Ghai always paid close attention to music in his films, which is why many of them are still audience-favourites.

He has directed, written and produced many blockbusters.

Ghai with his portait in his office at Whistling Woods International.

industry, as well as from corporate India. The song they had recorded played in the background as Bachchan delivered a few dramatic lines on stage. Newspapers and magazines called it the grandest mahurat ever.

Ghai still did not have all the dates he needed from Bachchan, and he wanted them in big chunks, since Bachchan's character was integral to most of the scenes. To complicate matters, it was now clear to Ghai he needed more than a hundred days from Bachchan so he could do more detailing and better framing.

'Sir, I think I need one hundred and thirty days,' he told Jain, but the latter was noncommittal.

Ghai began to worry. The old wounds of *Krodhi* were beginning to reopen. He only had seventy days from Bachchan so far. How was this going to work?

He spoke to Bachchan and urged him to speak with Jain.

'Subhash, what can the poor chap do?' Bachchan said. 'He has to worry about other producers as well.'

Ghai could see his relationship with Bachchan was not going to be what he had hoped for. He considered speaking to Bachchan's wife, Jaya, who was from FTII and whom he knew well, but he was unsure. He could quarrel with Dilip Kumar and complain about him to his wife, Saira Banu, but he did not think he could take such liberties with Bachchan.

Besides, his timing would have been awful. Bachchan was going through a difficult phase in his life outside the industry; he had joined politics and had become entangled in the controversy about the Indian army's acquisition of Bofors guns. His health, too, was suffering. Reluctant to add to his worries, Ghai ploughed on.

Any concerns he had disappeared when he saw the scenes they had shot. He had always maintained that Dilip Kumar had no peer. But, watching *Devaa*'s rough prints, he came to believe that Bachchan was the finest actor in the industry, ahead of even Dilip Kumar, especially now that the veteran actor was well into his second innings.

'Amit was perfect,' says Ghai.

This promise of brilliance pushed him to ensure there were no compromises in making *Devaa*. He returned time and again to Jain's office, asking about Bachchan's dates. He was not proud of having to nag Jain, but he did not know what else to do.

'If I had to compress a hundred and thirty days of work into seventy, there was no way I could make the film I wanted,' he says.

He turned to some of Bachchan's friends for advice. They were happy he was making a film with the star and couldn't wait to watch it, but the only counsel they had for him was: 'You will need to change your ways. You will have to work according to what Amitabh wants.'

Ghai began to feel nervous. How much could he change his ways? And if he did, would he be able to make his kind of film? When shooting resumed, he again brought up the issue of dates.

'Let's see, we will do something,' said Bachchan.

When Ghai reached home, Rehana asked why he was looking downcast, unlike his usual post-shoot ebullient self.

'This film will not work,' Ghai said despondently. The shoot was great and Bachchan was brilliant, but he couldn't shake off the sense of foreboding that had gripped him.

Rehana told him not to be stupid. If the script was good, the shoots were great and Bachchan was brilliant, what could possibly go wrong?

'I was not being stupid, I was afraid,' says Ghai.

Krodhi, too, had had a great script, so good that it had taken only one narration for Dharmendra to say he would not only act in the film but also produce it.

The fear that he would deliver a dud with *Devaa* took hold of Ghai. Given the high expectations from his collaboration with Bachchan, his career would be in peril if the audiences rejected the film. He phoned Bachchan to ask for a meeting and went over to his house.

'Things are not going according to the plan,' Ghai told Bachchan.

Bachchan was surprised but remained his usual calm and cultured self. 'Why, Subhash?' he asked.

Ghai said his health was suffering and he felt a constant pain in his left arm because of stress. 'This will not turn out to be the film we want to make.'

Bachchan asked him what he thought they should do.

This was a moment of reckoning. Ghai had to dig deep to make himself say the words: 'We should not make this film.'

Bachchan said it was, as the producer, Ghai's decision to make or not make the film.

'Maybe I have created unnecessary stress for myself,' said Ghai. 'But right now, I do not feel up to it. Maybe we will make another film together later. This is my loss.'

The very next day, Bachchan, a true professional, returned the signing amount.

The shelving of *Devaa* made a splash. Journalists said there had been an ego clash between the two titans of Hindi cinema. Others said success had gone to the filmmaker's head. Ghai was shocked to read the articles. He issued a statement to say he had cancelled the film because it was not turning out to be financially viable. No one was to be blamed for it. Indeed, Bachchan had been fantastic in the few shoots they had done and Ghai would consider it a privilege to work with him on another film. But of course, journalists were happier peddling their own theories.

Ghai was devastated. *Devaa* had not only been his dream, it had become his life. Now he was caught in a vacuum and he did not know what to do. Not just him, his entire unit was sunk in an almighty gloom. It was like they had suffered a collective miscarriage, which was not far from the truth.

'Start another film soon,' Rehana told Ghai, 'or you will go mad.'

Ghai took her advice and moved on.

So did Bachchan, presumably. He never said one bitter word about Ghai or about the experience of *Devaa*. And he remained gracious as ever. When Ghai invited him to give the mahurat clap for *Saudagar*, he accepted. After giving the clap, he said it was not too long ago that he was on the other side of the clapboard. To Ghai, that felt like a slap on the wrist, but all in good humour.

The two of them occasionally spoke about working together again, but somehow, they never did. Ghai moved from one project to the next and started producing films for other directors. Bachchan went through a lean phase in the 1990s, but for some reason, he did not approach Ghai to make a film together.

They keep meeting here and there. Bachchan has visited Ghai's film school, Whistling Woods. He remains a big box office draw. But times have changed, and Ghai has never found the right subject to do the actor justice.

In 2012, nearly a quarter century after the debacle of *Devaa*, Ghai happened to visit Bachchan at his house, Jalsa. Sure enough, this made headlines. 'Subhash Ghai breaks the ice with Amitabh Bachchan,' said a newspaper.

'I want to tell people there was no ice to be broken. It is just that Amitabh's and my paths crossed when the timing wasn't right. There was never any ill feeling. I blame myself for not changing my ways. If only I had been more tolerant and accepting, I may have made the biggest film of its time, possibly of all time. I feel bad about it, but I moved on,' says Ghai.

Devaa was doubly painful for Ghai. Its shelving denied him of a chance to work with not only Amitabh Bachchan but also with another legend of Hindi cinema: R.D. Burman.

Burman was to score the music for *Ram Lakhan* while L–P were busy with *Devaa*. When *Devaa* did not happen, L–P came into *Ram Lakhan*.

'I do not know if RD ever forgave me. I do hope he did. Just like not working with Amitabh was entirely my loss, so was not getting to work with RD,' says Ghai.

15

Ram Lakhan: The Small Big Film

When *Ram Lakhan* was released in January 1989, film analysts said it was the perfect example of a textbook script. It had something for everyone, and the film ran to packed theatres.

The irony is that at no stage did Ghai have a complete script for the film. He and his team, led by screenplay writer Ram Kelkar and dialogue writer Anwar Khan, wrote the scenes as shooting progressed. The dialogues for nearly every scene were written on the set.

That's understandable: Ghai was on the rebound; and, as it goes with heartbreak sometimes, he sought a balm for his aches with this film. Moving away from the grand canvas and sweeping storyline of *Devaa*, he decided to make a small, light film. That *Ram Lakhan* ended up becoming a big film came as a bit of a surprise to the filmmaker. It grew on its own, fuelled by the addition of characters that sometimes even Ghai could not control, and by extreme improvisation.

While Ghai was planning *Devaa*, Tolu Bajaj, a distributor, came over to the Mukta Arts office for lunch. Bajaj wanted to produce a film but did not have a story.

'Stories are easy,' Ghai told him. 'Making a film is the difficult part.'

To demonstrate his point, he cooked up a story right there at the lunch table, about a wronged mother's revenge. She has two sons, one good and the other a bit of a ne'er-do-well. She is proud of the good son and dotes on the other. The brothers, despite their different approaches to life, have a strong bond and love each other dearly. Together, they get justice for and avenge their mother.

Bajaj loved the story.

Around the time Ghai started work on *Devaa*, he had also begun setting up his brother, Ashok, as a producer. Ashok Ghai had done duty as the chief assistant director on *Karz* and *Krodhi*, and as the executive producer on *Karma*. He understood that his film would start only after *Devaa* but requested Ghai to at least get the story in place so some of the work could be done while *Devaa* was being filmed. That way, there would be no fallow period between the two films.

Ghai thought of the wronged mother's vengeance and phoned Bajaj to ask if he was making it into a film. Bajaj said filmmaking was proving to be a more difficult occupation than he had imagined. Ghai asked if he could use the story for a film to be directed by Ashok. Bajaj said it was Ghai's story and he could have it back anytime he wanted.

Suneha Arts, a sister concern of Mukta Arts, was set up to produce Ashok's film. Ghai worked on the story a bit and named it *Ram Lakhan*, after the two brothers. He set up a separate unit for it—internally called the 'B Unit'—which had A-list talent such as screenplay writer Ram Kelkar and music director R.D. Burman.

After deciding to shelve *Devaa*—among the more difficult decisions of his life—Ghai took comfort in the story of the mother and her two sons. He told Ashok they had to start the film immediately if he was to avoid going into depression. He went to Khandala to develop the story further and returned fifteen days later with the fleshed-out plot and sub-plots of *Ram Lakhan*. It was just a few pages, but had everything he needed to begin.

It wasn't a startlingly new story and had been brought to the screen several times before. One of the earliest versions was Mehboob Khan's

Aurat (1940), about an indomitable woman (Radha, played by Sardar Akhtar) and her two sons, one good (Ramu, played by Surendra) and the other bad (Birju, played by Lala Yaqoob). Mehboob Khan remade *Aurat* as *Mother India* (1957), with Nargis as Radha, Rajendra Kumar as Ramu and Sunil Dutt as Birju. Yash Chopra's *Deewar* had Nirupa Roy playing the mother with one good son (Shashi Kapoor as Ravi) and one grey (Amitabh Bachchan as Vijay). In all three films, the mother had a softer spot for the errant son. In fact, Nirupa Roy's character in *Deewar* says in as many words that she had always loved Vijay more.

Ghai believed in giving his audiences stories they were already somewhat familiar with—not too much, just a little bit, so they could identify with the characters and events easily, instead of feeling alienated and wondering what on earth was going on. The secret lay in giving the story a unique touch and treatment. *Mother India* is similar to *Aurat* because it is a remake, but totally different from *Deewar*, just as *Deewar* is different from *Ram Lakhan*. *Mother India* is set in a village and is peopled with farmers battling drought and usurious moneylenders. *Deewar* is a city film, in which one son is a cop and the other a smuggler. In *Ram Lakhan*, both sons are policemen, but with sharply different ethics. In this modern-day Ramayana, Lakhan believes it is the age of Ravana, not Rama. Both brothers witness their mother's pain and ignominy, but it makes Ram more honourable and ethical while having the opposite effect on Lakhan. Ram thinks of his uniform as a sacred responsibility; Lakhan thinks of it as the key to the treasuries of corrupt people.

Ghai frequently turned to the Ramayana and the Mahabharata for inspiration for his stories. The reincarnation plot in *Karz*, the shades of Radha and Krishna in *Hero*, the reformed dacoit in *Devaa*, these were all drawn from the two epics. Not only are the epics rooted deep in people's consciousness but they are also two of the finest stories ever told, with fascinating plots and diverse, full-bodied, colourful characters. Ghai had grown up on a steady diet of tales from the Ramayana and the Mahabharata, as told by his mother.

'If you are making an Indian film, you have to be well-versed with Indian history and mythology,' says Ghai.

The production of *Ram Lakhan* remained under the Suneha Arts banner and Ashok continued in his role as producer. Ram Kelkar, who had a strong social ethos and understanding of families, stayed on as the screenplay writer. But there were a few changes. Some members of *Devaa*'s unit said they had been promised a Ghai film and insisted on being a part of whichever film he was directing after *Karma*. This was all good-natured, but Ghai found himself in a quandary. He had promised *Devaa*'s unit a Subhash Ghai film and he felt he owed them one.

A significant change was L -P replacing R.D. Burman in *Ram Lakhan*. Ghai wrote a letter to Burman, explaining the circumstances and promising that they would work together soon. For Burman, who in the late 1980s was grappling with the troughs of an otherwise stellar career, this would have been quite a setback.

Ghai, to his great regret, never did get to work with Burman, whose music he admired immensely. But he feels no guilt. After *Devaa*, he needed to go back to the comfort of people he knew well and with whom he gelled, to a unit that was one big family on the set. L–P and Anand Bakshi, on whom Ghai relied heavily not only for the music score but also other advice about the story and characters, were important parts of that family.

Together, the four of them indulged in all sorts of experiments. The song 'My name is Lakhan' was originally meant to feature only Anil Kapoor. But when they were recording the song, Ghai said that this was a character-first song (as opposed to lyrics-first, music-first or dance-first); it was meant to reveal Lakhan's character, but for that, Radha had to be in it.

Anand Bakshi wrote Radha's lines and L–P composed them on the spot.

But, Ghai wondered, was Lakhan complete without Ram?

So they wrote Ram's lines and composed that part of the tune.

Ghai wasn't done. What about the mother? The mother had to be in it too, he said.

Bakshi came up with lines for the mother, quietly throwing up his hands in exasperation; he told L–P they better move fast lest Ghai bring even more characters into the song.

For the tune itself, Pyarelal lined up seventy-six rhythm instrument players, making this one of the rare songs that has none of the mainstays of Hindi film music: brass, violin, saxophone, flute, trumpet or harmonica—not even in the interludes.

For '*Bada dukh dina*', they lined up eighteen sitars and twelve flutes. The usual for a song was two to four sitars and one to three flutes. When the song's tune was complete, Laxmikant said only Lata Mangeshkar could do justice to it. But, those days, Mangeshkar was upset with L–P and the composer duo was working with Anuradha Paudwal and Kavita Krishnamurthy instead.

Undaunted, Ghai landed up at the studio where Mangeshkar was recording a song and told her about this new masterpiece his team had come up with. She was nice and warm to him, but said she was too tied up. Ghai came back and insisted that Laxmikant accompany him to meet Mangeshkar. He did, and Mangeshkar relented and agreed to sing the song.

'"*Bada dukh dina*" is *Ram Lakhan*'s heart and soul,' says Ghai.

Ghai needed to be around people who trusted him completely, who would make themselves available round the clock, week after week, month after month.

Two of those people—no surprises here—were Jackie Shroff and Anil Kapoor. Ghai spoke to them together at his home; he was down with fever at the time. The two actors were unabashed in their delight when they heard the story and did not hesitate even for a second before accepting the lead roles in *Ram Lakhan*. Both were middling stars at the time—they had tasted success, but they were not part of the top echelon that still belonged to Bachchan, Jeetendra, Dharmendra, Rishi Kapoor, Shatrughan Sinha and Mithun Chakraborty. Anil Kapoor, the more versatile actor, became Lakhan, whose character was more nuanced, and had both negative and positive shades. Jackie Shroff became the upright older brother, Ram. This was one of those films in which casting the male leads was a no-brainer.

Getting the right actress to play the mother was crucial. Her role was as central as Dilip Kumar's in *Karma* and *Vidhaata*. *Ram Lakhan* is Sharda's story from the beginning to the end, though she goes away on a pilgrimage in the middle to give her sons space to carry the story towards the climax. She is the custodian of the urn that contains the ashes of her husband, the boys' father. This urn is the hook that binds the story together and triggers the events of the climax, when Lakhan discovers it in his mother's trunk.

Incidentally, the urn wasn't there in the original pages that Ghai had brought back from Khandala. After two schedules had been shot, Ghai and his writers felt the need for a hook to hold together the sprawling story. And they came up with the urn.

Ghai narrated the story of *Ram Lakhan* to Rakhee, who had made the swift transition from playing Amitabh Bachchan's love interest in *Barsaat Ki Ek Raat* (1981) to his mother in *Shakti* (1982), and other mature roles thereafter. While writing the mother's character, it was she who Ghai found himself thinking of from time to time. He admired her as much for her acting as for her face.

'Rakhee's face is strong and sparkling. Her eyes emanate power,' he says.

Ghai told her Ram and Lakhan's mother was strong as well as soft.

'So is she strong or soft?' she wanted to be clear.

Ghai said that the audiences no longer expected the mother to be an abla naari (a helpless, suffering woman). Sharda loves her sons and indulges them, but there is also a grim side to her. When her husband dies, she does not cry. After the funeral, she takes a bath, and the water flowing down the drain looks dark red, as if she has bathed in blood. She keeps the urn containing her husband's ashes safe until her enemies are brought to book. Determined to avenge her husband, she nurtures her sons as weapons. She breaks down only when she learns of her younger son's treachery. Sharda's pratigya (vow) and the bloodbath have shades of Draupadi from the Mahabharata.

Rakhee needed to know no more. She agreed. Ghai was delighted. Inspired by her personality and star power, Ghai developed the character further. He always wanted all his actors to have the best role in his movie, different from anything they had done before, and Rakhee was no exception.

Amrish Puri had played the villain in *Vidhaata*, *Hero* and *Meri Jung*, but he had portrayed a different character in each: a mafia don in the first, the dreaded convict Pasha in the second, and a crooked lawyer in the third. In *Ram Lakhan*, he is Bishambhar, a feudal, property-hogging, narcotics-transporting criminal who is never far from his precious dibba of paan.

Anupam Kher switched from being Doctor Dang in *Karma* to Devdhar Shastri, a religious-minded grocer who is a devout vegetarian, to the extent that he even bans his assistant, Kashi Ram, from speaking the word 'anda' (egg). Shastri keeps quarrelling with Lakhan, and bantering with Kashi Ram, played by Satish Kaushik.

The three of them and Radha, Shastri's daughter and Lakhan's romantic interest, have their own subplot, and they improvised like crazy. They created entire scenes that were not in the screenplay, which anyway was fluid. The scene in which Lakhan comes to Shastri's shop to buy 'vegetarian eggs' and puts real eggs on Shastri's seat which he then disastrously descends on was created entirely on the set.

'Comedy is done best when it is not rigidly scripted and planned,' says Ghai.

That year, Kher and Kaushik jointly won the Filmfare award for best performance in a comic role for *Ram Lakhan*.

Ghai first met Madhuri Dixit in Kashmir, where he was staying in a hotel and looking around for locations to shoot *Karma*. Director Sohanlal Kanwar was also in Kashmir at the same time, shooting *Awara Baap* (1985), written by Ram Kelkar and starring Rajesh Khanna and Meenakshi Seshadri. Ghai had worked with Kanwar and went to visit him on the set. There he ran into Khatoon, a hairdresser who had worked for *Karz*. She told Ghai about a young girl who had a small role in the film.

'She has a nice face, you will like her,' she told Ghai.

Ghai thought it was one of the scores of recommendations he received every week. But he had time on his hands and asked Khatoon if she could bring the girl over to have lunch with him.

Madhuri Dixit came with her mother, Snehlata, and Khatoon. They told Ghai about Dixit's fledgling acting career. She had played the lead in *Abodh* (1984), which had not done well, and now the offers coming her way were only for second or third leads.

Ghai detected a magnetism in Dixit's face. She reminded him of Suchitra Sen, the famed Bengali actress known to Hindi audiences for *Devdas* (1955), *Mamta* (1966) and *Aandhi* (1975). Hers and Madhubala's faces are generally considered to be perfect for Indian screens.

But Dixit was shy and weak. It's how Ghai remembers her back then. Still, he invited her to visit the Mukta Arts office in Mumbai. Dixit came to the office with her mother and sister, Rupa. It was during this meeting that Ghai became convinced of Dixit's potential and decided to mentor her.

A production house needed to have new people under its wings to counter the dominance of stars. However, Ghai was already deep into the making of *Karma* and wouldn't start a new film until after this was done. He told Madhuri and her mother that he could offer her a five-year contract under which she would be trained for a year or more and then work in three films with Mukta Arts. She could do outside films with the banner's permission.

This was Mukta Arts' standard contract with newcomers. It also included a clause that if the newcomer became a star and did endorsements, they would donate a fifth of the endorsement fee to the Mukta Arts Workers' Welfare Trust. All actors and actresses, while signing up, thought this was a fine gesture, but few wanted to honour it once they became stars.

Dixit signed the agreement and her training, which included, among other things, lessons in acting, dancing, make-up, hairdressing, what to wear on social occasions and what to an evening party, began. Ghai told the Dixits that Madhuri should not accept any random films that could hamper her progress as a leading lady. He suggested that if she had already signed up to do a small role in a film, she should quit it, returning the signing amount. Madhuri and her entire family trusted Ghai and followed his advice.

Meanwhile, Ghai requested Rakesh Nath, Anil Kapoor's secretary, to manage Dixit's affairs as well. Nath agreed.

The song, '*Maine rab se tujhe maang liya*' in *Karma* was originally planned differently. Jackie Shroff and Sridevi would chance upon a film unit from Mumbai shooting a song, and imagine themselves to be singing the song. The other pair, from the shooting, would sing the first few lines, until Jackie and Sridevi took over.

Ghai wanted the other pair in the song to be unknown faces. Someone suggested the new girl who had just signed a contract with Mukta Arts. Ghai thought it was a good idea, and flew in Dixit. He was happy with her performance, brief though it was, but he later deleted that part because he wanted her to be perceived only as a leading lady, not as someone who made brief appearances.

Soon after, Dixit was offered the lead in *Uttar Dakshin* (1987) opposite Jackie Shroff and Rajinikanth. The film was written by Ghai and directed by his former chief assistant director, Prabhat 'Kuku' Khanna.

While he was busy with *Karma* in Mumbai, Ghai received a call from Saroj Khan. Since the climax song of *Vidhaata*, Saroj Khan had become a Mukta Arts regular, choreographing all the songs of *Karma*. She was calling from Chennai, where she was choreographing the song '*Laila mar gayee*' for *Uttar Dakshin*.

Saroj Khan, never one to hide her emotions, did not sound pleased. Madhuri Dixit, the new girl, she said, could not dance.

Ghai was astonished. Dixit had trained for years in Kathak and had also performed on stage. Saroj Khan did not doubt that, but she was not looking to have Kathak in '*Laila mar gayee*'. Filmi dance was a different art form.

Ghai flew down to Chennai and saw Dixit dance. It was obvious she wasn't getting the hang of it. Ghai spoke to her after the shot and asked what the problem was.

'Sir, I know Kathak, but I am not able to get the expressions and gestures Saroj ji wants,' she said.

Ghai realized it was nothing but her shyness and inhibition. To be a successful leading lady in Hindi films she would have to shed those and learn the grammar of film dancing.

'All you need to do,' he told her, 'is watch Saroj's eyes and face. Filmi dance is about the eyes and face and adaa, more than the movement of the body. You have nice eyes and a nice smile. You need to put them to use.'

That would have given Dixit confidence and shown her the way.

'There are some people who are born to work, Madhuri is one of them. The thing she loved most was her work; everything else was duty,' says Ghai. 'When she danced, her passion shone through. She would be unrecognizable from the girl she was moments before.'

After Dixit signed the contract with Mukta Arts, Ghai made a short video featuring her. In different parts of the video, she was a traditional girl and a modern one, and some parts had her dancing. Rakesh Nath took the video to eight of the top producer–directors, along with a letter from Ghai, saying he had signed Dixit up for his next film and she was going to be a star. If the other producer–directors wanted to cast her, they should send Mukta Arts a cheque for ₹5,000.

All eight sent the cheques. Among them were Feroze Khan, who cast Dixit in *Dayavan* (1988), and N. Chandra, who had been told about her by Anil Kapoor and wanted her for *Tezaab* (also 1988).

Soon after, Mukta Arts took out a massive announcement in *Screen* magazine, presenting Madhuri Dixit as the girl who would be queen, one who had already been signed up by eight producers. The industry sat up and took notice, not only of what was said but also how—even the announcement of a new film in *Screen* used to occupy no more than a page or two; Dixit was splashed over six.

Ghai's involvement in Dixit's career went beyond the films she did for Mukta Arts. When Saroj Khan, who choreographed '*Ek do teen*' showed him the song, Ghai said it was good, but had only long shots. Dixit could hardly be seen in it.

'Put in close-ups. It should be Madhuri's song,' he told Saroj Khan.

The song was shot again, and became one of Dixit's most famous dance numbers, making her the country's favourite 'Ek Do Teen Girl'.

When the time came to choose Radha, Devdhar Shastri's daughter, in *Ram Lakhan*, Dixit was the easy and obvious choice. Radha, in many ways, was Madhuri: trusting, innocent and obedient. Radha presented quite a contrast to Lakhan's clever and street-smart ways.

Did Madhuri also happen to have the right name, or the right first alphabet in her name? Over the years, a perception has gained ground that Ghai likes his leading ladies to have names beginning with M: Meenakshi, Madhuri, Manisha, Mahima.

He dismisses it as nothing more than coincidence.

'My wife is Mukta, and my daughters are Meghna and Muskaan. Meenakshi, Madhuri and Manisha were their original names, we did not give them those names,' he says.

He did convert Ritu Chaudhary into Mahima, though, for *Pardes*.

'Yes, we did give Mahima her screen name, because there was already an actress called Ritu Shivpuri. But Mahima chose the name herself,' says Ghai, and goes on to add, 'and I did not change Katrina and Aishwarya to Matrina and Maishwarya. I do not believe in superstition. I believe in karma. Actions can rewrite destiny.'

Ghai liked being involved in the songs and dances in his films. Influenced by the likes of V. Shantaram, Guru Dutt and Manoj Kumar, he believed that songs were great tools of storytelling. Many directors were comfortable leaving the filming and editing of songs to the choreographer. But Ghai controlled the camera for songs just as he did for other scenes, and also edited the songs himself.

One day before '*Bada dukh dina*' was to be shot, Saroj Khan invited Ghai to come and watch the rehearsals. She was kicked about the song and wanted to make the dance a masterpiece.

Ghai came, saw the dance, and blew a fuse. The steps, expressions and gestures made it look like a mujra (a courtesan's dance). The song was about Radha, a young girl from a conservative, traditional family, fearlessly declaring her love for Lakhan before his elder brother—in Indian culture, the relationship of a girl with her intended husband's elder brother is a sacred one—and she would be doing so before people who were trying to humiliate her. The song was a helpless girl's tale of woe, not a celebration of sexiness by a siren.

'You seem to be so focused on the dance that you have ignored the story,' Ghai told Saroj Khan. 'A song and dance is irrelevant without the story.'

The choreographer was understandably upset. She had worked hard on the song for ten days. It was supposed to be shot the next day.

When filming began, Ghai made Dixit sit on the carpet and started shooting the song without any dance steps. Saroj Khan was so upset she walked out of the set and stationed herself in the canteen. She instructed an assistant to tell Ghai to choreograph the entire song himself.

Ghai chuckled. He understood this was a tantrum; Saroj Khan was a genuinely nice person. He told the assistant to tell her to relax and that he would summon her when the song needed dance steps. Till then, she could stay in the canteen and chew paan.

He spent two days filming the mukhda and filled it with Dixit's close-ups. She stayed on the carpet, a veil covering her head and forehead, and sang with her eyes and smile. She gets up only after half of the first antara is over.

On the third day, as Radha finally rose to her feet, she needed dance steps. Ghai set up a long shot with a trolley to capture the background dancers while a beautiful sitar piece played out. He told his chief assistant director, Shashi Wadia, to call Saroj Khan back to the set. She did come back, but spoke to Ghai only through Wadia.

Once the song was done, Ghai edited it and booked a theatre for the trial. He told Wadia to tell Saroj Khan to go and watch the song. She did, and came straight to Ghai's house from the theatre.

'Subhash ji, I'll never argue with you again,' she said, touching his feet. 'I could not have imagined that this song would look so good on screen.'

Ghai told her she was a wonderful dancer and choreographer, but this was cinema. 'I have to think about the entire film, story and characters as a whole.'

They remained good friends till Saroj Khan's death.

Ram Lakhan had one of the most eclectic collection of villains in any Hindi film ever. Amrish Puri, a Ghai regular returning to the unit after missing out on *Karma*, was supported by Paresh Rawal, Raza Murad, Annu Kapoor, Anand Balraj, Gulshan Grover, Sonika Gill and Lalita Kumari. Each stood out because of their distinct characters and lines.

Ghai had meticulously planned the characters of Ram, Lakhan, and their mother—he had some three pages of notes on the brothers and a bit more on the mother. For the villains, however, he and the team did plenty of improvisation while shooting.

Paresh Rawal, as Bhanu, is his older brother Bishambhar's shadow, constantly echoing his views. Ghai made Bhanu literally echo his brother by repeating the last bits of whatever Bishambhar had just said.

The brothers' constant companion is Shiv Charan, Bishambhar's wife's brother, played by Annu Kapoor, who is perpetually ingratiating towards his brother-in-law.

Kesariya Vilayati, played by Gulshan Grover, was not in the story initially. His character had to be written because Grover insisted on being in the film. Although Ghai told him there was no role for him, Grover was adamant. He was ready to play even a sidekick, he said, but Ghai felt he was too good for that.

After *Karma*, a lot of people wanted to work with Ghai and went to great lengths to show their keenness. This was a sharp contrast from the days right after *Krodhi*.

Grover came to Ghai one day, in costume, with long hair and a beard. Ghai broke into laughter. 'Why have you come looking like a joker?' he asked.

'Not a joker, sir, look at me,' said Grover. 'Don't I look like a good villain?'

Ghai admired his eagerness so much he wrote in a new character.

When they were shooting, he made the impromptu decision to have Kesariya Vilayati refer to himself as a 'bad man'. Grover was to say it frequently through the brief role he had in the film. Ghai thought it could be like Ranjeet's 'Once in a blue moon' in *Vishwanath*. There was something chilling about a bad man unabashedly calling himself just that. The impact of that brief role was such that Grover is still remembered as Bad Man.

Raza Murad was Sir John, a 'chairman villain' like Sir Judah in *Karz*. 'You have given Gulshan a hit line, what about me?' he asked Ghai, somewhat miffed at this perceived slight.

Ghai had already given Sir John a different look with white hair, a white beard and dark glasses. One of his eyes was made of stone, so he had to turn his head more than normal to be able to look on that side. But now he wanted a line too. Ghai and his team came up with, '*Khelne do, khelne do, hum baad mein khelenge* (Let them play, our turn will come later).' Murad was told to not react much, only to remain grave and speak this line.

Sonika Gill was Vivienne, Sir John's right hand, the posh villainess with a heart of gold to go with her short golden hair and sea-blue eyes. She looked exotic and sophisticated to the Indian eye.

Anand Balraj played Bishambhar's son, Debu, just returned from abroad. He got a surfeit of English lines: 'Debu from America', etc.

The one thing about *Ram Lakhan* Ghai planned meticulously was its mahurat. Ghai wanted it to be even grander than *Karma*'s and *Devaa*'s mahurats. He booked all the rooms in Hotel Fariyas in Khandala and invited the who's who of the film industry for a three-day getaway. Everyone—producers, directors, stars and distributors—came. Dilip Kumar gave the mahurat clap.

It was a constant party, morning till night, with the songs of the film playing everywhere in the background. The songs had of course already become huge hits. *Ram Lakhan* was the first Hindi film to have its music released on CD.

People said the party was like a big wedding.

This was designed to lift the unit's spirits after the *Devaa* disappointment and assure them that Mukta Arts would continue making bigger and better films. It recharged everyone in the unit, from the cinematographer, writers and editors to the sound recordist, the lighting people, production managers—people who are all crucial in the making of a film.

In the switch from *Devaa* to *Ram Lakhan*, Ghai learnt an important lesson: one should never be overambitious and try too hard to make a magnum opus. The self-imposed stress spoils things. Ghai had wanted *Krodhi* and *Devaa* to become milestones in the history of Indian cinema; instead, they had brought him anxiety and worry.

Ghai and his unit made *Ram Lakhan* as if they were playing a game. Ghai was back to his merry ways on the sets, telling stories, singing songs, mingling with the unit and generally having fun with everyone. He felt confident and secure again. He was no longer playing in a professional league where he had to be proper, measured, calculated and parliamentary. He felt free again. This was the therapy he needed to get over *Devaa*.

'*Ram Lakhan* is a film that made itself, it just happened,' he says.

After *Devaa* was shelved, three distributors had walked away from *Ram Lakhan*. They saw it as a big step down for Ghai. However, all three came for the film's silver jubilee party. Over drinks, they admitted that they had, to their own detriment, misunderstood the potential of *Ram Lakhan*.

The film was such a big hit at the box office that it propelled Anil Kapoor and Jackie Shroff into the top echelon of stars. Kapoor is still remembered as Lakhan; and Shroff proved his mettle as an actor with a thoughtful, mature performance. Rakhee transformed the image of the Hindi film mother—and went on to reprise the role with aplomb in *Karan Arjun* (1995).

The showstopper, though, was Madhuri Dixit. Coming just eleven Fridays after *Tezaab*, the big hit of 1988, *Ram Lakhan*, the mega hit of 1989, established her as the biggest challenger to Sridevi's crown as the reigning female superstar, and one of the finest dancers ever. Two minutes into '*Bada dukh dina*', as Dixit gets up from the carpet for her first dance steps, she does so with such confidence and grace, it is like she is telling the world: 'Watch me, and remember the name.'

16

Saudagar: Clash of the Titans

Ram Lakhan was possible because the actors trusted the director and gave their best to help him execute his story and vision, even though it was clear to everyone that there was no final, bound script.

Saudagar, which was released in 1991, had a complete, fleshed out, bound script though. It was voluminous, like an ancient text, and had nearly two dozen important characters vying for attention and scenes. Perhaps, somewhere in his heart, Ghai had still not given up on his dream to make a *Devaa*, and that may have motivated him to move from *Ram Lakhan*'s family affairs to a project of epic proportions.

'If I was to be a truly big and successful director, I had to be able to make big films,' he says.

As usual, he did not want stars. So, he reused his strategy from *Vidhaata* and looked at *Saudagar* as a story about two generations—a pair of old men, sworn enemies, whose grandchildren fall in love—eliminating the middle generation that would have been portrayed by reigning stars.

The offspring of two warring clans falling in love with each other was not a new plot; it has been around at least from the times of Shakespeare, whose *Romeo and Juliet* has spawned countless adaptations. But Ghai gave it a twist.

Usually, the stories of young lovers from feuding families led to the lovers running away—in *Bobby* (1973) and *Love Story* (1981) for instance—and/or meeting with a tragic end—*Ek Duuje Ke Liye* (1981) and *Qayamat Se Qayamat Tak* (1988). In Ghai's story, though, the young lovers decide not to flee or end their lives but to end the feud and reunite their families by exchanging places. Else, they won't marry; that's how much they love their families.

Ghai wanted to give *Saudagar* a wide canvas, so he chose Ashok Mehta, the cinematographer for *Ram Lakhan*, once again. He had picked Mehta to shoot *Devaa* after he watched Aparna Sen's masterpiece *36 Chowringhee Lane* (1981), which Mehta had shot.

For *Karz*, *Vidhaata*, *Hero* and *Karma*, Ghai had worked with Kamlakar Rao, who was a technical wizard and a camera engineer. But while working with Mehta on *Devaa*, Ghai found that his own concept of cinematography changed completely. Mehta raised the bar of artistry and creativity with every shot. With Rao, Ghai had done a lot of cuts and zooms. Mehta focused more on lighting and paid immaculate attention to properties. He engaged with the art director and set designers to improve his frames. When Ghai saw the rush prints of *Devaa*, he became aware of a new kind of photography.

When *Devaa* was shelved, Mehta was one of those who migrated to *Ram Lakhan*'s unit. It was when he shot its first schedule that Ghai sensed it might not end up being the small film he had in mind. Always unhurried and indifferent to what other pressing engagements the actors might have had, Mehta made every frame better than Ghai had imagined it. He had a way with low-key lighting and could shoot in the flame of just a candle, or even a lit matchstick.

Distributors didn't appreciate Mehta's art as much because the frames would not be properly lit in the theatres of small centres, but Ghai just loved it.

'Kamlakar was a master technician, Mehta an artiste. K.K. Mahajan was my first teacher of cinematography, Kamlakar helped me grow as a director, and Ashok taught me aesthetic,' he says.

Ghai reunited with his writing partner from *Devaa*, Sachin Bhowmick, his usual choice for larger-than-life films, to script *Saudagar*. He also roped in Kamlesh Pandey, the dialogue writer who had recently worked on the blockbuster *Tezaab* and the delightful *Chaalbaaz* (1989).

Pandey had a sound grip over the epics, which were an inevitable part of Ghai's storylines. Together, they settled on the title, *Saudagar*. However, Rajshri Productions had made a film in 1973 by the same name, starring Amitabh Bachchan and Nutan. So Ghai approached the Barjatyas, seeking permission to use the title, and Rajshri, the nice folks that they were, graciously agreed, without fuss.

For the next five months, the three writers discussed and developed the story and characters. After each discussion, Ghai would write the draft himself on paper in his own hand. They delved deeper into the story of the two old men. They are friends when young, and clash because of a dilemma, a misunderstanding and pride. The second generation carries the feud forward. Matters only worsen with the passing of years.

The two old men were given contrasting personalities to accentuate their differences and add a sharper edge to their conflict. One becomes a rich, suave businessman who flies around in a helicopter; the other is the rustic head of a village. One is proud and haughty, the other down to earth.

Around this time, Ghai went to attend a wedding in Delhi. After lunch, he went to the bathroom where he bumped into Anand Bakshi. The lyricist asked Ghai how the story was coming along and whether the title had been chosen. Ghai said he had finalized *Saudagar*.

Bakshi nodded and grunted. As he washed his hands in the sink, he said, '*Saudagar, sauda kar* (Trader, do your trade).' Then, as he wiped his hands on the towel, he added, '*Dil le le, dil dekar* (Give me your heart in trade for mine).'

Ghai had the mukhda of his title song right there in the men's room. Back in Mumbai, he took it to Laxmikant and told him it was crafted while Bakshi washed his hands in a sink. The composer said he would work on it in the shower.

After *Ram Lakhan*, Ghai could have got several top stars by just crooking his finger. But he zeroed in on two stalwarts who had settled nicely into their second innings—Dilip Kumar and Raaj Kumar—and decided to get two newcomers to play the third generation lovebirds.

Newcomers not because he wanted to show off to the world his ability to turn them into stars, but because they would add depth to the story by appearing vulnerable and incapable of ending the age-old feud between the mighty patriarchs. They would be rabbits before lions, sparrows before eagles, minnows before whales—always an interesting confrontation that adds to the drama and piques viewers' curiosity about how the task would ever be accomplished.

When Ghai narrated the story to Anand Bakshi, the latter suggested he get absolutely fresh faces. 'They will create their own power on screen if you write the characters well, this story needs that power.'

Till then, Ghai had been considering taking fledgling actors who were a film or two old, but now he made up his mind to take absolute newcomers, and wrote the characters accordingly.

But first, he wanted the oldies in the hut.

Dilip Kumar heard the story—the plot and broad storyline—and liked it. As usual, he said it was a good beginning and needed more work. 'Do you think you can pull it off?' he asked.

Ghai said he did.

'Have you thought it through?'

'Yes.'

'All right, then,' said Dilip Kumar.

It was as simple as that.

As Ghai was preparing to leave in his car, Dilip Kumar stopped him. 'Listen, who plays the other friend?'

Ghai hesitated. It was common knowledge that the two Kumars—Dilip and Raaj—had been at loggerheads since their last outing together in *Paigham* (1959).

Both had taken on new screen names upon entering the industry: Yusuf Khan became Dilip Kumar when he debuted in *Jawar Bhata* (1944) and Kulbhushan Pandit became Raaj Kumar with *Rangeeli* (1952). Dilip Kumar was the first among equals in the 1950s and 1960s. When he slowed down in the 1970s and took a five-year gap between *Bairaag* (1976), his last film as a romantic lead, and *Kranti* (1981), the start of his second innings in mature roles, Raaj Kumar picked up speed, appearing in a multitude of films. The 1980s saw him rule the mature protagonist's space in potboilers, from *Bulundi* (1980) to *Police Public* (1990). Both actors were known for having their own quirks and few would have described working with them as a cakewalk. At parties or public events, they were seen to assiduously avoid each other.

Ghai had a relationship with Dilip Kumar and believed he would be able to persuade him to do *Saudagar* opposite Raaj Kumar, but he did not want a discussion right then. As he rolled up the car window—power windows were not yet standard—he mumbled, 'Raaj Kumar,' and sped away.

He wondered if Dilip Kumar would phone him or summon him, but he heard nothing. Finally, a few days later, he went back to Dilip Kumar on the pretext of discussing some aspects of the story. They talked of this and that for a while, and then, inevitably, the subject of Raaj Kumar came up.

'Think about it,' Dilip Kumar cautioned him. 'Shehzada [crown prince] is not an easy man to work with.'

In his heart, Ghai knew no one else would be able to match Dilip Kumar in a parallel role. He stood his ground. He had fallen in love with his story and characters and wanted to go ahead.

Dilip Kumar said it was up to Ghai, but that Shehzada should be spoken to as soon as possible.

Ghai phoned Raaj Kumar. This was the time when a call from him would have been the event of the day for most actors. Unsurprisingly, Raaj Kumar immediately came on the line and invited Ghai over to his house in the evening.

The two men had never met before. Raaj Kumar turned out to be a fine host. He brought out a bottle of whisky and glasses himself, and, while they drank, urged Ghai to try the accompaniments, pointing out the specialty of each. He was a warm person, and, like many of his screen characters, a bit theatrical. He spoke with the same deliberate pauses that elicited applause in theatres. As on screen, he used 'jaani' quite a lot in real life as well, often referred to himself in the third person and used the royal 'we'.

Actors are not fools; they know why a director has called out of the blue. Raaj Kumar would have known what was coming, but he waited until after dinner to broach the topic of Ghai's visit.

'Chief, I have heard good things about your *Ram Lakhan*,' said Raaj Kumar.

Ghai thanked him, and said he had a new project. He narrated the story of *Saudagar*, adding that he wanted him to play one of the two patriarchs. Raaj Kumar's first question was who would play the other role.

Ghai raised his glass, held it in the air right in front of his face, and blurted out: 'Dilip Kumar.'

Raaj Kumar raised his own glass to his lips slowly and took a long sip. Ghai dug into the snacks and started talking about the importance of having two stalwarts in the film. It was the story about two towering personalities, two lions in the jungle. The actors had to live up to the characters; not everyone could do justice to the roles.

Raaj Kumar remained thoughtful for a while. Finally, he raised his glass in a toast, and said, 'Look, Jaani, after me, if there is anyone I consider a good actor, it is Dilip Kumar. You are thinking on the right lines. Let there be a clash of two lions, the world will watch. Let me know when your script is ready.'

Ghai let out the breath he'd been holding. He was heartened by the fact that both men had stressed on the script.

Raaj Kumar asked if he had spoken to Dilip Kumar. Ghai said he had.

'So, what did he say?'

'He said if there is any actor who can do justice to this role, it is you,' said Ghai.

This was a convincing tactic. But, as in love, you cannot always be completely truthful in filmmaking.

Ghai told Dilip Kumar that his and Raaj Kumar's roles would match in significance and length. Dilip Kumar said that was how it ought to be. His own role would not come out well unless Raaj Kumar's character was also equally powerful.

'And don't worry about me and my comforts,' he said, 'look after Shehzada.'

Ghai was so overwhelmed he could have kissed Dilip Kumar's feet right there. He took out the note every actor had to sign. The money slot was blank. He asked the thespian how much it should be.

'I don't remember how much you paid me for *Karma*.'

Ghai told him.

'Don't I deserve an increment?' Dilip Kumar asked.

Ghai laughed and added to the *Karma* figure before writing it in.

'The whole discussion took a minute; there were no agents, no secretaries around,' says Ghai.

Next he went to visit Raaj Kumar at his farmhouse, forty kilometres outside Bangalore. Since this was the first time they would be working together, Ghai was willing to go the extra mile. He gave Raaj Kumar the note and said he wanted to pay him the same amount as Dilip Kumar because he wanted to treat them equal in every way. But that amount turned out to be lower than Raaj Kumar's standard fee. The actor said he wouldn't settle for anything less than what he commanded from others producers. Ghai agreed to pay him the market price but told him that he would raise Dilip Kumar's fee to match Raaj Kumar's.

When the script was ready, Raaj Kumar invited him to dinner at the Naval mess in Mumbai's Colaba area. It was an unusual setting for a script narration, but Ghai did not want to make a fuss. With several other tables occupied and chatter in the air, he narrated the script over pegs of whisky.

No sooner had he finished than Raaj Kumar shot back, 'What am I doing in this script?'

Ghai once again explained his role and its importance.

'I am not doing anything,' protested Raaj Kumar. 'It is all about Dilip Kumar.'

They drank more whisky.

Ghai understood actors by now—how their minds worked, what rattled them, what made them insecure. He weighed his words carefully.

'Let's do one thing,' he said, 'I will leave these pages of the story with you. Please read them during the day tomorrow.'

Raaj Kumar did not take kindly to that. 'Are you implying I did not understand what you narrated just now?'

Ghai said that perhaps his narration had not been up to scratch, or perhaps Raaj Kumar was too focused on Dilip Kumar's character to grasp his own role adequately.

Three days later, Raaj Kumar phoned him to ask what he was up to. Ghai said he was at home and not doing much. Raaj Kumar came over to his house. He confessed to not having slept the previous two nights, staying up to read the pages Ghai had left with him, thinking them over, and making notes.

Ghai waited patiently while Raaj Kumar detailed his discomfort. He raised sixteen issues with the narrative.

Ghai was on top of his story by now and addressed all sixteen points with ease. Most of the questions were related to Dilip Kumar's role, anyway. Simple stuff, such as: 'When he rebukes me, why do I say what I say?'; 'Will this make me look like a bad guy?'; 'Will Dilip Kumar get more sympathy from the public?' His last question was about which of the two died in the end.

Ghai said he had not figured that part out yet.

'But that is critical,' said Raaj Kumar, 'The one who dies will walk away the hero.'

Ghai said he would tell Raaj Kumar once the details were worked out. He understood that it was Raaj Kumar's insecurity taking the form of questions—he was daunted by the prospect of going toe-to-toe against Dilip Kumar after three decades.

'Here is a promise,' Ghai reassured him, 'once the film comes out, everyone will say that the two of you have done equally well.'

Raaj Kumar shook Ghai's hand and said he would leave it to the director to do justice to his role.

It was now up to Ghai and his team of writers to keep this promise. It was not so difficult in this case. This was not a fight between good and evil. This was the story of two friends whose friendship had turned to hatred. Both men were good in their own ways, and innocent of anything heinous. It was a matter of pride and misunderstanding, which would be cleared up.

Most actors get concerned with what the others in the film are doing. Dilip Kumar, of course, was an exception and often talked about developing other characters and giving them more play. Aamir Khan is another.

'I admire Aamir Khan,' says Ghai. 'He always puts the story, script and characters first, even if it gives him a smaller role. He asks questions only to understand the script and the situation. Once that is done, he is a team man.'

Incidentally, Aamir Khan came to Ghai's house when *Saudagar*'s cast was being chosen. After exchanging pleasantries and inquiring after each other's well-being, Aamir said he had heard that Ghai was working on a new project and was looking for someone to play a young lover. He said he would be delighted to work with Ghai.

Ghai was pleasantly surprised by Aamir's magnanimity. The young actor was already a star, having hit it out of the park with his debut, *Qayamat Se Qayamat Tak*. In an era where some of the biggest hits were filled with double entendre, violence and bizarre storylines, the film had turned the tide of filmmaking, reviving romance and young love as bankable subjects.

But it was that success that deterred Ghai. He thanked the actor and said, 'It is sweet of you. But you are too big a star. The romantic hero I need is someone who is completely unknown to viewers and rather nondescript. The film actually revolves around two grandfathers. The young man's role will not do justice to you.'

Aamir thanked him for explaining things so well and took his leave. At the door, though, he said if either the role or Ghai's mind were to change, he would be available. Ghai said he would definitely come to Aamir if he did not find the right newcomer.

Thirty to forty young women and as many young men walked into Mukta Arts to audition for *Saudagar*, but none matched Ghai's idea of the young lovebirds, Radha and Vasudev. What he was looking for in Radha was fresh, unblemished beauty, not a face that needed make-up. He needed someone who, when she woke up in the morning, had glowing skin and shining eyes merely after washing her face with water.

Instead, what he was getting were girls who wanted to be Sridevi or Madhuri Dixit, and young men who wanted to look like Salman Khan or Jackie Shroff. It would show not only in their look but also in their manners, starting with the way they did namaste. Their role models were great, but not what Ghai needed. The aspirants came without doing any research on the roles they were auditioning for.

Someone suggested Karisma Kapoor, Raj Kapoor's granddaughter, who was breaking the family taboo of women not working in the movies. Ghai was friends with her father, Randhir Kapoor, and of course, her uncle Rishi. He had seen her grow up and always thought of her as a niece of sorts. He felt he would not be comfortable directing someone who was like his own daughter.

'It was a stupid reason, I realize it today, but back then those were my sensibilities,' says Ghai.

Meanwhile, Rakesh Shrestha, an ace photographer who knew Ghai was looking for a new face, sent him photos of a girl from Nepal. The girl in the photos was wearing a cap and looked nothing like what Ghai had in mind.

A while later, the journalist Meena Iyer phoned Ghai and said the daughter of one of her friends from Nepal wanted to meet him. When Ghai realized it was the same girl whose photos Shrestha had sent, he said he didn't think she would suit the character. But Iyer was insistent. It was a Sunday evening and Ghai had dinner guests, but he told Iyer to tell the girl to come over.

When the doorbell rang, he opened the door himself, to find a young girl dressed in simple, everyday clothes, with loosely tied hair. She had everything he was looking for: beauty, innocence and shining eyes.

She introduced herself as Manisha Koirala. Her mother was there, too. Ghai invited them to his study for a quick chat. Koirala did not say much. Her mother said Manisha had been in the running to play the lead in *Prem* (1995), but at the last minute Shekhar Kapur and Boney Kapoor had chosen a girl called Tabu. Manisha and her mother were going to Delhi the next day. Ghai said he, too, would be in Delhi soon. The three of them agreed to meet at the Hyatt Regency, where Ghai would be staying. Then Manisha and her mother left.

As Ghai rejoined his dinner guests, one of them asked who the pretty young lady was. Inexplicably, Ghai heard himself reply, 'That's the heroine of *Saudagar*.'

A couple of days later, Ghai flew to Delhi and checked into the Hyatt. The next morning, he received a flower—a rose—with a card saying 'Welcome'; it was unsigned. After that, he got a rose every hour. Eight roses later, Manisha and her mother arrived with a bouquet of the same kind of roses.

'Did you get our other flowers?' they asked. 'Welcome to Delhi.'

As they chatted, Ghai switched on a little video camera, as he had done when Jackie Shroff came to meet him for *Hero*. He observed Koirala as she spoke about her early life and family. She was born in Nepal into a political family, but her early years were spent largely in India, first living in Varanasi with her maternal grandmother, and studying there and in Delhi. She had done a bit of modelling and, just for fun, acted in a Nepali film, *Pheri Bhetaula*.

Ghai said he would like to sign her for his film but she would have to take a few screen tests. He also told her not to lose heart if she was not picked; it would only be because she did not match this particular character, not because she lacked anything.

Koirala aced the tests and Ghai put her into a six-month training course for acting, dancing, make-up, horse riding, the works. She signed a five-year, three-film contract with Mukta Arts, just like Madhuri Dixit had.

A buzz was now inevitable around Koirala. People began to say she was the next Madhubala. Ghai told her to forget anything she heard and focus on learning her craft.

Ghai was known to be impulsive on occasion and given to making emotional decisions. His determination to use only new actors for the young lovers in the film was met with scepticism on several fronts. Distributors, when they could not get through to Ghai, tried to press his production executive, Sudesh Gupta, in the hope of getting better-known stars into the film. When Gupta requested him to look for other actors and actresses, including established ones, to play the young lovers of *Saudagar*, Ghai pointed to the film's initial poster which had a flower, and the line: 'Love blossoms under terror'. He asked Gupta whether the heroine should be a flower or a tube of cosmetic cream.

Gupta understood that his reasoning would not move Ghai when it came to the heroine, but he persevered, and asked if they could at least take a star for the young man's role.

Gupta's wish nearly came true. A time came when Ghai, in the absence of suitable candidates, began to wonder if he should speak to Aamir Khan and ask if he would still be interested.

However, one day, his chief assistant director Shashi Wadia phoned him at home to say a young fellow had come to the Mukta Arts office and that Ghai should meet him for a few minutes. 'He has a good face,' Wadia said.

Ghai told Wadia to send the follow over. The young man came and introduced himself as Vivek Mushran.

'Have you done any acting?' Ghai asked.

'No sir,' said Mushran.

'Any dancing?'

'No sir.'

It was like a replay of Ghai's conversation with Jackie Shroff at the time of making *Hero.* The difference was that where Jackie was strikingly handsome and had an aura, Vivek had an innocence that shone through.

Ghai asked him what made him think he could be in such a big film.

'I'm counting on you,' he said. 'I've heard you can make anyone an actor.'

Ghai burst out laughing. 'That's not how things work!' he said. 'This is an important role in an expensive film. What was it that motivated you to try?'

Vivek said, he too, was wondering the same thing.

His disarming vulnerability and openness made Ghai consider him seriously. That's how young men in the villages in the hills could be, he thought: unscarred by the ways of the big city. He screen-tested Mushran and signed him up.

Sudesh Gupta fell further into despair. At least, Manisha Koirala clearly had the makings of a star, Vivek Mushran not so much.

Meanwhile, Ghai went ahead and announced his line-up for *Saudagar*.

Newspapers and magazines labelled the pairing of the two Kumars as a recipe for certain disaster. Some said the film would take at least four years to make, others opined that it would never be made, that it would end up being another *Devaa*.

All these dire predictions seemed to be coming true when the first shooting schedule began.

For the first schedule, the unit went to Manali, where *Saudagar*'s Sanatanpur and Palinagar villages were created. Raaj Kumar had said he wouldn't be able to shoot for the first two days after reaching Manali because he would need to rest and recover from the trip. Ghai told him to come to the location after he had recovered. Meanwhile, he told Raaj Kumar, he would be shooting Dilip Kumar's scenes.

Competition with a peer is something that doesn't lose its edge even after decades. Raaj Kumar forgot all about his need to recover. As soon as he had checked into his hotel in Manali, he found out where the shoot was going to be and landed up there.

He sat in a tent some distance from where the cameras were set up and watched as Dilip Kumar delivered his lines. As the scene progressed, Raaj Kumar's expression changed. He accosted Ghai during the lunch break.

'Subhash, this is serious,' he said. 'I heard Dilip Kumar speak Haryanvi! What language do I speak?'

Ghai said Rajeshwar, Raaj Kumar's character, spoke proper Hindustani. An educated man who, for a time, was running a business overseas, he couldn't possibly speak a rural dialect.

'But now that he is back in India, can't he speak Haryanvi?'

'No,' Ghai said, 'your character is too proud to speak a rustic dialect. He ridicules Veer Singh, Dilip Kumar's character, for being uneducated and not being able to speak Hindi properly.'

'But,' Raaj Kumar protested, 'this is a contest I will lose before it has begun. Dilip Kumar will steal the show with his dialogues. I can't do this film.'

This was terrible. A hundred and fifty people of Ghai's unit had landed in Manali for the twenty-day schedule. This was just the second day, and one of the two lead actors was saying he wouldn't do the film. Usually in the face of crisis, Ghai either became aggressive and angry or calm and collected. This time, he took a deep breath and calmed himself with thoughts of the divine force.

'If you are not convinced by what I say, let's shelve this film,' he told Raaj Kumar. 'I will book your tickets to Mumbai for tomorrow.'

The unit members who heard this were stunned. The film had already made news. Distributors were onboard. Ghai told Raaj Kumar he had to finish the day's schedule, since the entire unit and Dilip Kumar were already on location and cameras had been set up; they could discuss the matter after pack-up. Raaj Kumar, simmering, returned to his hotel room.

Dilip Kumar sensed something was amiss. 'Do one thing, Subhash,' he said when Ghai explained the situation to him, 'let Shehzada speak Haryanvi lines.'

Ghai was resolute. This was about making a film while respecting the integrity of the story and script; not a game of one-upmanship between Dilip Kumar and Raaj Kumar.

When Ghai reached Raaj Kumar's hotel room in the evening, a bottle of whisky stood on the table, waiting. Ghai was heartened to see two glasses, which signalled that there would be a conversation and not a verdict without a hearing in Raaj Kumar's royal court.

'Sir, can I join you?' asked Ghai.

'Of course,' said Kumar and gestured for him to sit. He seemed to have thought things over in the six hours since his outburst.

'Subhash, you said I could trust you,' he began. 'You said you will keep the two of us equal in every way. We shook on this.'

'I did, and I will keep my promise,' said Ghai.

'You didn't tell me he was going to speak Haryanvi and I was not,' said Kumar. 'How are the two equal?'

Ghai explained that just as he hadn't discussed the particulars of Dilip Kumar's role with Raaj Kumar, he hadn't told Dilip Kumar what clothes or shoes Raaj Kumar would wear in the film, or what dialect he would speak in. The decision to have Veer Singh speak Haryanvi was a recent one, made as the screenplay evolved, because it suited the character of the rustic, uneducated villager. Also, Dilip Kumar had spoken Awadhi with much success in the blockbuster *Gunga Jumna* (1961) in which he played a villager-turned-dacoit.

'Let me tell you one thing, sir,' Ghai told Raaj Kumar. 'Nobody in my unit can believe that you were worried about Dilip Kumar's lines. They say the earth shakes when Raaj Kumar speaks his dialogues.'

That soothed Raaj Kumar somewhat, but he was still not entirely convinced. Finally, Ghai told him he could speak Haryanvi if he was adamant. 'However, think of the effect it will have on your character,' he said. 'In my screenplay, you are royalty. Can we have a king speaking a rustic dialect?'

This gave Raaj Kumar pause, and he stopped protesting. They ate dinner together. Afterwards, around half past midnight, Ghai went to meet Dilip Kumar, and told him Raaj Kumar was not yet fully convinced, but seemed to have calmed down.

'That's just like him,' said Dilip Kumar. 'First he will create an issue and then come around. So, are we shooting tomorrow?'

'We are shooting, come what may,' said Ghai.

He woke up at six in the morning for the seven-thirty shift. Before leaving the hotel, he left a note at the reception for Raaj Kumar: 'Raaj ji, I am leaving for the shoot. Remember, you play a lion in this film. I want to see whether the lion stays or goes away. I hope to see you at the location.'

Around nine-thirty, with the shooting in full swing, a car drove up to the location and stopped. Raaj Kumar stepped out, shoes first, like he did in his films. Ghai gestured to his unit and everyone clapped. When it was Raaj Kumar's turn to face the camera, Ghai handed him his dialogues—which were in high-brow Hindustani—and the actor took them without a word.

In that first schedule, Ghai avoided the confrontation scenes between the two patriarchs. Instead, he filmed their friendship song, *'Imli ka boota, beri ka ped'*, during which they are seen playing Holi. While Raaj Kumar's make-up was being done, he kept turning his head to see where all Dilip Kumar was dabbing his face with colour.

'Raaj ji,' Ghai told him with a chuckle, 'please turn this way and let us do your make-up.'

Raaj Kumar took the plate of colour and turned it over on his head. It was all in good humour.

Thereafter, the unit named the two veteran actors Chunnu and Munnu—names given to toddlers in Hindi-speaking areas. The entire unit called them by those names. One could hear the production managers saying: 'What is Chunnu's schedule today?' or 'When is Munnu arriving?' By the end of that schedule, even the tea boy would say: 'Chunnu Sa'ab's tea is ready.'

Once, Saira Banu happened to hear this and asked who Chunnu was.

'Your respected husband!' replied Ghai.

As Raaj Kumar came around to seeing Ghai's interpretation of the script and understood his way of working, it was Dilip Kumar's turn to go into a sulk. In ten years of their working together, this was the first time Ghai had got into a heated argument with the veteran actor, replete with raised voices, much to the surprise of those around them.

As the shooting progressed in Manali, Ghai wrote a new scene to make full use of Dilip Kumar's acting abilities. The young lovers have exchanged places: Rajeshwar has been spending time with Veer Singh's grandson while Rajeshwar's granddaughter has become a quasi-member of Veer Singh's family. They have pricked the old men's conscience and reminded them of their old friendship and their song: '*Imli ka boota beri ka ped*'. In the scene, both Rajeshwar and Veer Singh are plastered. Veer Singh, with a somewhat slurred speech, comes to the river that divides the two villages and hurls a monologue at Rajeshwar, whose mansion is just on the other side, well within earshot. Endearingly drunk and with one foot on a boulder, Veer Singh chides, mocks and challenges Rajeshwar, in the manner of old friends' banter. Rajeshwar, equally sozzled, does not say a word in response. He merely takes out his rifle and shoots in the air, safely away from where Veer Singh is standing.

On the day the scene was to be shot, Shashi Wadia told Ghai that Dilip Kumar was in discussions with Kamlesh Pandey, the dialogue writer, and wanted to see him.

'Everything all right?' Ghai asked.

'I don't think so,' said Wadia.

The moment Dilip Kumar saw Ghai, he said he wasn't going to do the scene. When Ghai asked what was wrong with it, the actor said it made no sense for one man to deliver two pages of dialogue while the other said absolutely nothing at all. Ghai explained that the scene was an important step in breaking the ice that had formed between the two friends over thirty-five years. That is how he had envisioned it in the screenplay.

This appeared to agitate Dilip Kumar further. 'I have been working for ages,' he said, 'but this is the most ridiculous scene I have ever come across.'

That hurt Ghai's creative pride. His voice rose to match Dilip Kumar's. 'I can tell you that when the history of Hindi cinema is written, this scene will be counted among the best ever.'

They quarrelled some more until, finally, Ghai left saying he and his unit would be ready to shoot the scene that evening, just before sunset. Two cameras would be mounted and waiting for the actor. Dilip Kumar shot back that there was no point in troubling the unit and mounting the cameras.

Ghai went ahead and set up the shoot.

Around four, Dilip Kumar arrived and made his way over the stones on the riverbed towards the cameras. He was visibly upset. When he asked for the scene, Ghai took out his pages and read them out while Dilip Kumar wrote it all down on paper in Urdu, as he always did, grumbling all the while.

Ghai asked for a rehearsal. Dilip Kumar agreed, but his dialogue delivery was forced; his heart was clearly not in it. Ghai offered to demonstrate what he wanted from the scene by acting it out himself.

'Why not! You do think of yourself as a good actor, don't you?' Dilip Kumar said cuttingly.

Ghai ignored the jibe, and put his heart, soul, body and throat into his performance. His voice rose to high pitches as his body swayed like a drunk man's. When he finished, the entire unit clapped and cheered.

Dilip Kumar was moved. He said he would give it a try, and went on to give a brilliant take. Ghai covertly gestured to his unit to applaud even more loudly than they had for him.

That scene did become a high point of the film, and reminded audiences of Dilip Kumar when he was at his peak.

In August 1991, *Saudagar* released to an enthusiastic response from audiences all over the country. The film fetched Ghai the Filmfare Best Director trophy, the only one of his career. While receiving the award, he said he did not think he deserved it, and was promptly criticized for not being humble. But he was genuinely surprised.

In those days, the awards people did not inform the winners beforehand, and the field that year was formidable. The nominees for Best Director included Yash Chopra for *Lamhe*, Mahesh Bhatt for *Dil Hai Ke Manta Nahin* and Randhir Kapoor for *Henna*. Ghai had expected Chopra to win.

Two months after the awards, he happened to meet Hrishikesh Mukherjee, who was the chairman of the jury. Ghai asked why they picked him. Mukherjee said Ghai was recognized for doing a true director's job.

Had *Saudagar*'s script been simply shot on film, it would have been a very different film, and a very long one—so voluminous was the script. For instance, take the death of Jackie Shroff's character, Vishal, which escalates the enmity between Veer and Rajeshwar. The script said he was bathing and chanting mantras. An assassin, lurking in the bushes, shoots a bullet into his chest. The scene was described with all the atmospherics and sounds.

In the actual scene, the audience sees Vishal bathing. The muzzle of a rifle appears on the screen. There is the sound of a gunshot, followed by a glimpse of the setting sun. In the film's pivotal murder, you see neither blood nor a bullet.

Another turning point in the film was the rape—a rarity for a Ghai film—and murder of Amla, played by Pallavi Joshi. Rajeshwar's grandson is in love with Amla and she has borne their child. Rajeshwar, who is unaware of the relationship, thinks it is a ploy to malign his family and rejects Amla's infant child. Soon after, Amla is abducted, raped and killed (by Chuniya—Amrish Puri—the true villain of the piece). This brings Veer Singh and all of Sanatanpur to confront Rajeshwar and his family. Veer Singh vows that he will not let anyone in Palinagar get married or have children. This is when Radha (Manisha Koirala) and Vasu (Vivek Mushran) realize their own love will never be accepted unless they pull off the miracle of reuniting the warring patriarchs.

Ghai shot the rape so subtly that it is over in seconds. All the audience sees is Amla being lured into a white Maruti Omni, with Amrish Puri and an accomplice already inside. The car's door slides shut. The frame switches to a wide angle showing the car going down a winding road along the side of a mountain. Amla's screams are heard, briefly, and moments later she is thrown out of the car, in front of an oncoming truck. The camera cuts to the sky as an eagle soars, letting out its high-pitched shriek.

Hrishikesh Mukherjee, an acclaimed director and editor, also praised *Saudagar*'s somewhat unusual narrative. The film begins with Mandhari, the narrator, played by Anupam Kher, showing paintings of Rajeshwar and Veer Singh with garlands around them. The audience realizes the two men are dead, but stays on to watch the story behind their deaths unfold over the next three hours. That was reminiscent of *Anand* (1971), directed by Hrishikesh Mukherjee himself, in which the opening scene tells viewers that the title character is no more.

Two days after *Saudagar*'s release, a Sunday, Ghai received an envelope containing a gold coin and a letter from Raaj Kumar. 'Thank you,

Chief,' it said. 'I hear that I stand out in your film and everyone is talking about my performance.'

Raaj Kumar was a gracious and well-read man. Once Ghai asked him why he ridiculed others so much. 'Our industry is full of talented people,' he said, 'not intelligent people. But they think of themselves as intelligent, and that makes me laugh.'

Raaj Kumar fell sick during the making of *Saudagar*. Reports said he had cancer of the throat. When Ghai phoned him to inquire about his health, he said, 'Jaani, we have cancer. We are Raaj Kumar; do you think we'll have a pesky little illness like a cough? But do not worry, we are going to make a good film.'

Saudagar became one of the milestones of Raaj Kumar's career. He made seven more films before cancer claimed him in 1996.

17

Khal Nayak: The Anti-Hero

As the youngest of three tennis-playing brothers from Chennai, Ashok Amritraj's achievements on the court were more modest than those of his brothers—Vijay and Anand—but he more than made up for that in later life. He became a successful producer in Hollywood with more than a hundred films in his portfolio. He and Ghai became friends in the 1980s and were close enough for Ghai to host a dinner in Mumbai to celebrate Ashok's wedding.

After *Saudagar* was out, Ghai took a small break to visit Los Angeles, the home of Hollywood, where he stayed with Amritraj. They attended a few filmi parties, where Amritraj presented Ghai as the Steven Spielberg of India. When Ghai spoke to Hollywood's directors, writers and technicians, they asked—with thinly veiled condescension—how films were made in India.

One day, out of the blue, Amritraj said, 'Subhash, why don't you make an English film here in Hollywood?'

Ghai, buoyed by his consistent success in India, was enthused by the notion of exploring foreign shores. He narrated a story idea that Amritraj liked. They registered it as *The Negatives*.

Amritraj discussed the project with Eddie Murphy and Omar Sharif through their agents. Murphy had gained stardom by playing charming, witty, street-smart characters. Sharif, considerably older, had

had starring roles in classics such as *Lawrence of Arabia* (1962) and *Doctor Zhivago* (1965). Both the actors liked the story and wanted to see the script.

Eddie Murphy would play a prisoner—funny and fast-talking, in keeping with his image—and Omar Sharif the investigating police officer who wants Murphy to disclose the details of his gang and activities. Murphy tells Sharif he is going to escape on a certain date, which he does, leading to a chase. While on the run, Murphy hides in a distant village where he meets a geisha, gets her pregnant, and flees. Hot on his trail, Sharif tracks down the geisha, who confirms that she is carrying Murphy's child. The officer waits for the birth of the child. When the child is born, Sharif spreads the word so that it reaches Murphy. Although his fatherly instincts are aroused, Murphy does not come to see his child. Sharif thinks he has lost and that Murphy was not human enough to care for his offspring. That's when the jailer tells him he is wrong, that Murphy is already back in his cell. When Sharif meets Murphy, the latter says he has indeed been pulled in by his longing for the child, but it won't last long, that he will escape again, and tells Sharif the date of his escape. That is where the film was to end. It was meant to be a fast-paced, ninety-minute chase thriller.

Hollywood movies have their own grammar. So, Ghai teamed up with a screenwriter in Los Angeles to develop the script. This was Ghai's first time working with a writer who did not have any of the hallmarks of Indian film writers: paunch, paan and pareshani (stress). Ghai's co-writer was particular about his fitness and used to ask for meetings at his gym at six-thirty in the morning. Keen to learn Hollywood's way of working, Ghai kept every gym appointment. The sentence he heard most often from his co-writer was: 'This is not going to work here.' The writer also took him to studios where Ghai could meet people and see how things were done.

After a month of this, Ghai decided Hollywood was not for him. In India, a film could be a one-man show, with the director as the boss. In Hollywood, the director was the first among technicians, who were all more or less equal. The division of labour was clear. All technicians had their own views and did their jobs themselves. The director was the custodian of the screenplay and made sure everyone stayed true to it, but his role in making a film remained well-defined and specific. He did his job, others did theirs. Some super-successful directors in Hollywood did become auteurs, but it probably took twenty years of consistent success.

That was not Ghai's way and he sensed conflicts in the offing. 'When I made a film, I wrote, I directed, I edited, I crafted every scene, I worked closely with the cinematographer, I filmed songs, I weighed in on the music score and background music, I oversaw costume design, and I mixed sounds,' says Ghai.

In that, he was far from unique; it was how Raj Kapoor, Manoj Kumar, Vijay Anand, Yash Chopra and many others worked.

Back in India, a magazine article caught Ghai's attention. It talked about the reality of villains, presenting them as tragic heroes. Villains had wealth, power and brains, but they never got the one thing they desired the most. Most of them would fall in love with a nice and simple girl only to find their love unrequited. That would lead them either to redemption or destruction.

The article inspired Ghai to want to make a small arthouse-cinema-type film, focused on the villain, that would take him back to his roots in an FTII headed by Ritwik Ghatak. He redrafted 'The Negatives' as a chase from Nashik to Mumbai. The convict's love for his mother was what the police officer would leverage to put him back behind bars. It was going to be a low-budget, experimental project.

Ghai discussed the role of the convict with Nana Patekar, who had made a name for himself as a fine actor by playing edgy characters in *Ankush* (1986), *Salaam Bombay* (1988), *Parinda* (1989) and several others. He had also turned director with *Prahaar* (1991). He was perfect for the part and keen to do the film. However, after a few meetings, where Patekar hinted that he had his own style of working and liked to be in control of his scenes and lines, Ghai got the same feeling that had made him drop the Hollywood project.

In a discussion at the Mukta Arts office, Ghai's team suggested making the story into a commercial film. All it needed was a heroine, a few other characters, and music. The idea had immediate appeal for Ghai, who anyway wanted his films to be seen by the masses. He turned to Ram Kelkar for his intuitive understanding of emotions for the screenplay. Kamlesh Pandey stepped in once again to write the dialogues. Together they made some changes to the story.

The police officer got a lady love, also a police officer, whom the convict kidnaps and falls in love with. The convict's mother's character developed into one who loves him dearly and indulges all his misdeeds, never once questioning or rebuking him. Until the climax, that is. A truly bad man was added as the real villain. Songs waltzed in; the heroine performed a loving number for her man and a seductive one to lure the convict, among others.

They came up with the title, *Khal Nayak*, designed to convey the film's message that there is a hero (nayak) lurking inside every villain (khalnayak).

It found few fans outside of Ghai's inner circle.

Distributors phoned to say it was a lousy title, like that of a cheap Hindi jasoosi upanyas (detective novel), several notches below weighty titles such as *Saudagar*, *Karma* and *Vidhaata*. Ghai told them not to worry: every child in the country would know the meaning of 'khal nayak' after the movie was released.

Once news about Ghai's new project got around, many leading men called him to say they were keen on working with him. Anil Kapoor came over to banter. He said he was going to shave his head to show that he could be a really good bad man. But Ghai did not think he would suit the character. In his mind, the khal nayak, Ballu Balram, was a near-psychotic man who treated every situation as a game, someone who was a self-proclaimed villain. Ballu's tragedy was that he was forced by circumstances to leave his mother whom he loved dearly, because she chose her husband over her son. This separation was a source of constant pain for him. But Ballu was not quite the villain he painted himself to be. He craved for love.

When Ballu finds Ganga, the police officer's lady love, something stirs inside him and he feels emotions he has not felt before. A gradual change takes place in him and he almost turns into a lover (the assumption being that lovers are nice people who want the world to be a better place). On the film's canvas, Ballu goes from being an all-black character (he kills a politician in his first scene) to having shades of grey, to becoming an almost white knight in the end.

While discussing the character of Ballu, the writers—Ghai, Kelkar and Kamlesh Pandey—often talked about Birju of *Mother India*, how he was the perfect villain-hero in Hindi cinema. And then it struck them: why not have Sanjay Dutt—whose father, Sunil Dutt, had so memorably played Birju—play Ballu Balram?

Ghai did not have the fondest memories of working with Sanjay Dutt during *Vidhaata*. To end the discussion, he said he would consider Dutt for the title role only if he came to his house and asked for it. Pandey called Dutt and told him to go to Ghai's house and somehow persuade him. This was a role that could transform his life and career.

Dutt had strayed somewhat after *Vidhaata*. He had taken a break from films for a while and resurrected his career with *Naam* (1986), which was produced by Rajendra Kumar for his son Kumar Gaurav. Although the film did little for Kumar Gaurav, it gave Dutt the boost he sorely needed. However, his track record on either side of *Saajan* and *Sadak*—both of which came in 1991—was filled with flops.

Dutt took Pandey's advice and visited Ghai at his house. He spoke of *Vidhaata* and how it had helped him grow as an actor. He said that

Ghai had been one of the most important persons in his life and he was willing to go to great lengths to make sure they worked together again. As he spoke, Ghai observed that Dutt's face had matured nicely over the years. He looked like a man who could take matters into his own hands and could charm any woman. He came across as a vulnerable tough guy—the combination that always worked on screen.

Ghai and his team of writers had crafted the khalnayak as a unique hero. His left eye is nearly always covered by unruly locks of hair, he tilts his neck sideways while speaking, he looks up (into the camera, which was stationed at a height) while speaking. His demeanour is usually mocking, but can turn menacing in a split second.

The more Ghai thought about Dutt, the more he began to look the part.

'Sanjay is a charmer, like Shah Rukh. When he is with you, you will think the two of you are a team,' says Ghai.

He told Dutt it would not be an easy role, he would have to surrender himself to the film and the director. Dutt agreed, and did surrender himself.

Jackie Shroff was the obvious choice for the nayak (hero), Ram Sinha, Ganga's love interest. It was an extension of the character of Ram from *Ram Lakhan*, the principled and upright police officer.

Anupam Kher, too, asked Ghai if there was a role for him in *Khal Nayak*. If there wasn't, Kher mock-threatened, he would not allow the film to be made. Ghai promised to do something. When Kher asked him about the heroine, Ganga, Ghai admitted to briefly considering Madhuri Dixit—she still had a third film to do with Mukta Arts in her contract—but felt deterred by her stardom. She had become a big star, too big for Ghai, perhaps, and fallen out of touch with him. He said he was considering a few leading ladies, of whom Urmila Matondkar was the frontrunner. She looked full of youth and freshness and had proved her dancing ability with *Narasimha* (1991).

But Kher would have none of it; he said it had to be Dixit.

'Yaar, she is too big a star now,' said Ghai.

'That she may be,' said Kher, 'but you better be a professional and speak to her.'

Ghai went to meet Dixit and narrated the story in a few quick minutes. He was pleasantly surprised when she readily agreed.

The Sanjay Dutt who played Ballu Balram in *Khal Nayak* was as different from the young man who had portrayed Kunal in *Vidhaata* as chalk is from cheese. The lad in *Vidhaata* was a raw and careless actor who had to be coaxed and coached before every scene. He was far more interested in hanging out with his friends. The man who signed *Khal Nayak* was committed and passionate about his work, whether the shift was at nine in the morning or at midnight. The only time he wasn't on call was when he was in the gym.

It was when the climactic courtroom scene of the film was being shot that the unthinkable happened. Sanjay Dutt was arrested in connection to the Mumbai blasts of 12 March 1993, an act of terror that had shaken the country's financial capital and destroyed the communal harmony that the people of the city had always maintained. Ghai was close to Sunil Dutt, Sanjay's father, who had informed him of reports that Sanjay apparently had in his possession a weapon connected with the incident. Ghai received the information with concern, but was not alarmed. He knew about the younger Dutt's fondness for guns and hunting, but could not imagine any of it was illegal. Dutt, too, denied any such thing. Ghai was shocked when he learned that the police had arrested the actor upon his return from Mauritius, where he had been shooting for G.P. Sippy's *Aatish* (1994). Pictures of Dutt in police custody were splashed all over the newspapers, looking eerily like stills from *Khal Nayak*. Although he was shooting for several films at the time, it was *Khal Nayak* that bore the brunt of people's ire—his role in the film was too close to what had happened in real life. Many headline writers found the film's title quite handy in their editorials and reports. Luckily for Mukta Arts and its distributors, it was not long before Dutt got bail and came back to complete the shooting, so the film could release in August.

Between Dutt's arrest and the furore around '*Choli ke peeche*', Mukta Arts managed to save a fair amount of money.

'We had to spend very little on *Khal Nayak*'s publicity,' says Ghai.

All of Ghai's films had fascinating villains, from Lion in *Kalicharan* to Chunia Chand Chaukhan in *Saudagar*. But his leading men were seldom all-white characters themselves. Most of them were classic anti-heroes who, to different degrees, had dwelled on the dark side at one time or another because of circumstances; be it Kalicharan, Vishwanath, Govinda, Vikramjit, Shamsher Singh, Jaikishan, or the three convicts in *Karma*.

For *Khal Nayak*'s Ballu Balram, the mitigating circumstances—mainly poverty and joblessness—are less compelling. He kills many, and with abandon. Though he gets a haircut and shave before expressing his love for Ganga; once spurned, he goes to a big party though he knows that she is in police custody for saving him. He is likeable in parts, but remains essentially pretty bad until the last few minutes of the film, when he arrives in the courtroom in the middle of a trial to save Ganga.

In that, Ballu was a sort of culmination—a pinnacle, so to speak—for Ghai's bad-good-bad men. He finally lifted the villain to the status of the title character, the hero.

Thus far, the music for all Ghai's films had been with HMV, who were a keen partner, but seldom loosened the purse strings when it came to paying for the rights. Still, Ghai had not thought about changing music companies—music rights were not such a money spinner then—until, one day, a massive cake arrived in his office. The message on it said: 'Saudagar Sauda Kar'. It was from Ramesh Taurani of Tips Music Company.

When Ghai phoned to thank him for the cake, Taurani asked for *Khal Nayak*'s music rights. '*Price aapki, music hamari* (Any price you want),' he said.

Ghai spoke to HMV, whose bosses, sitting in Kolkata, said they would not be able to pay more than what they had for *Saudagar*. Getting back to Taurani, Ghai quoted four times what HMV would have paid. Taurani agreed without hesitation.

'This is a lottery,' Ghai told his unit, but he had already begun to feel the pressure of the transaction, and passed it on to his music team of L-P and Anand Bakshi. The music had to live up to the price.

'It was under that pressure that "*Choli ke peeche*" was born,' says Ghai.

He first heard the tune in Mount Abu, Rajasthan, where he was scouting for locations. He had stopped his car beside an obscure paan shop on the road and sent his driver to fetch a pack of cigarettes. As he rolled down the car's window, a mellifluous tune caught his ears. It was a young boy dressed in a traditional Rajasthani outfit playing his iktara (a single-string instrument played with a bow).

Ghai gave the boy ₹10 before his car moved away. The driver was puzzled. 'Didn't you have change, sir?' he asked. A ₹1-tip would have been generous.

'You have no idea what I have got for this money,' said Ghai. It was probably the cheapest deal in the history of music.

Back in Mumbai, Ghai met Laxmikant and hummed the tune for him, saying they should make a song of that. Then he went to have lunch at Madhuri Dixit's house. As they chatted about the film, Ghai told Dixit he had found a fantastic tune and hummed it while drumming on the dining table. He asked her to hum along, making a tuk-tuk-tuk-tuk sound, like the sound of flour mills in villages. They had a good laugh.

Later, in the evening, Ghai went back to Laxmikant and told him how Dixit's sound effects had enriched the tune. The composer, ever responsive to ideas, added it. This is the 'Ku-ku-ku-ku' one hears in the opening chorus before the lyrics kick in.

When Anand Bakshi heard the tune, he asked Ghai what kind of song he wanted. Ghai said he wanted a risqué song. After all, the woman singing it was keen to be picked up by a gangster. She had to be seductive yet earthy. The other reason, Ghai explained with a chuckle, was that Tips had paid a lot of money and the song had to click with the masses.

In many parts of the country, there is a time-honoured tradition of groups of women singing suggestive folk and wedding songs at gatherings and ceremonies. The lyrics are often abusive and always borderline vulgar. Some songs are in the form of a series of questions and answers. On occasion, an older woman, the village aunty, becomes bold and teases young girls with innuendos and gestures.

This was the format Ghai and Bakshi discussed for the song. At nine that evening, Bakshi phoned Ghai and said, 'Subhash, get a pen and paper.' Ghai knew his song was ready.

The first two lines were: '*Choli ke peechhe kya hai, choli ke peeche / Chunri ke neeche kya hai, chunri ke neeche* (What's hidden in the blouse, what is it that's hidden / What's under the chunri, what is it that's hidden).'

Ghai burst into a laugh. 'Bakshi Sa'ab, you will get me into trouble. Let's drop this,' he said.

But Bakshi would have none of it. 'Wait, it will all come back on track and become honourable. You just write,' said Bakshi. '*Choli mein dil hai mera, chunri mein dil hai mera; ye dil main dungi mere yaar ko, pyaar ko* (What's in the blouse is my heart, what's under cover is my heart, it's my heart that I'll give to my lover, to my love).'

'What a manoeuvre, Bakshi sa'ab,' Ghai said, and wrote on, all the while thinking there was no way he was going to use those lyrics.

Bakshi explained that that was the pattern: the older woman's questions are suggestive and aggressive, but the younger one stays on the straight and narrow in her responses.

Ghai took the lyrics to L-P and they slotted nicely into the tune; no surprises there, Bakshi's lyrics always fit right into tunes. They recorded it in the voices of Alka Yagnik for Madhuri Dixit and Ila Arun for the older woman.

But who would be the raunchy older woman? Satish Kaushik met Ghai one evening and they talked about it. Aruna Irani's name came up, but given her star power, she would need a full song to herself, and maybe a meatier role. Kaushik suggested Neena Gupta. She was a capable artiste and agreed to the role, though she didn't have much to do in the film apart from the song and a couple of scenes. The song itself, though, turned out to be a challenge.

When she first heard the song, Saroj Khan was crestfallen. What dance steps could possibly go with those lyrics? Ghai's advice was simple: 'Do not listen to the lyrics, listen to the melody and beats.'

On the first day of shooting the song, Dixit fell ill. So, Saroj Khan and Ghai decided to shoot the song's end chorus and Neena Gupta's parts. In the couple of scenes she had in the film, Neena Gupta's character, Champa, is shown to be the one who taught Ganga dancing. Obviously, she had to be an accomplished dancer herself.

During the rehearsals, Ghai felt that Neena Gupta's dancing wasn't competent. He told Saroj Khan that most, if not all, of her lines would have to be tight close-ups of her face; it was up to the choreographer to make Champa's face dance.

Saroj Khan, of course, had vowed not to argue with Ghai after *Ram Lakhan*. She accepted the challenge. The knowing smirks and mocking expressions on Neena Gupta's face became one of the highlights of the song. She is also seen sitting, holding a chillum, while others dance. It is only towards the end of the song that she does a few steps—simple ones. For someone who had taught Ganga to dance, it was precious little movement, but Ghai and Saroj Khan pulled it off, thanks in no small part to the dazzle Dixit created in the rest of the song.

Saroj Khan did perhaps her best work on '*Choli ke peeche*', making it an extremely sensual number that flirted with the boundaries without once crossing them. It won her the Filmfare award for best choreography.

No one involved with the making of the song expected the outrage that followed.

'We only wanted to make a nice folk number,' says Ghai.

Ten million audio cassettes of the soundtrack were sold in the first ten days of its release. The Indian music industry had not seen anything like it; audio cassettes were being sold in black at a premium. The country was firmly in the grip of 'choli' fever. The shivers followed soon enough.

Thirty-two organizations called for a ban on the film because of the song. But Mukta Arts refused to remove the song from the film; there was way too much riding on it. A lawyer from Delhi filed a case saying his four-year-old child was singing the song and, as a result, losing the moral compass. Arvind Trivedi, who had played Ravan in the popular television series *Ramayan* and had become a member of Parliament, gave the example of '*Choli ke peeche*' at a meeting on censorship. He was quoted as saying: 'Today, they are asking what lies behind the choli. Tomorrow, they will actually show what lies behind.'

Ghai went around explaining to anyone who would care to listen that the song was rooted in folk traditions and ought not to be considered vulgar, that people should wait to see how it was woven into the narrative and how it looked on screen. Not many listened.

As a last resort, Ghai arranged a special screening of the unreleased film for Bala Saheb Thackeray, the Shiv Sena leader, whose voice carried a long way in political circles as well as social ones. Thackeray liked the film a lot and was surprised that people were calling for a ban on it. He came out publicly in support of *Khal Nayak* for its message about the scourge of terrorism and its depiction of a principled officer reforming a misguided young man.

Thackeray's support appeared to turn the tide. All the members of the censor board watched the film in full strength and passed it with minor cuts. '*Choli ke peeche*' itself got small cuts.

When the film released, a leading newspaper called the song one of the finest pieces of art in commercial cinema. It was adopted in dancing schools across the country for its eleven different rhythms.

Incidentally, Ghai's favourite song from the film is '*O maa tujhe salaam*', resonating with the mellifluous tones of Jagjit Singh.

Like most Ghai films, *Khal Nayak*, too, got a large-scale premiere in India, in thirteen theatres in Mumbai and eleven in Delhi. Some of the top directors, among whom were Mahesh Bhatt, Shekhar Kapur, Vinod Chopra, J.P. Datta, Randhir Kapoor and Mukul Anand, accompanied Ghai to the premiere in Delhi. Although one would have thought this was an indication of the goodwill Ghai enjoyed in the industry, the events that followed showed otherwise.

A few months ago, Saawan Kumar Tak, a producer–director who gave sporadic hits, had met Ghai at a party and said he was making a film called *Khal-Naaikaa* (the female anti-hero). This was a departure of sorts for Tak, who was known for titles such as *Souten*, *Sanam Bewafa*, etc.

Ghai had chuckled and said Saawan Kumar had every right to name his film whatever he wanted so long as it wasn't registered by anyone else, and Ghai certainly did not own the title 'Khal-Naaikaa'.

Several months later, in June 1993, Mukta Arts announced that *Khal Nayak* would be released on 6 August. Within days, Saawan Kumar Tak announced that *Khal-Naaikaa* would hit theatres on the same day. *Khal Nayak*'s distributors got worried: theirs was the much bigger, more expensive film and it had far more riding on it. They had more to lose from the confusion arising out of the similarity of titles.

Ghai spoke to Tak and said there was no point in both films losing business, but Tak stood his ground, saying he had informed Ghai about his title. That he had, but the date of *Khal-Naaikaa*'s release had come as a shock.

The matter went to the Film Makers' Combine, the industry body that settles such disputes. An overwhelming 80 per cent of the members saw nothing wrong with Tak's releasing his film on the same day as *Khal Nayak*.

'I realized that day that my success had turned many people in the industry against me,' says Ghai.

Those people did not stop there. Once the two films released, word got around that *Khal-Naaikaa* was a better film and also a bigger hit. Dilip Kumar spoke to Ghai and laughed the whole thing off. More such incidents were in the offing, he said, because the industry was tired of Ghai's successes.

People were also annoyed by the leeway Ghai got from distributors and actors alike. Distributors were willing to pay more for his films. *Ram Lakhan*, for instance, commanded 30 per cent more than another film which also had Anil Kapoor and Jackie Shroff in lead roles. Most actors were also happy to work with Ghai for less than their market rate.

To compound matters, Ghai's parties were the biggest in town. It was a matter of prestige to be invited, and an affront not to be on the invitee list. Obviously, not everyone could be invited, because even the biggest party halls in town had finite capacities. A genial senior producer once told Ghai to definitely send him an invitation to all his parties even though he wouldn't attend. He explained that his wife looked down upon him if he was not invited to Ghai's parties.

As the numbers poured in, it became clear that *Khal Nayak* was a blockbuster and among the fastest money spinners the industry had seen. It opened up the overseas market for Hindi films as well, drawing huge crowds in the theatres of the USA. According to reports, mounted police had to be called to control the crowds in Los Angeles, the home of Hollywood, where Ghai had chosen to shelve 'The Negatives'.

18

Pardes: The Home and the World

For a film to be a hit, it has to not only be good but also come at the right time and match the mood of the times. Some films, of course, are ahead of their time. Not hugely successful when first released, they acquire cult status as the years roll by. Raj Kapoor's *Mera Naam* Joker (1970), Kundan Shah's *Jaane Bhi Do Yaaro* (1983) and Ghai's *Karz* (1980) are some such films.

Pardes got its timing spot-on. In the India of the mid-1990s, time was moving at a faster pace than before. Economic liberalization had gained momentum. Mobile phones were taking their first slow steps. With the rise of the internet, satellite television and easier means of travel, the West had come closer to home. The Indian mind was struggling to find an equilibrium between the value systems of the East and West.

It was out of this turmoil that *Pardes* was born.

In the Hindi film industry of that time, some new talent was emerging. One such talent was Mukul Anand, who had directed a bunch of small and big films. Although not all of them were hits, they had proved his technical finesse. He had emerged as Amitabh Bachchan's favoured director: together, the two had done *Agneepath* (1990), *Hum* (1991) and *Khuda Gawah* (1992).

Around the same time, Mukta Arts, now a corporate entity, was thinking of spreading its wings a little bit by producing films made by directors other than Ghai.

Ghai spoke to Anand, who said he would be happy to direct a film for Mukta Arts if Ghai wrote it. They agreed on a story of three brothers, of whom the older two interpret their mother's ideals differently and take divergent routes in life. They clash when it comes to shaping the life of their youngest brother. *Trimurti* (1995) became the first Mukta Arts production to be directed by someone other than Ghai.

As a director, Ghai did his best work when given a free hand. So, he decided not to come in Anand's way either. He would occasionally drop in on the sets for tea and a bit of a chat, but not much else. He stepped in only for the big decisions.

One of those decisions was to replace Sanjay Dutt, who was playing one of the two older brothers (the other brother was played by Jackie Shroff, and the youngest brother by Shah Rukh Khan). After they had completed a schedule, Dutt said he had a court hearing coming up and would resume shooting upon his return. The court sent him to prison for a year and a half.

Several names came up for consideration as Dutt's replacement. One of them was Aditya Pancholi, who had built an on-screen image of the tough guy. But Ghai chose to go with Anil Kapoor, whose versatility and range had impressed him time and again.

Soon after, Kapoor started getting threatening calls from an unknown number. He went to the police and the calls were traced to a hotel room and eventually to Pancholi. Kapoor did not press charges when Pancholi said he was driven by the disappointment of not getting to work in *Trimurti*.

Disappointment, mixed with panic, was what Ghai felt when he saw the first ten reels of *Trimurti*. He had refrained from watching its rush prints till then. When he did, he found them technically brilliant, but ordinary in content. Mukul had interpreted and visualized the screenplay very differently from how it was intended. Ghai was certain the film would flop. He tried to salvage it, reshooting parts, incurring expenditure and delays. But that ship had sailed and was bound to sink.

Trimurti released in December 1995, when Ghai had taken the star cast and director of the film to New York on a holiday. While they were busy having fun, news came that the film was an unmitigated flop. That evening, they went to a pub. Anyone who saw them would have thought they were celebrating.

Shah Rukh Khan, speaking in the general direction of the others in the pub, said loudly: 'Bhaisaab, our film has flopped.' Then he corrected himself and said, pointing to Ghai: 'Actually, not mine, *his* film has flopped.' Anil Kapoor jumped in, and said, pointing to Khan and Ghai: 'It is *their* film that has flopped, I came in way too late.'

They bantered on, with Ghai and Shroff joining in, and the others in the pub wondering, blank-faced, what the lot was up to.

While Mukul Anand was making *Trimurti*, Ghai had embarked on a directorial venture of his own: *Shikhar*. It was about love in the time of an India–Pakistan war. In the manner of war movies, it was meant to be a grand affair, comparable to *Devaa*.

Jackie Shroff, the oldest of the three brothers in *Trimurti*, and Shah Rukh Khan, the youngest, were also in *Shikhar*. Shroff was playing an officer of the Indian army who falls for a young Kashmiri woman, to be played by a newcomer. The woman is in love with Khan, who gets captured by the Pakistani forces and taken prisoner. Shroff goes to rescue him. All this while a war is on between the two countries.

A.R. Rahman was composing the music for *Shikhar*, as Ghai thought he could no longer deal with the acrimony between Laxmikant and Pyarelal. Their quarrel had peaked during the making of *Trimurti*.

The two composers refused to speak to each other, leaving Ghai to constantly run from one to the other to get the music score completed.

One day, Ghai was travelling in a car in Mysore and wondering how he was going to deal with the L–P situation. A separation from them was not going to be easy for Ghai, given how close he was to them and how big a role the two composers, along with Anand Bakshi, had played in his films.

The music on the car stereo pulled him out of his contemplation. The driver had put on the cassette of *Roja* (1992). Ghai had heard about Roja and its music composer, A.R. Rahman, but had not really listened to the songs. Now he sat entranced. He asked the driver to rewind and play the songs again and again. He listened to the sounds, the beats and the orchestra.

Back in Mumbai, he phoned Rahman and said he wanted to meet him. Rahman was warm and welcoming. Ghai flew down to Chennai for the meeting. They discussed *Shikhar*. Ghai said he would pay Rahman the same price as L–P.

Rahman said, 'Let's work together, Sir, the price comes later.' He said he used to play the tunes of *Hero* and *Karz* on his synthesizer and was keen to work with Ghai.

They recorded two songs for *Shikhar*.

A grand mahurat took place in an open ground in Suraj Kund, outside Delhi. The location was chosen to get a healthy presence of international media, given the India–Pakistan theme of the film.

But *Trimurti*'s failure shook Mukta Arts. People in the industry and the media saw it as a sign that Ghai's run as a successful filmmaker was over.

'Subhash Ghai is history ... He is trapped in a bygone era ... He cannot make films that work in the nineties ...' they said. In their glee, they missed the little detail that Ghai had not directed *Trimurti*.

It reminded Ghai of the time right after *Krodhi*, when he had similarly been written off. Mukta Arts had made some money from *Trimurti* because of the high prices distributors had paid. Ghai decided not to keep any part of the profit and passed the money on to the distributors. This further alienated his peers in the industry, who complained that he was setting the wrong precedent. Distributors, they said, did not cough up more money when a film was a big hit and must not be compensated for a flop. But Ghai valued the distributors' goodwill more than his popularity among peers.

This was not the time to splurge on a large-scale war movie, Ghai decided. Distributors would not cough up enough to cover its cost, forget profits. He dropped the idea of making *Shikhar* and, instead, decided to make a 'small' film with a third of the budget.

The Tandons were the promoter family behind Tandon Corporation, which at one point of time was the world's largest independent producer of disk drives for small computers and word processors. Ghai was friends with the family. Once, while he was staying with them in New York, Sirjang Lal Tandon, the head of the family, opened a bottle and with it his heart to Ghai, as they talked late into the night.

Tandon's was one of the more prominent migrant success stories. He, however, had a secret sorrow. In their thinking and conduct, his children were American, not Indian, he felt.

'I have earned a lot of money here,' Tandon told Ghai, 'but I lost my children.' His dearest wish was to have his youngest son marry a nice Indian girl rooted in an Indian ethos.

Ghai spent a little more time with the Tandons, observing them and listening to them. And he decided to marry 'only a good Indian girl can save my family' idea with 'the matchmaker gets the girl'.

Pardes was born.

It was about preserving Indian values under the onslaught of migration and westernization. It was, like *Ram Lakhan*, about two families, but they were not at war over property; theirs was a tussle of values.

At its core, *Pardes* is the story of Ganga, a young woman from semi-urban India who gets engaged to Rajeev, the son of Kishori Lal, an affluent Indian-origin businessman in the US. The match is made possible by Arjun, an orphan whose relationship with Kishori Lal's family is complex. Kishori Lal refers to him as a foster son and Rajeev's aunts talk about him as a sort of servant. Rajeev calls him a friend but treats him like a sidekick, often showing him his place and telling him off for trying to interfere in his relationship with Ganga. Only Ganga shows Arjun respect and quarrels with him as one would with a dear friend.

In its subject, look and feel, treatment, attitude and ethos, the film was going to be unrecognizable from all the other movies Ghai had made till then. So, he put together a completely new team for it.

Neeraj Pathak joined forces with Ghai to write the screenplay and Javed Siddiqui came on board for the dialogues. Pathak was a young and upcoming talent who had recently made a mark on television and Siddiqui had done pathbreaking work for the classics *Shatranj Ke Khilari* (1977) and *Umrao Jaan* (1981), before redefining the lingo of the modern NRI film with the dialogues of *Dilwale Dulhania Le Jayenge* (*DDLJ*, 1995).

Ghai also made a big departure in the editing department, moving away from Waman Bhosle and Gurudutt Shirali. The duo had sculpted most of his films but the world was changing. A new editing technology, called Avid, had just arrived in India. Mukta Arts was one of its early adopters.

Editing a film is a non-linear process; you need to switch between scenes and sequences and move parts from one place to another. In the old editing system, this cutting and splicing took a lot of time and effort and created room for error. Avid made it quicker and simpler to cut, copy and paste clips, as one does with word processing. That made it easier for the director to change his mind and the editor to follow the director's vision in real time, without having to start all over again.

Bhosle and Shirali said Avid was not their cup of tea. So, with a heavy heart, Ghai got Renu Saluja to edit *Pardes*. Saluja had proved her abilities with classics such as *Ardh Satya* (1983), *Jaane Bhi Do Yaaro (1983)*, *Bandit Queen* (1994), *Parinda* (1989), and many others. She had been quick to master Avid.

Saluja played a big role in making the two halves of *Pardes* as distinct as their locations. When the action moves from India to the US after the interval, the cuts are faster and the background soundtrack is Western. The audience's first views of the country are as seen from a helicopter while English pop music plays in the background. The pattern and the treatment of scenes in the second half capture the pace and rhythm of the West and are in contrast with the tranquility of India as seen in the first half.

When Ghai finalized the climax, which lasts twenty minutes, Saluja asked for five days to show him her own version. When Ghai saw it, he was so impressed that he chose to keep her version and discard his own. She had taken the same scenes and presented them from Ganga's point of view.

Shah Rukh Khan had signed a three-film contract with Mukta Arts, starting with *Trimurti*, and was keen to work in a film directed by Ghai himself. Even though Ghai explained that the story of *Pardes* was about Ganga, Khan readily agreed to be Arjun, a decision that might have given him a few sleepless nights while he was shooting for the film.

With *DDLJ*, one of the biggest hits of Hindi cinema, Shah Rukh had emerged as the super cool romantic hero who could look into any woman's eyes with an intensity that convinced her that he loved her and only her.

'No intensity, Shah Rukh,' Ghai told the young hero when they were preparing for *Pardes*, 'and no love; not for Ganga. Friendship and affection, yes, but no love.'

The idea was to keep the audience guessing how the hero and heroine were going to get together. Even in the climax, Arjun insists that he does not love Ganga and asks her to go back home.

Arjun's non-hero persona is further emphasized by his attire. He wears loose-fitting trousers, not branded denims. And he wears shirts with suspenders. No tees for him.

In contrast, Rajeev is the Americanized scion of Lal's business empire. Tall, well-dressed and handsome with an aquiline nose and a well-defined jawline, he oozes privilege and arrogance.

Khan would argue with Ghai about wearing denims and tees which, he said, would give just the same effect as trousers and shirts, but Ghai would have none of it.

'No being a hero, Shah Rukh,' Ghai would say, 'nothing filmi.'

What bothered Khan more than the clothes was that Arjun was a bit of a wuss for the most part—subdued before Kishori Lal and positively cowed down by Rajeev. He did not think being shown to be weak did justice to his stardom and image. But, as Ghai explained to him, the orphan Arjun is deeply obligated to Kishori Lal for taking him in and giving him a livelihood. He cannot dream of defying his benefactor or his family. Ghai told Khan he would have to leave behind the romantic character of *DDLJ* and embrace *Pardes*'s orphan.

Khan, in spite of his apprehensions, brought all his passion, commitment and energy to the film. There was a shooting schedule in which the unit was divided into two, one working on the song '*Do dil mil rahe hain*', and the other on the action scenes of the climax. Without being asked, Khan would, in between shooting for the song, offer to go and help shoot the action scenes. He was always there, even if it meant filling up immigration forms for an overseas schedule, carrying the equipment, moving props, or assisting the production in any way.

'Shah Rukh was always ready to help the unit,' says Ghai. 'He had a staunch determination to succeed and did not worry about money, only about his work.'

The actor also oozed charm and befriended everyone in the unit with his natural ability to communicate with anyone and make them comfortable. 'He can talk to a tonga driver just as easily as to the Prince of Wales,' says Ghai. 'He knows what to say and he does it naturally, not in a tutored or affected manner. Anyone who talks to him for even a short while will come away convinced that he likes them.'

However, while they were shooting for *Pardes*, there was a bit of an edge between Ghai and Khan over how Arjun and the film were shaping up. With industry talk about Ghai having lost his touch, the actor probably felt that the film wouldn't work.

For the last schedule, Ghai needed a couple of days extra from Khan to film the song '*Ye dil deewana*'. They were in Las Vegas and, if they did not wrap up all the scenes, the entire unit would have to come back to complete the work.

Khan's wife, Gauri, was expecting, and he wanted to return to India as soon as possible. Ghai, of course, understood his compulsions, but knew that the cost of bringing the unit back would be prohibitive. He decided to shoot the song on the only remaining day that Khan was available.

Ghai was on location at six in the morning and had the camera set up. As soon as Khan arrived, they shot his close-ups, and then Ghai took him around to different locations to shoot other portions of the song, including a bungee jump. They finished the work by four that evening. After Khan left, Ghai filmed the long shots using a body double.

Khan left for India worried that the haste in which the song was shot might not have done justice to it. He was stunned when Ghai, back in Mumbai, edited the song and called him over to the editing room to see the results. Khan, his usual charming and generous self, hugged Ghai and said he could not have imagined the song would turn out so well.

'Sometimes, compulsions and restrictions bring out creativity,' says Ghai.

For the roles of Ganga and Rajeev, the unit of Mukta Arts clamoured for Madhuri Dixit and Salman Khan. Word in the industry was that both had liked the story. But Ghai was adamant about having newcomers.

The beating heart of *Pardes* is the character of Ganga. She is the kind of girl who, on seeing airplanes fly by, becomes wistful about going overseas, but also holds the traditional values of her family intact in her heart. She runs through green fields with abandon, her chunni flying, but still keeps track of Kishori Lal's medicines—even though they have just met. She tells Arjun that new relationships are not made by breaking old ones, and she takes a firm stand against her husband-to-be when he badmouths Indians and is violent with her.

In fact, in the original announcement, the film's title was *Ganga*. But a producer sent Mukta Arts a legal notice saying he owned that title.

Ghai, hoping to sort the matter out, asked the producer how much of his film had been made.

'Four reels,' said the producer.

'And how long have you been making it?'

'Two or three years, but that does not mean you can take away my title.'

Ghai had nothing to say after that, and he changed his title to *Pardes*.

When he began looking for Ganga, Ghai was certain it had to be an actress with no existing image in the audience's mind.

At first glance, Ritu Chaudhary looked like the antithesis of Ganga. She had first been noticed when she was overshadowed in a Pepsi commercial by Aamir Khan and Aishwarya Rai. Thereafter she had gone on to become a video jockey on a music channel.

She looked and spoke exactly like what she was, a model and veejay. Her preferred language of conversation was English and it was with difficulty that Ghai could steer their meeting into Hindi now and then.

But there was something about her eyes, and once Ghai had seen those eyes, he saw nothing else. All he noticed was how, while speaking, her eyes went from being cheerful to serious to sombre to mischievous.

'Ritu could speak volumes with her eyes,' says Ghai.

During the screen test, Ghai observed that she had poise, and she could flirt with the camera—and the camera flirted back. She laughed with abandon and delivered her lines without a hint of self-consciousness.

'Sir,' Ghai's chief assistant Shakir Khan protested, 'we have got so many tall and beautiful women who are keen on this role.'

But Ghai did not want a tall woman. Ganga was the ringleader of the half-a-dozen children in her extended family. She could not be tall and statuesque and also look playful and innocent. Ghai was certain Ritu was the right woman for the role.

The hitch was that there was already an actress called Ritu (Shivpuri) who had done a few films, of which *Aankhen* (1993) had been a big hit. Ritu Chaudhary needed a new screen name.

She spoke to her mother and they came up with Mahima, which Ghai approved. He got Khatoon, Madhuri Dixit's hairdresser who had first introduced the actress to Ghai, to not only do Mahima's hair but also help her understand what to expect during shoots and tutor her a little in the ways of the industry.

Kabir Lal, who replaced the peerless Ashok Mehta as cinematographer, did wonders with Mahima's face. Lal was a master of close-ups and knew his lenses inside out. He was also particular about the raw stock.

Those were the days when movies were shot on film, not digital cameras. Most cinematographers used the same raw stock of film from the beginning to the end. But Lal used to procure four different kinds of raw stock and used different ones for different scenes.

Several actors, including a few from the US and UK, auditioned for the role of Rajeev. But Ghai chose Apurva Agnihotri. He looked every bit like how Ghai imagined Rajeev. He turned out to be so good that many thought he was an NRI actor.

Even after he had finalized the cast, Ghai's team pressured him to consider Salman and Madhuri for the parts. Sudesh Gupta, who had pressed Ghai to take known faces to play the young lovers of *Saudagar*, said distributors were willing to pay a lot more for *Pardes* if it had three stars instead of one. It was tempting for a production company whose previous film had flopped, but Ghai said he would rather not make the film than have stars play Ganga and Rajeev. He promised his team he would make up for *Trimurti* with *Pardes*.

Pardes became the first Subhash Ghai film in a decade and a half to have music by someone other than Laxmikant–Pyarelal. Ghai's first choice was Rahman, but the composer had become too busy after *Shikhar* was shelved. So he turned to the team of Nadeem Saifi and Shravan Rathod.

Nadeem–Shravan were the most successful composers of the first half of the 1990s. Beginning with their breakthrough album, *Aashiqui* (1990), they gave hit after hit—*Saajan* (1991), *Phool Aur Kaante* (1991), *Dil Hai Ke Manta Nahin* (1991), *Sadak* (1991), *Deewana* (1992), *Hum Hain Rahi Pyar Ke* (1993), *Damini* (1993), *Raja* (1995)—and won three consecutive Filmfare awards in 1991, 1992 and 1993.

Nadeem was an instinctive genius. He carried around with him a kettledrum or dugi, which he played with the palm and fingers of one hand. Sometimes, on seeing lyrics on paper, he spontaneously started singing a tune while drumming on his dugi. Shravan's strength was orchestra. This being their first time working with Ghai, they were quite excited. They had scores of tunes and could offer Ghai twenty to choose from for each song.

'Nadeem bhai, Shravan bhai,' Ghai told them, 'all your songs have been hits, you guys are great. But please don't play any tunes for me. I cannot choose from a bank. There is something about my songs that you need to know. All my songs are part of the narrative and take the story forward. My songs have narrative, melody, orchestra and voice.'

He wanted them to spend time to understand the subject, story, characters, situations and the visuals that were going to be in the song. The orchestration had to express the drama of the situation and narrative as a whole. 'Together, we will develop the music score,' Ghai told the music director duo.

Some reviewers called *Pardes* Nadeem–Shravan's best album and marvelled at how different it was from their other work. This distinctiveness can partly be attributed to Ghai's taking the matter of orchestration in his own hands and entrusting three ace musicians. He had learned much from the master, Pyarelal, and taught himself more by studying books on music.

To execute the orchestration, he roped in Tabun Sutradhar, a whiz on the keyboard; Naresh Sharma, who was a master of arranging music; and Surender Sodhi, a composer. The three of them, Shravan and Ghai would sit together to arrange the orchestra for the tunes according to the narrative and situation, occasionally doing away with the composer duo's signature sounds.

For '*Do dil mil rahe hain*', a standout melody because of its gentle and soothing notes, the team rehearsed for four days and designed the dynamics of the orchestra. When they wrote the full orchestra, it required seventy-five musicians. But Ghai was not happy with the effect: he thought the song's rhythm was slow and it had too much orchestra.

The evening before the recording, he phoned Anand Bakshi, who was full of praise for the tune.

'Do you think the rhythm should be fast or slow?' Ghai asked Bakshi.

'The song is slow, so the rhythm should be fast,' Bakshi suggested.

This convinced Ghai further that the rhythm needed to change. On the day of the recording, he reached the recording studio ahead of time. Tabun Sutradhar was fiddling with his keyboard. They were going to make ten or twelve tracks and mix them up for the recording. Sutradhar had already prepared two percussion tracks when Ghai found him.

'Tabun da,' said Ghai, 'that percussion track you just played, let me sing to it.'

It sounded wonderful.

When Shravan arrived, Ghai told him he would like to keep only the two percussion tracks in the song and no dramatic orchestra. He felt the dramatic orchestra would disrupt the soulful nature of the melody. Shravan, an amiable man, agreed.

Of the seventy-five musicians who had turned up for the recording, only ten were needed to record the song; the others were paid and sent away. Strings—mainly violins—kick in only towards the end, lifting the vocals and the entire tune. That's the song you hear.

For '*Yeh dil deewana*', which expresses the conflict between Arjun's heart and mind and the resulting turmoil, Ghai wanted elaborate orchestration. The song was recorded in a rush, over fourteen hours in the course of a single day, in a tiny studio in Andheri; the big ones were all booked and Ghai's unit had to leave for the US the next day.

Sonu Nigam, who sang it, was an emerging talent then. Ghai told him to put everything into the singing even if it made his throat bleed. Nothing less could do justice to the ebb and flow and the aggression of the orchestra. Here was a man—Arjun—who was striking his heart, literally, and fighting his feelings. Nigam sang the alaap first, in which he gave it his all, then the antara, and finally the mukhda. The word dil, which he sings with emphasis and a thump, was recorded separately.

'*Yeh mera India*' was another track that became an anthem of sorts. The film was released the year India turned fifty, in 1997, and had everyone singing 'I love my India'.

'India' is a difficult word to place in a song; it does not lend itself easily to a metre. The song was made possible only because of Anand Bakshi's masterstroke of using the word bindiya in the previous line.

Pardes was made within budget, on time, and recorded at least 80 per cent occupancy in theatres for forty weeks running. And it clocked a golden jubilee, though not all critics were kind in their reviews.

When the film completed a hundred days in theatres, a significant milestone that used to spark celebrations, Mukta Arts published posters announcing the feat. Ghai took one of those posters to Shah Rukh Khan's house. Some of the star's friends, including Aditya Chopra of Yash Raj Films, were present and they all praised *Pardes*.

After *Pardes*, Ghai wanted to quickly start his next venture, *Taal*. He wrote a letter to Mahima Chaudhary, explaining that *Taal* was a dance-oriented film and, as she had not yet mastered dancing, he was considering other actresses to play the lead.

Chaudhary had a three-film contract with Mukta Arts, but the three need not have been consecutive. Madhuri Dixit, for instance, had the same contract. She did *Ram Lakhan* and *Khal Nayak*, but was not a part of *Saudagar*. Ghai's letter to Chaudhary explained this and said she would be considered for the film that would be made after *Taal*.

Chaudhary, riding high on the success of her debut film, did not take this kindly. When she received the Filmfare award for Best Female Debut, she thanked everyone but did not mention Mukta Arts or Subhash Ghai.

One day, Sudesh Gupta brought a news clipping to Ghai that Mahima Chaudhary was going to the US to do a stage show. Gupta pointed out that, under her contract, Chaudhary had to pass on 20 per cent of her earnings from the stage show to the Mukta Arts Workers' Welfare Trust.

Ghai said Chaudhary was probably upset, but Gupta should send her a letter asking her to speak to Ghai about it. When there was no response to the letter, and no call came, Gupta sent the actress a notice. In response, her lawyer sent a much longer notice, saying his client was being harassed, and that she had not been in the right frame of mind when signing the contract.

Ghai felt it was better to back off. He told Gupta to forget about the contract and send a message to Chaudhary wishing her luck.

19

Taal: The Symphony

After *Pardes*, Ghai felt he had nothing left to prove. Having an able team at Mukta Arts to handle the day-to-day legal, financial and business aspects had allowed him the freedom to concentrate on the creative side. He had made all kinds of films with all sorts of actors and technicians and played a hand in every aspect of filmmaking.

What else was there to do? What new story could he tell?

Over time, he had found himself turning inwards, and becoming more reflective and introspective. For years, he had been listening to tapes of Acharya Rajnish (Osho) and reading his books. He had found a new perspective to life through them, different from established thought and, therefore, heretical to some.

A child of a traditional home who had grown up reading and listening to stories from the epics, Ghai heard with interest and curiosity as Osho called himself God. Not only himself; Osho said any human being who could stay great for a hundred years was God. He did not believe that life was about suffering, self-denial or sacrifice; it was meant to be a celebration, full of happiness, dance and music.

Although Ghai never became Osho's disciple—he felt blessed to be a filmmaker and did not ever consider renouncing the world—the Acharya's teachings helped him deal with the vicissitudes of life and calmed his mind during phases of turbulence. What's more, his teachings helped Ghai give expression to his spirituality every now and then.

For instance, in *Krodhi*, a criminal tells a saint that man invented two useful words thousands of years ago, God and Fate. The first kept him on the path of goodness and the second helped him deal with failure.

After *Pardes*, as Ghai grappled with the question of what might be next, he looked back on his journey. From the crime dramas, *Kalicharan* and *Vishwanath*, to modern India's existential dilemmas in *Pardes*, it had been quite the adventure. But the one story Ghai felt he had never told was of young love, the kind that strikes during the transition from the teenage years to adulthood. Even if some of his stories, such as *Saudagar*, featured young love, they were about much more, and spanned lifetimes.

For his next project, he decided to make a musical love story laced with spirituality. After all, music was first born in bhajans, choirs, shlokas and the epics, and, for many believers, the strongest, purest kind of love is what you feel for God.

Taal (1999), Ghai's last film of the twentieth century, was a landmark for him in more ways than one. It marked the culmination of his pursuit of excellence within the boundaries of commercial cinema, and also his coming of age as a spiritual person. At the heart of the story were Osho's words: Do not fall in love, rise in love. This idea was woven into a narrative based on the perennial tussle between the servants of Lakshmi, the goddess of wealth, and the devotees of Saraswati, the goddess of knowledge, wisdom and the fine arts. Music was integral to the narrative, starting with the tranquil notes in the mountains and leading up to the cosmetic beats of glamour on television.

To develop the story of *Taal*, Ghai turned to his old friend, Sachin Bhowmick, and Javed Siddiqui. When the plot was ready, he told A.R. Rahman, 'I have written a musical film for you.'

Rahman was delighted.

'My story,' Ghai went on, 'is the body of the film, your music will be its soul. The two must grow together.'

Rahman had recorded two songs for *Shikhar* before the film was shelved. One was 'Tera nahin jawab o rabba', and the other '*Ishq bina kya jeena yaara*'. Ghai absolutely loved 'Ishq bina'. He told Rahman he was going to use it in *Taal*, but the film would obviously need many more songs. Besides, every note of the background score had to express an emotion.

The progression of the music had to be like that of the story and the heroine Mansi's character—tranquil to turbulent to explosive. Beginning with the ghatam (clay pitcher), it would move to the dugi, tabla, dholak, drums, octopad, and finally rise to a crescendo and round off with the timpani.

'Rahman, you are the hero of the film,' Ghai said. 'I have cast no one so far.'

The narrative of *Taal* derives its music from Chamba in Himachal Pradesh. The compositions had to be rooted in the hills of the north. Lyrics were not a problem; for Anand Bakshi, Himachal was like the back of his hand. The task was to blend his lyrics with Rahman's modern, global sensibilities.

Ghai started sending Rahman cassettes and CDs of North Indian folk music. When the two got together, he would play the same music on one pretext or another. He did not want to offend Rahman by coming on too strongly. But he soon realized that the composer was not a man to be offended in matters of music. He had an open mind and was eager to learn new styles and compositions. An ace musician, sound engineer, recordist, singer, composer and keyboard wiz, he quickly grasped what *Taal* needed.

Still, he was not cut from the same cloth as Anand Bakshi. The lyricist did not speak much English; he preferred Hindi and Punjabi. Rahman, at that time, knew little Hindi, and of course no Punjabi.

Bakshi, based in Mumbai, did not like to travel and refused to go to Chennai, where Rahman's studio was located. The two met only once, when Rahman was in Mumbai and Ghai took him to Bakshi's house.

The meeting lasted an hour, an hour that felt like an age. Neither Bakshi nor Rahman had much to say after the initial pleasantries. They sat in silence, which was broken only when Ghai tried to make conversation. After a while, Bakshi brought out his harmonium and asked Rahman to play some tunes he had made for *Taal*. Rahman said he hadn't made any yet. They had some tea and snacks and sat in silence. Ghai felt like he was trying to arrange a match between a Punjabi and a Tamilian.

That silence eventually produced music so lilting it refuses to grow old.

If Ghai was the bridge between Bakshi's north and Rahman's south, Sukhwinder Singh would become the pillars that held up that bridge.

Singh had begun his career at the age of eight, singing on the stage in his hometown Amritsar. He later joined Laxmikant–Pyarelal's team and became a music arranger. In the early 1990s, he found moderate success as a playback singer in Hindi and South Indian films. A sabbatical followed during which he travelled to the US and UK to hone his craft. He came back to a shower of awards for '*Chhaiyya chhaiyya*', Rahman's terrific number for Mani Ratnam's *Dil Se* (1998).

Singh understood the layered complexity of Rahman's music as well as the simple metre of Bakshi's lyrics and helped bring the two together. Ghai used to call on him all the time and Singh always delivered, with improvisations of his own.

'It was the case of a Tamilian trapped among three Punjabis,' chuckles Ghai.

The mellifluous music flows seamlessly through the narrative. The film is a story of perceived betrayal in love, and Ghai wanted a song to state that upfront. He explained the situation to Rahman and Bakshi: a folk singer of Chamba and his troupe are singing. The music had to reflect the setting: a sylvan village ensconced by mountains and forests, sounds of earthen pitchers, chants and bells from temples, and a tune from heaven itself.

Rahman composed a melody and played it on his computer for Ghai using dummy words in Tamil. The tune was lovely, but Ghai wondered how Bakshi was going to replace the Tamil words. The legendary lyricist, even after all the years of working together, could however, still surprise Ghai. After spending some time listening to the tune, he wrote: '*Kariye na kariye na koi vaada kisi se kariye na / Kariye kariye, o kariye kariye to vaada fir todiye na*' (Don't, don't make a promise to someone / And if you do, do make sure you don't break your vow).

The lyrics were perfect and needed no smoothening from Sukhwinder Singh or Ghai.

'A great song like this is the result of the composer, lyricist, musicians, choreographer, actors and the director coming together harmoniously,' says Ghai. 'In the eye of the public, though, the songs belong to the stars.'

Rahman worked nights, from about nine in the evening to seven or eight in the morning. Ghai was used to working days, but he told Singh that they would have to make changes to accommodate Rahman's genius. He was also careful not to have *Taal*'s music sound like L -P's or R.D. Burman's. Had L–P done '*Taal se taal mila*', it might have been a dholak-based rhythm. Instead, for the opening strains, Rahman used the sound of droplets of water, followed by Sukhwinder Singh's 'Tum tanak tum ta na na' laced with an alaap in a female chorus and modern percussion, rounded off with the flute.

Ghai had briefly dozed off the night they were composing this part in Rahman's studio in Chennai. The composer went away to offer his midnight prayers. When he came back and played this strain, Ghai woke up with a start and screamed in jubilation: 'That's the one!'

It is such a layered composition that few artists can truly replicate it in stage shows, though there is no dearth of those who try.

'*Ishq bina*' has three different tracks and required three different female singers. Rahman was always patient with singers and worked within their abilities and limitations. He would let them sing what they could and, during the mixing, work miracles.

For all the songs, Ghai would drag Sukhwinder Singh to Chennai. Late at night, in Rahman's studio, they would listen to the tunes. Ghai would do rough translations of the lyrics for Rahman—for instance, his translation for '*Taal se taal mila*' was 'beat and beat, let them meet'.

Singh had many outstanding improvisations to offer. Ghai would suggest changes as well. Rahman was a patient man who understood that this teamwork was essential to bridge the chasm between north and south. He bore everything with a smile and remained a team player to the last recorded note.

The first cuts of all the songs were in Sukhwinder Singh's voice, which created interesting creative conundrums.

'*Kahin aag lage lag jaye*' was recorded in Mumbai. Rahman happened to be in the city, so Ghai took him to his studio. Bakshi hadn't written the lyrics yet. Since it was a dance song, they wanted to first make the groove—the rhythm plus the tune. That night, as usual, Rahman made the groove and took a break to offer his prayers. Ghai and Sukhwinder Singh decided to use the break time by fiddling around with things. It was half past midnight. The moment they switched on Rahman's computer, the groove started to play. Ghai asked Singh to take the microphone and sing something in Punjabi.

'But what should I sing?' asked Sukhwinder.

Ghai wrote the first four lines of the song on a piece of paper as the groove played on the computer. Singh sang the lines for the mukhda and used random Punjabi words for the rest of the groove. He was still in the middle of it when Rahman came back. Ghai and Singh looked sheepish, but Rahman was intrigued.

'That sounded quite nice,' he said, with a smile. 'Let's hear it again.'

Singh sang again, this time with even more of a Punjabi punch.

'God alone knows what Sukhwinder used to consume on those nights,' says Ghai. 'Singing at unearthly hours, he used to achieve impossible notes. No other singer could touch him.'

By morning the mukhda was ready, and Ghai went to sleep. He woke up a few hours later and rushed to Bakshi's house with a cassette of the rough tune. Bakshi heard it and took a long drag on his cigarette—a sure sign that the gears of his brain were shifting into place. He wrote out the rest of the song and Ghai rushed back to the studio.

The final cut of '*Kahin aag lage lag jaye*' had to have a woman's vocals. But Singh had hit such high notes in the first cut and sung at such a high scale that they were left wondering who could match them. Finally, Ghai phoned Asha Bhosle.

'Rahman and I are stuck,' he said. 'Can you please come this evening? You alone can do this song.'

Bhosle agreed. One of the best singers in the history of music, she gave a special something to the song. For the antaras, of course, they needed to mix a chorus with her voice.

For '*Nahi saamne*', the lyrics were written first. Ghai told Bakshi it was a song of separation, parts of which would also serve as the background for a montage. Bakshi took a long drag on his cigarette and asked Ghai to come back the next day. The song was ready when Ghai visited Bakshi again.

The night Rahman was composing the tune for it, he took his usual prayer break. Probably feeling guilty for making Ghai and Singh wait, he switched things on quickly once he was back and started playing a tune on his keyboard, in piano mode. He looked up at Ghai and found him nodding vigorously. As Singh sang, Ghai signalled to him to pause at a place where Rahman had given a long drumbeat and sing an alaap saying 'preyasi' (beloved). It was well past midnight, Singh's golden hour. He took the note and carried it high and higher, and on and on he went. Ghai wanted to interrupt, but Rahman gestured to him to let Sukhwinder go on. This was an artiste expressing himself.

When Anand Bakshi heard the song, he loved it, but said it could not be in Sukhwinder Singh's voice. Singh was singing for Vikrant Kapoor in other songs and '*Nahi saamne*' was to be filmed on Manav. The two characters were so contrasting they could not sing in the same voice.

Ghai and Rehman tried many singers, including Hariharan, but no one could match Singh's 1 a.m. vocals. Finally, they called upon Hariharan again, who pulled it off the second time. However, that bit—'preyaseeeeee'—was beyond any other singer and was retained in Sukhwinder Singh's voice.

Ghai and his team of writers created the character of Manav Mehta as an embodiment of the spiritual elements of love: a combination of shringar ras (beauty, love, romance) and bhakti ras (devotion, divinity). He is an unsual romantic hero, to say the least.

Manav is a rich kid, who, having lost his mother at the age of eleven, has spent much time away from his family. He likes to be on his own so he can see the realities of the world and connect with people.

When Mansi, whom Manav loves, wants to go to a temple, he says he doesn't visit temples, though he won't stop her from going. He says God is inside him. 'What is God?' he asks, in one of the most unusual romantic conversations to have been part of a Hindi film. 'God is about truth and faith. Some people find God in books, some in idols, and some in a flame of light. I see God in myself.'

Manav's lack of fear is remarkable. Accused of furtively taking photos of Mansi and her sisters, he owns up to it with a disarming innocence. When he happens to phone Mansi's home at the exact time that her father, Tara Babu, is berating her, he asks for the father and tells him that his love for Mansi is true and his commitment unwavering.

He talks of, and believes in, his inner truth and the purity of his love is his strength.

None of these sound like a sermon in the movie because these profound messages are woven into an emotional narrative and delivered with conviction by young and innocent people.

'We are different people,' Mansi tells Manav.

'Yes, it is different people that come together,' he says.

She calls him obstinate. He calls himself truthful.

There is a memorable scene in which Manav's uncle shouts at him and throws a glass tumbler that shatters on the floor. Calmly, with deliberate pauses, Manav shatters seven tumblers one by one, and asks his uncle, without raising his voice, if that makes him seven times more right. He goes on to say, in the same calm manner, that all the family members now opposing his relationship with Mansi will one day be appearing in family photos around her.

Hindi film audiences were used to love stories in which the hero got into high-voltage confrontations with his parents, delivered thunderous dialogues and blistering ultimatums. Manav, confronted by his father, says he will do nothing to bring disgrace to his family. 'No tamasha, no chhotapan (pettiness), no violence,' he says, and goes on to add that one day his father himself will bring Mansi home. He says the same thing to Mansi's suitor, Vikrant Kapoor, that one day the latter will send Mansi to Manav; and to Mansi, that one day she will come to him—all because God is inside him and his love is true.

It was an uncommon character and difficult to fathom for most people, perhaps even for Akshaye Khanna, who played Manav.

Akshaye's father, Vinod Khanna, a megastar of the 1970s and 1980s, was friends with Ghai. Khanna had produced *Himalay Putra* (1997) to launch Akshaye, but the film had not quite served its purpose. Father and son came to meet Ghai to see if he had a role for Akshaye. Vinod Khanna did most of the talking. Akshaye listened intently.

Afterwards, as Ghai developed the character, he found himself thinking of Akshaye's piercing eyes. When he was ready for a narration, he called the young actor over and told him the story and the character.

New actors usually lose interest in a narration early on and their mind wanders as they begin worrying about the director's track record, the film's chances of succeeding, the budget, their co-stars and other things. Khanna listened to every word. When Ghai finished, he said it was a great story.

'But, sir,' he said, 'what am I doing in it? My character has nothing to do.'

'You are not doing anything, and you are doing everything,' said Ghai. When he saw the confused expression on Akshaye's face, he added helpfully that it was a commercial film in which he would play Mahatma Gandhi.

Ghai explained that Manav was different from all the other lovers in the history of Hindi cinema. He did not fight for his love; he knew that his love would triumph, eventually. This was a young man filled with spiritual calm. Even when he danced, his face and eyes did most of the dancing.

Khanna was still in two minds. Like any young man aspiring to make it in films, he wanted to do action, romance, and everything else that being a hero entails. But he agreed to play Manav. Maybe because his father told him to. Maybe because, if you were an actor in Hindi movies in the 1980s and 1990s, you did not say no to Subhash Ghai.

Unless of course you were Govind Arun Ahuja.

Govinda was the ultimate everyman star of the 1990s. After shooting to nationwide popularity as a dancing sensation with *Ilzaam* (1986), a tale of crime and love, he had found his groove in dramatic comedies, several of them directed by David Dhawan. However, although he had delivered several hits and was universally loved for his comic timing and admired as a dancer, respect as an actor had eluded him.

One day, he came to Ghai's house. Ghai was in the early stages of developing *Taal*, which he intended to announce on 24 October 1997. He announced all his movies on 24 October, the date of his wedding to Rehana. The plan was to start shooting *Taal* in early 1998 and release it the following year, probably in August—an eighteen-month cycle of shooting, dubbing, editing and sound-mixing before the final release.

Govinda was candid about the purpose of his visit.

'Sir, I have done many hit films, I am doing well, but I want to do good films,' he said.

Ghai started to smile at his innocence. 'You are an extremely talented person,' he said, 'you have given more hits than me.'

'True, but you make good films,' Govinda continued. 'I have come to ask you for work. I can give you any dates you need, and I will be happy with any price you pay.'

This was extraordinary. Of all the big stars, Govinda alone could have done this. Ghai thanked him and promised to develop a character for him.

Now that he had Govinda's face, body and abilities for visual clues, Ghai wrote the character of Vikrant Kapoor, Manav's rival for Mansi's love, as a great dancer. Vikrant spots Mansi's potential when she is down and out, and makes her a star.

On a visit to Govinda's home, Ghai saw a picture of the actor performing on stage. The camera had frozen him three inches above the ground in the middle of a swirl. Govinda's mother told him that her son was a wonderful classical dancer. Taking the cue, Ghai made Vikrant the practitioner of a dance form that combined the classical with the contemporary.

When the first draft of the script was ready, Govinda came over for a narration. Ghai spoke passionately for an hour, ending with the climax sequence: Vikrant does a sort of taandav, Lord Shiva's dance of anger, when he realizes Mansi is still in love with Manav, but in the end he tells her to go to Manav.

Govinda heard politely, and kept saying '*Achcha hai* (Nice)'. After several 'achcha hai's, Ghai knew something was troubling the actor.

'Think it over,' Ghai said. 'If you have any suggestions, I'd be happy to hear them.'

Govinda said he would come back soon. He returned the next day with his filmmaker brother, Kirti. This time, Govinda was more open about his reservations.

'Subhash ji, I feel like I am only a character actor in your film,' he said. 'If the girl goes to Manav in the end, I will lose the image of the hero.'

Ghai asked him if he thought that only the one who got the girl was a hero. He pointed out that some of the most memorable heroes in Hindi films were those who sacrificed their love or died without getting the girl.

Nevertheless, Govinda was insistent that Vikrant should get the girl in the climax. 'He is a good man,' he said, 'the girl should stay with him.'

Ghai said that was not possible. 'This film is different from the ones you usually do,' he told Govinda. 'It will make you a legend.'

Govinda turned to his brother for advice. Ghai sat and watched as the brothers chatted with candour and without guile. One said Ghai was a great director, the other that he was legendary. One predicted that *Taal* would be a special film, but the other remained doubtful about its performance at the box office. Kirti told Govinda the film could do wonders for him, but it might also confuse his dedicated audience, who thronged to theatres to see Govinda do comedy and songs.

'*Tu dekh le bhai* (Think about it, brother),' said Kirti.

When they paused, Ghai spoke up. 'You should not do this film,' he told Govinda. 'I thought you would be excited, but you are sceptical.

If you have such strong reservations, you will not put your heart into this role.'

'Sir,' Govinda asked, 'will you feel bad if I do not do this film? I know I came to you to ask for a chance to work with you.'

'No,' said Ghai, 'it's okay.' He promised to think of another project that might be more to the actor's liking.

'Thank you very much for your understanding,' said Govinda.

'Don't worry about it,' Ghai said.

Now Ghai was worried. One of the film's three pivotal characters had just fallen off the map. No one other than Govinda could have done justice to Vikrant Kapoor the way Ghai had visualized the character. Ghai and his writers debated rewriting the character and how that might affect the script. Finally, they retained Vikrant's arrogance and pragmatism, but changed him from a dancer to a music conductor.

Ghai spoke to Anil Kapoor and told him Govinda had backed out.

Kapoor erupted in good-natured whingeing. 'Subhash ji, you always treat me as a spare wheel,' he complained. 'First *Trimurti*, now this.'

Ghai told him not to ask too many questions. 'If you agree, I will write the character to suit you. He'll be a music conductor of the calibre of Yanni.'

'How can you think I won't do it?' said Kapoor. 'Have I ever said no to you?'

'We don't have the time to do workshops and internalize the character,' said Ghai. 'On the sets, do as I say.'

Kapoor, of course, trusted Ghai far too much to question him.

For every shot, Ghai would plan the scenes imagining how Kapoor would do it, and then demonstrate it to him. Kapoor did as Ghai showed him, but he was in fact imitating himself, as transmitted through the director.

Mansi is a girl nurtured by the first rays of the sun and the music of the mountains. Her entire family is immersed in music, and worships the goddess Saraswati.

Where on earth were they going to find such a girl?

A lot of actresses were discussed during Ghai's sessions with his team. When someone suggested Aishwarya Rai, Ghai's immediate reaction was sceptical.

Rai had finished as the runner-up to Sushmita Sen in the Miss India beauty pageant and had then been crowned Miss World 1994. She was a sought-after international model. Like many of her predecessors, she had been trying to find a place for herself in the film industry, but hadn't met with much success.

She had made her screen debut in 1997 with *Iruvar*, a landmark Tamil film directed by Mani Ratnam. The same year, she appeared in her first Hindi film, *Aur Pyaar Ho Gaya*, which received a lukewarm response from viewers and critics. The Hindi film industry was quick to dismiss the former Miss World as cosmetic and wooden, not much more than a beauty queen.

Film producer Murli Manohar was friends with Ghai. His wife, Sunanda, was producing *Jeans*, with Aishwarya and Prashanth in the lead. Manohar organized a showing for Ghai, who came away unimpressed.

'Forget *Jeans*,' Murli Manohar told Ghai, 'watch *Iruvar*.'

Rai had a double role in *Iruvar*: one of them was a simple village girl called Pushpavalli and the other a modern actress named Kalpana. Since this was a Tamil film, her voice had been dubbed over by another actress. But Ghai was struck by a scene in which Pushpavalli is going away in a train, leaving her husband behind. Dressed in a simple, cream-coloured saree, with her hair parted in the middle and a bindi on her forehead, she is standing at the door of her train compartment, saying farewell to her husband. As the train begins to move, she bursts into tears.

Ghai felt that Mansi was lurking somewhere in that scene. He asked Saroj Khan who the best dancer was among his team's wishlist for the role of Mansi.

'It is Aishwarya, without a doubt,' said the choreographer. 'She is outstanding, and she has grace.'

But what about acting ability?

Ghai met Rai in Mumbai and told her about *Taal*. He also played '*Ishq bina*' for her. When she said she was keen on the role, Ghai placed his cards on the table.

'You probably know already,' he said, 'that the industry does not have a high opinion of you as an actress. But opinions and perceptions can be altered. We'll have to make a few changes, and we will begin by destroying you first.'

Rai was still trapped in her image as a Miss World—something many filmmakers were trying to leverage and exploit. Mansi, on the other hand, was the antithesis of Miss World, untouched by the city and television and modern life. Her father and other members of their family made musical instruments and sang folk songs on the radio and gave public performances. She enters the cosmetic world of glamour and fame much later in the film.

'I will make you Miss World, but not just yet,' Ghai said.

Rai said she was ready.

Ghai used up every resource at his disposal—characterization, script, make-up, costume, cinematography and, above all, music—to create Mansi. This is a character that evolves, not unlike the gradually building notes in a saptak, from the purity and innocence of a simple girl from the hills to a star singer–dancer. The film's music bears witness to this transition as the tranquil rhythm of '*Taal se taal mila*' slowly gives way to the anger of '*Kahin aag lage lag jaye*', before returning to the folksy melody of '*Ishq bina*' in the climax.

Ghai gave Rai the sketches for each stage of her character.

Films are typically not shot in a linear fashion; scenes are shot at random according to the availability of locations and actors. If the action sequence of the climax is supposed to take place in the same location as a romantic song and with the same actors, the two can be shot in the same schedule. The written script is just a sequence of events, not a reliable guide to what comes up next for an actor. This was why Ghai always believed in giving narrations to his actors and technicians, along with sketches, paintings and storyboards.

'That is how you find the artiste in every actor and every technician,' he says.

The same narration, sketches and paintings were given to Mickey Contractor, who did Aishwarya Rai's make-up, and Neeta Lulla, who designed her costumes. They curled her hair and made her wear all kinds of dresses, from flowing whites to television tights and Osho's wine-coloured robes. She looked perfect in all of them.

Contractor was the best and most expensive practitioner of his art. 'I will pay you whatever you want,' Ghai told him, 'but you are not going to apply any make-up on the heroine in the first half.'

Contractor understood immediately, and he was delighted. 'I know what you mean,' he said.

He did the kind of make-up that did not make Rai look made-up.

The actress's beautiful green eyes, when seen through the lens, were not the most suitable to portray a virginal beauty of the mountains. So Mansi was given dark brown contact lenses. Mansi's make-up, too, evolved in stages, going from nothing to completely cosmetic: from untouched rain-kissed freshness to lipstick, to kohl, to hair, to texture, to drama, to the Miss World look. It required immense control from Contractor.

'*Kahin aag lage lag jaye*' is the first song that presents Mansi as a singing–dancing star. Contractor and Lulla were told that this was where Mansi becomes a new woman; she should look like a medieval European princess emerging to greet her subjects. They told Ghai to leave them alone with Rai for a few hours.

When he was finally summoned to the make-up room, Ghai's first glimpse of his heroine was through the half-open doors as he approached. The effect Contractor and Lulla had created was stunning.

Ghai replicated this on film in the song's opening shot where the viewers first see Mansi in the make-up room.

As much as Contractor and Lulla did for Mansi, she was also a creation of Kabir Lal, the cinematographer, who had grown in confidence with all the awards he won for *Pardes*.

Lal was exceptionally skilled and loved presenting the leading ladies in all their radiance. His ambient lighting was great, but he truly excelled in close-ups. For evidence, look no further than the many backlit shots of Mahima in *Pardes*. The entire unit used to chuckle when the time came to shoot the heroine. 'Kabir babu will now come to life,' the other technicians would jest.

Given Rai's ethereal beauty and screen presence, and the changes Mansi's character goes through with the passages of time, Lal raised his game several notches for *Taal*.

'Kabir is an instinctive artiste. Aishwarya owes him a lot,' says Ghai.

Lal was up for all the demands Ghai made on him. For the song '*Taal se taal mila*', Ghai thought of shooting in real rain and asked the cinematographer if that was possible. Lal was thrilled with the idea. The artificial rain that a shooting unit arranges is confined to a small area. With real rain, you can shoot till the infinity reading of your focal length. Around 125 people put on raincoats to shoot the song out in the open. The unit froze, but the results were great.

When *Taal* was released, critics said it was different from other Ghai films, that it was long and loose, that it was not as good as *Pardes*. That was expected; each Ghai release was usually greeted with the verdict that the previous one was better. One well-known critic devoted most of his review to Brownie, Manav's dog.

Some people were more charitable. The film was good, they said, but it was missing the large drums of *Ram Lakhan* and the larger-than-life villains of *Karma* or *Kalicharan*. True, but *Ram Lakhan* had come ten years earlier, *Karma* thirteen, and *Kalicharan* twenty-three years ago. The world had changed in the interim, and so had Ghai and his films.

From the Friday of its release to Sunday, *Taal* seemed to generate more interest in theatres in the US and UK. A theatre in New Jersey, which was showing *Taal* on four of its twenty-two screens on Friday, kept adding screens until all twenty-two were showing it on Sunday. 'We never saw so many people turn up for one film,' the theatre owner told Ghai. Hollywood's trade magazine, *Variety*, reported *Taal* in its top twenty box office hits that year, a first for an Indian film.

The Tuesday after the film was released, Ghai put up banners on theatres with the reviews and appreciation *Taal* had got overseas. Slowly, the film picked up in India and went on to be declared a hit.

Instead of celebrating it as a success of Indian cinema overseas, the Mumbai film industry said, '*Jungle mein mor nacha kisne dekha* (If a peacock dances in the jungle, who's seen it)?'

Ghai was used to critics not praising his films. He chuckles at how difficult it was to pick even one line from a review for promotions. But, he says, many of those same critics watch his films with renewed interest on DVDs in their homes now and praise them to him when they meet. Ghai reminds them of their past criticism, but few remember it.

Roger Ebert, a well-regarded film critic in the US, saw *Taal* in a theatre in India. His review carried the usual curiosities about India, Indian films, their songs, and the way Indians express love. He also said, 'There is an innocence in this pure entertainment that Hollywood has somehow lost.'

Taal was screened at the Chicago International Film Festival, the longest-running competitive film festival in North America, and at Ebert's own Overlooked Film Festival, now known as Ebertfest. Ebert introduced the film to two thousand Americans in the audience, saying: 'I think Americans must see how beautiful this film is.'

Ghai sat among the festival's audience and watched his film with subtitles. The viewers laughed and cried at all the right places, clapping with delight every now and then. In the end, they gave it a standing ovation.

English composer Andrew Lloyd Webber watched *Taal* in a small theatre in the UK and got so enchanted by the background score that he asked his friend Shekhar Kapur about the music director. Kapur introduced Lloyd Webber to Rahman, and together they wrote the Broadway musical *Bombay Dreams*.

Back home, as *Taal* gathered momentum at the box office, opinions in the film industry were revised as people took cues from one another. From Friday to Monday, Ghai's phone remained silent. From Tuesday, it began to ring off the hook with congratulatory calls.

'Opinions changed with the box office collections of every show,' says Ghai.

If reports said the matinee show was lukewarm, people would say they 'knew it', the film was no good. If collections picked up in the evening show, they would say the audiences were tolerating the flaws. If the night show was full, they would say there were indeed some good things in the film. If the next day shows were house full, they would say they had loved the film and known all along that it was a surefire hit.

'That is the fun of being in our industry,' says Ghai.

20

Yaadein: The Disconcerting Memories

The story goes that the closest Alexander the Great came to tasting defeat was against King Porus. When the vanquished Porus was presented before Alexander, he was asked how he should be treated. Porus replied: 'Like one king treats another.'

That is the line Ghai uses while describing the way he treated directors who made films for Mukta Arts—with the respect and courtesy one director should show another.

Mukul Anand, when he was starting work on *Trimurti*, the first Mukta Arts production not directed by Ghai, asked how much control Ghai would like to have. Ghai said he would limit his engagement till the finalization of the script. After that, it was up to Anand, the film's director.

On one occasion, while *Trimurti* was on the shooting floor, some of the unit members told Ghai the film was going off on a tangent. For instance, it was intended to establish Mohan Agashe, who played Kuka, as one of the industry's premier villains, now that Amrish Puri had started to play positive characters from time to time. However, Kuka was so loud that he became a caricature of the formidable villain the script had envisaged him to be. Ghai, though, intervened only after ten reels were done.

'Technically, Mukul was better than me. But content is different from technique. Content is more about the fabric of the story and the psychology of characters,' says Ghai.

In the later productions of Mukta Arts directed by others, Ghai became even more fastidious about giving directors their space. This worked well in the case of passionate, mature directors: Prakash Jha (*Rahul*, 2001), Anant Balani (*Joggers' Park*, 2003), David Dhawan (*Ek Aur Ek Gyarah*, 2003), Abbas-Mastan (*Aitraaz*, 2004 and *36 China Town*, 2006), Nagesh Kukunoor (*Iqbal*, 2005 and *Bombay to Bangkok*, 2008), Sangeeth Sivan (*Apna Sapna Money Money*, 2006), Rituparno Ghosh (*Noukadubi/Kashmakash*, 2011) and some others.

Ghai's involvement in these films was minimal between the script and final editing. For instance, Kukunoor, who had started with a bang by making *Hyderabad Blues* (1998), was going through a lean phase when he came to meet Ghai. He had not tasted much success with *Rockford* (1999), *Bollywood Calling* (2001) and *3 Deewarein* (2003). He narrated two or three concepts to Ghai, which were all right, not spectacular. He left saying he would come back another day with more ideas.

He reappeared after only a few minutes, saying there was another idea he forgot to talk about. It was about a deaf-mute young man aspiring to play cricket for India. Ghai approved it on the spot.

Once the script was finalized, Ghai stepped in only to discuss the ending, the title and the pre-release publicity. Kukunoor was not sure about the title, so Ghai suggested that the film should be named after its central character. He also suggested a modification in the ending to include Iqbal's mother and sister so they could share his triumph.

The film turned out well and won the National Award for Best Film on Other Social Issues. However, there were no good stills to make its posters. Finally, Ghai chose a still in which the lead actor, Shreyas Talpade, was looking at the sky, with his arms raised in triumph. Talpade's face was not visible in this photo, but Ghai decided to go with a faceless hero. It worked.

Ghai arranged fifteen trial shows of the film for his celebrity and journalist friends, followed by dinner. He put a feedback logbook at the venues. He had his team cull out comments from this logbook and used them to promote *Iqbal*.

For *Noukadubi* (Bengali, *Kashmakash* in Hindi), Ghai left it completely to Rituparno Ghosh, the feted director of Bengali and Hindi cinema. After the script was ready, Ghosh went back to his base in Kolkata. A year later, he presented the complete film to Ghai.

Giving directors a free hand did not always bear the desired results though, especially where the directors were raw and still not on top of their game. Some films turned out to be different from the script, because the directors interpreted scenes and characters differently.

But Ghai was unwavering in his approach. Creative independence was the one thing he had craved while, early in his career, he was making films for other producers—and he was not about to deny that freedom to Mukta Arts' directors. He would hand them the script and tell them to show him the final print when it was ready. He did not want to be breathing down their necks. That would have made the directors nervous, given Ghai's formidable reputation as a maker of hit films.

When Ghai discovered that a film had strayed from the script, he tried to fix things during editing. That did not always make the directors happy, but Ghai, as the producer, had a responsibility towards the distributors, who always paid good money for Mukta Arts productions.

Creative freedom made sense otherwise too. Filmmaking is a democratic art. Ten directors working on the same story and script will turn in ten different films and they can all be good and successful as well. It was prudent to welcome other perspectives. After the year 2000, and especially after its initial public offer and listing on stock exchanges in 2001, Mukta Arts was producing a large number of movies and it would have been bad business to have all of them looking like Subhash Ghai films.

In fact, Ghai himself could not afford to keep making trademark Subhash Ghai movies, he had to constantly reinvent himself. Filmmaking is different from other professions in that a doctor or engineer or a craftsman presumably gets better by doing pretty much the same things over and over again. A filmmaker, having made a hit, cannot make the same film again and expect it to be successful.

'There is no failproof recipe. The best directors and the biggest producers make flops. You have to respect writers, directors and actors, and you let them express themselves,' says Ghai.

Though the film industry is known to worship formulas—say, lost and found, which has been used in innumerable films—the good films using the same formula can be starkly different from one another. For proof, look no further than *Waqt* (1965), directed by Yash Chopra, and Manmohan Desai's *Amar Akbar Anthony* (1977). Both could be made because Chopra and Desai had the freedom to make their films their own way.

Ironically, Ghai struggled to strike a balance between his responsibilities as a producer and his creativity as a director. Producer Ghai and Director Ghai could seldom treat each other as one king should treat another. They often got entangled in the same fracas that is at the centre of *Taal*—the tussle between Lakshmi and Saraswati.

The year 2000, when Ghai turned fifty-five, was significant for him and for Mukta Arts in many ways. Ghai had started work on *Kalicharan* in 1975 and had now completed a quarter century as a writer–director, arguably the most successful of them all in the eighties and nineties. He had directed eleven box office hits. The twelfth—*Karz*—was not a big hit but had received much acclaim and its cult had grown with the passing of years.

As the world sought to come to terms with the fear of turbulence that could be caused by Y2K, Ghai grappled with his own inner turmoil. He found himself frequently wondering: what next?

This professional question was tinged with changes in his personal life. Meghna, Ghai's older daughter, was growing up and coming of age. The younger one, Muskaan, arrived in 2001.

Having moved away from crime dramas to women-oriented family affairs with *Pardes* and *Taal*, Ghai wanted to go the whole hog and make a film about a man's relationship with his three daughters after their mother dies in an accident. The first daughter has an arranged marriage, the second marries a man she loves but the marriage breaks up soon after, and the third does not believe in love but falls for the son of her father's employer. Ghai intended it to be a small film, the likes of which Hrishikesh Mukherjee and Basu Chatterji excelled in. And he wanted the film to have the message that you should treat your children as friends once they come of age.

Randhir Kapoor's daughter Kareena Kapoor had debuted with *Refugee* (2000), following in her older sister Karisma's footsteps to break the family tradition of women not acting in movies. *Refugee*, which was also the debut of Abhishek Bachchan, Amitabh's son, had not quite smashed the box office, but Kapoor had shown enough spunk for every expert to predict a bright future for her. She was keen to work with Ghai and bagged the role of the youngest daughter. For the role of the young man she loves, Ghai was thinking of calling Akshaye Khanna when he ran into Rakesh Roshan at a party.

Rakesh Roshan was a second-generation film professional. His father, Roshan, was the legendary music composer of *Barsaat Ki Raat* (1960), *Taj Mahal* (1963), *Chitralekha* (1964) and others. After Roshan died in 1967, his son Rakesh went on to achieve middling success as an actor in the 1970s and 1980s, without establishing himself as a solo lead who would ensure a good initial on the opening weekend. His fortune changed when he turned director with *Khudgarz* (1987).

Rakesh's son, Hrithik, had played a significant role as a young boy in *Bhagwan Dada* (1986), which was produced by Rakesh Roshan and directed by his father-in-law, J. Om Prakash. At the time Rakesh Roshan met Ghai in 2000, he had made a film to launch Hrithik as a leading man. Roshan told Ghai the film was in the final stages of post-production work and he would like Ghai to see it.

The next day, Ghai went to Rakesh Roshan's editing room and saw *Kaho Naa... Pyaar Hai*, without the background music, which was still being mixed. He liked it. He thought the film would do well and that Hrithik was good in it.

The day after, Hrithik Roshan came to meet Ghai at his house. 'Papa told me you liked my work and asked me to visit you,' he said.

Ghai told Roshan he had indeed done a commendable job while playing a double role in his very first film as the hero. There was a role Ghai could offer him in *Yaadein*, but it was a small role that would be nowhere close to the significance of his two roles in *Kaho Naa... Pyaar Hai*. 'It is your decision whether you want to do it,' said Ghai.

An immensely respectful young man, Roshan said he would be keen to do any part in Ghai's film, even if small, because he was sure he would get to learn a lot. Ghai was only too happy to have him. The Roshan family, too, was delighted that their boy was working with Ghai.

Although he was the third generation of a film family, Hrithik was shy and unfledged, like all newcomers. Ghai tutored him a little on how to face the media, how to answer questions during an interview, how to speak on television, and helped him prepare responses.

They shot the first schedule of *Yaadein*, of eight or nine days.

Two weeks later, *Kaho Naa... Pyaar Hai* released and rewrote box office history. Hrithik Roshan became such a big star that all others began to appear pale in comparison.

When the second schedule of *Yaadein* was being shot in the Surya hotel in New Delhi's New Friends Colony, word got out that Hrithik was around. Thousands of people gathered outside the hotel for a glimpse of the young star. The frenzy could be compared with Rajesh Khanna's heyday in the early 1970s.

Everyone connected with *Yaadein* was thrilled at Hrithik's overnight stardom. Everyone except Ghai. To the bafflement of distributors who wanted to now pay more for *Yaadein*, he said it was a small film that did not deserve such a high price. To the astonishment of his team of writers—Aatish Kapadia, Anuradha Tiwari and Amrik Gill—he said they should perhaps drop Roshan from the film.

Yaadein, in Ghai's mind, had no room for Hrithik Roshan the superstar. Jackie Shroff was the biggest star in it. Two of the women playing his daughters were unknown. The third, Kareena, had been chosen because hers was the love story in the film that made things happen. She was just a film old and hadn't attained stardom. Her love interest had to be of a similar stature. The film was, after all, the story of a man and his daughters, the love story was not its centrepiece.

The team of writers disagreed with Ghai. Instead of dropping Roshan, they said, it would be better to use his stardom. 'It is a not a bad role he is doing,' they said.

'It is certainly not a bad role,' said Ghai, 'but it is not significant enough for a superstar. How will we do justice to his stardom and meet people's expectations?'

'Let's make the role more significant,' said the team.

The business managers at Mukta Arts agreed with the writing team. 'You cannot drop Hrithik,' they said, 'our film's price has gone up.'

In the end, Producer Ghai, too, was tempted, and trumped Director Ghai. He and the team rewrote the script. The original had Roshan making his first appearance around the interval, similar to how Anil Kapoor did in *Taal*. The script was redrafted to narrate the entire story from the point of view of Roshan's character, Ronit Malhotra.

Ronit was made a friend of Raj Singh Puri, played by Shroff. He was given much more footage, and got added to the beginning, middle and end. The father was still the central character, but a little less central than in the original.

'For the first time, I became disloyal to the script,' says Ghai. 'This was a big mistake.' He edited the film himself, to make sure the revised script worked.

For the pre-release publicity, Rahul Nanda, the publicity designer, came up with a beautiful, evocative poster of the father and his daughters. The second poster had the extended family. There was also a third poster, which was dominated by the young couple, Hrithik Roshan and Kareena Kapoor.

Ghai said the film was not Hrithik and Kareena's story, so there was no need for the third poster. But he was told there would no harm in putting a few copies of the third poster here and there to help the initial collections. The posters were sent to distributors clearly stating the hierarchy: the father and daughters were the main show, the young couple could be used if there was space.

When the film released—in June 2001—it was the third poster that dominated theatres and other walls. The focus had moved completely away from the story of the father and his daughters. As a result, audiences came expecting to see Hrithik's next big outing after *Kaho Naa... Pyaar Hai*—and were bitterly disappointed.

'"Initial" is the game that has destroyed many films,' says Ghai.

In the first week, box office collections overseas were fine, because the right posters had been used and audiences came to see a Subhash Ghai film; Hrithik was not yet a big draw for them. But, in India, the collections were weak.

Industry wags, tired of Ghai's knack of making hits, pounced on *Yaadein*. Once again, they said Ghai had lost his magic touch. Critics also berated the film for its many product placements.

Taal, too, had product placements, but they were woven into the narrative more seamlessly. Given how well the film had presented Coca-Cola, several brands sought placements in *Yaadein*. Only half of those were accepted—their offers were too big to refuse—but they stood out in the narrative. The uncharitable asked if *Yaadein* was a feature film or an ad film.

Eventually, *Yaadein* turned in a profit, but it did not enhance Ghai's reputation as a producer–director. Today, television channels say they get a high repeat viewership for *Yaadein*, perhaps this father–daughters story finds a greater resonance in today's urban culture. Consequently, *Yaadein* is a film that has grown younger over the years. But, in 2001, it did not get the kind of viewer appreciation to which Ghai was accustomed.

He decided to move away from the women-oriented stories of his last few films: *Pardes*, *Taal* and *Yaadein*. He wanted to make a big war film, similar to *Shikhar*, which he had shelved after *Trimurti* tanked. He announced *Motherland*.

The announcement made news for its star cast: Dilip Kumar, Amitabh Bachchan, Shah Rukh Khan, Aishwarya Rai, Preity Zinta and Mahima Chaudhary. You couldn't possibly put more star power as well as acting ability into a film. Ghai narrated the subject to the leads and worked on the script for a long time. He also recorded three songs for the film. This was his second attempt, after *Shikhar*, to make a war movie.

For one reason or the other, the film kept getting deferred. Shah Rukh Khan was busy with other films and was not able to start work on *Motherland*. After more than a year of working on the script and other pre-production aspects, Ghai came to know that Khan would need another year to finish his other commitments.

By now, Ghai was restive. He was going through a low phase in his career after all the negative noises around *Yaadein*. He wanted to quickly start another movie. And he wanted to make a grand film. He chose to shelve *Motherland* and move on to *Kisna*.

21

Kisna, Yuvvraaj and Beyond

Kisna: The Warrior Poet (2005) is a film close to Ghai's heart. This is the film on which he worked harder than he did on any other, he says. With the benefit of hindsight, he thinks maybe that was not such a good thing. He was at his best when making a film with an unencumbered head and heart, improvising, innovating and having fun on the sets. While making *Kisna*, he was trying to prove the point that he could make a grand film, never mind what had happened to *Motherland*.

So grand was his vision that he decided to make two versions of *Kisna*, one in Hindi and the other in English. 'When you are at the peak, you want to fly,' says Ghai. And he left no stone unturned. This would be his path to break open the overseas market for Mukta Arts. He had nothing left to achieve in India, now was the time to make it big outside.

For the subject, Ghai decided to give his audiences a peek into how India was, and how Indians were, before Independence. This was a tale of dharma versus karma—the path of righteousness versus the path of duty—playing out against the backdrop of India's struggle against the British rule.

Ghai roped in Farrukh Dhondy for the English screenplay. Dhondy had done notable work on British television for shows such as *Tandoori*

Nights, Channel 4's first Asian comedy series. He was based in London and Ghai had to make several trips to the city so they could work together. But these trips were nothing in comparison to Ghai's travels to find the right actors. For the role of Catherine alone, he conducted more than a hundred auditions to find the right British face, before deciding on Antonia Bernath.

The screenplay was a balancing act between the sensibilities of Indian and Western audiences. Every scene had to be written in a way that would help both Hindi as well as English audiences to understand and relate to the narrative. However, since *Kisna* was to be a big leap into the overseas markets, every scene ended up being underplayed to suit Western audiences.

For the first time, Ghai roped in two different composers for a movie. A.R. Rahman was to score the Western music-based songs and Ismail Darbar, known for *Hum Dil De Chuke Sanam* (1999) and *Devdas* (2002), came in for the Indian classical raga-based ones.

'Perhaps the shelving of *Motherland* was playing on my mind,' says Ghai. 'I was going to make a really big film. Every frame, every shot had to be grand.'

Somewhere along the way, he might have ended up focusing more on the form and perhaps a little bit less on the content. He sensed that when the first copy of the film was out. After the trial show, Rehana asked Ghai how he liked it, and was stunned to hear her husband's response. It would be a stroke of luck, Ghai said, if the film did well. She had not seen him so downcast at the prospects of any of his films, and this one he had worked especially hard on.

Now, with the benefit of the intervening years, Ghai realizes it was not a good idea to make two versions of *Kisna*. As the same actors gave two final takes, one for English and the other for Hindi, the pace and rhythm of the film ended up becoming a hotchpotch of Indian and Western sensibilities. The English version was meant to be slower in pace and the Indian one more dramatic. The film ended up being too slow for the Hindi audiences and too dramatic for the English ones.

The changing demography compounded matters. As India became the youngest country in the world with more than half its population below the age of twenty-five, the masses of 2005 might not have connected readily with the dilemma between dharma and karma.

Ghai was not surprised that *Kisna* flopped. Still, it depressed him. For the first time, the failure of a film affected him so much. Earlier, he would dust his hands off and move on to the next film, probably telling his team: '*Chalo ek chhoti si film banate hain* (Come, let's make a small film).' In time, that little film would of course grow and evolve and become a blockbuster.

This time, things were different.

Ghai had joined panels and committees of industry chambers and attended seminars and workshops on the future of India's media and entertainment industry. The consensus among all experts was that a massive boom was on the anvil. Every speaker and presenter talked about more corporatization, unbridled expansion, hundreds of television channels, and billions of dollars in revenues.

At these sessions, Ghai would ask where the human capital would come from. Would this boom be fuelled by accidental, instinctive talent? Would that be enough? Was there a need to set up a system to train and hone talent?

A stream of youngsters used to meet Ghai to seek his blessings and guidance. He often wondered what was to become of those youngsters. Who was going to look after them? They reminded him of his own struggles as a young man desperately seeking a toehold in the industry. He used to stumble from studios to offices since there was no platform to connect young aspirants with the movers and shakers.

These questions got fused with the 'what next' introspection that had been going on in Ghai's mind. What was going to be his legacy? Should he set up a big studio, on the lines of Raj Kapoor's R.K. Studio or Yash Chopra's Yash Raj Films? He asked his elder daughter, Meghna, if she saw herself as a writer–director someday. Meghna's answer was an unequivocal no. She saw herself more in the field of management. Ghai also wondered where the march of technology would leave the big-daddy film studios. Somewhere in his mind, these questions got fused together and led to the most logical answer. Ghai decided to set up a film school.

As usual, he turned to Dilip Kumar for advice. The thespian said a film school was a great idea, but it should be in Mumbai, in close proximity to the industry. The only such institute worth its name was the FTII, Ghai's alma mater, in Pune.

Next, Ghai spoke to Sunil Dutt, the actor-turned-politician who was Sanjay Dutt's father and had been like an elder brother to Ghai. Dutt, too, liked the idea of a film school and offered to help Ghai acquire land for it.

Vijay Choraria, who was active in the real estate and financial markets, knew Ghai. He came up with the idea of an initial public offer for Mukta Arts. 'Subhash ji, it will raise enough money to fund all your dreams,' said Choraria. Ghai was uncertain, but Choraria told him it was the right time. The stock market had the appetite for a production house with a strong balance sheet and ebullient projections.

Other winds were also blowing in the right direction. The government had recognized filmmaking as an industry. Aided by that, Ghai had led a campaign, through the Indian Motion Pictures Producers' Association, to start insurance coverage for films. Mukta Arts had suffered a financial damage when Sanjay Dutt had to leave *Trimurti*. Two elaborate sets had to be erected all over again and scenes were reshot with Anil Kapoor stepping into Dutt's role. Ghai did not want a repeat with *Taal*, which he was then making.

He met the New India Assurance Company, whose management was cautiously interested. Ghai told them about his experience with *Trimurti*. Of course, no insurance could cover the box office performance of a film, but production losses could be covered. The New

India people said they saw risks because of an absence of transparency and discipline in filmmaking. Ghai invited them to visit Mukta Arts and examine the company's books to their hearts' content.

They came and pored over Mukta Arts' accounts of the preceding ten years. Everything was spic and span. All the schedules had been followed exactly as planned. The New India people were so impressed that they started a new policy and called it Mukta Cine Insurance Policy, under which *Taal* became the first Hindi film to be insured. The insurance company used the same name, Mukta Cine Insurance, while covering other films.

In 2001, Mukta Arts became the first Indian film production house to go public and get listed at the stock exchanges. It was the culmination of a process that had started with the income tax raid on Mukta Arts' offices in the 1980s, after the pyrrhic success of the piracy-hit *Hero*. That had made Ghai set in motion a process to establish complete transparency and discipline.

Until *Taal*, Ghai could focus only on making films, to the exclusion of the business aspects. He had the luxury of having a strong team—led by his brother-in-law, Pravez Farooqi, and Sudesh Gupta—to take care of the business aspects. Farooqi, right from the beginning of Mukta Arts, looked after accounts, taxes and legal matters. Gupta liaised with the industry and distributors.

That left Ghai free to devote himself to the creative aspects, which was his 24x7 occupation, so much so that he did not accept any offer to shoot ad films or make shows for television. He came from an era in which creativity was not hampered by commerce. He had seen Laxmikant pay musicians from his own pocket when the producer did not have the money on a given day.

Things changed for Ghai after the listing of Mukta Arts.

Now, as the cynosure of shareholders' eyes, Ghai had to truly act as the chairman and chief executive. As shareholders demanded scale, he had to become more of a producer. Besides, though Ghai was new to being a businessman, he was not short on ambition. He wanted to make Mukta Arts an exemplary film company, above the usual problems of the industry. And he gave it his best shot: flitting from business meetings to creative meetings, from meeting distributors to the editing table, looking after distribution, watching the markets, announcing quarterly results, and addressing analyst meetings.

Accustomed to making one film in two years or so, now he had to think about making a few films every year. Mukta Arts ventured into the Marathi, Punjabi and Bengali language markets. Ghai set up Mukta Searchlight to make films that were high on concept and low on budget, such as *Joggers' Park*, *Iqbal*, *Rahul* and *Noukadubi/Kashmakash*.

'I was a 100 per cent writer-director till *Taal*, totally focused on the creative aspects. Afterwards, I became 80 per cent producer, focused on business,' says Ghai. He had to now think and work like a businessman. Films became projects, guided by market demand and distributors' preferences. Some of these films worked at the box office, but few of them were memorable.

'My life got divided. It was like bringing up many children at the same time; not all of them turned out well,' says Ghai.

Yuvvraaj (2008) turned out to be a spoilt child.

The tussle between Lakshmi and Saraswati, in Ghai's mind, had reached a crescendo after *Kisna*. He had started working on a small film, *Black & White*. The story of a Hindu professor who taught Urdu, and a terrorist, the film explored human relationships in the Old Delhi area.

People had seen enough 'Subhash Ghai-type' films, he felt; he wanted to give them something special, even if that meant making a film for only 30 per cent of the audience. He wrote *Black & White* with love and made it real, realistic, and a far cry from the old Ghai model.

The market was miffed. Ghai was told that a small and realistic film was an indulgence after the dismal showing of *Kisna*. Ghai said he was producing films by other directors that were doing well, but the market wanted him to direct one himself, a grand film that would start with a huge initial and be an unqualified success. That needed stars and a mindset that treated a film like a project.

Ghai fell in line. 'I surrendered myself to commercial terms,' he says.

He happened to meet Arbaaz Khan, Salman Khan's brother, who said Salman would be happy to work with Ghai. Ghai was delighted. Salman was a big star who could guarantee an initial. Ghai met him and they agreed to do a film together.

When Ghai mentioned this at the Mukta Arts office, it triggered shivers of excitement. Everyone said this film would mark the return of Subhash Ghai, the badshah of blockbusters. Ghai pulled himself out of his labour of love, *Black & White*, and started working on the new film with Salman Khan.

'Some films are made because they are needed,' he says.

He narrated a story to Salman Khan about a policeman and his relationship with a prostitute. Khan heard it with patience but said, 'Let's make a big film.'

Ghai was under pressure to start the film quickly. He rehashed the plot of a 1962 film, *Sautela Bhai*, starring Guru Dutt. It was about a man whose father wills all his property to his son from another wife. This is one of those films that never figures in any conversation about Guru Dutt's greatness.

Ghai added another brother to the plot and presented it to Khan, who loved it. Anil Kapoor and Zayed Khan came on board to play the other two brothers, and Katrina Kaif to play Salman's love interest. A.R. Rahman and Gulzar came in for the music and lyrics. The market exclaimed that this was a fail-safe crew.

The people at Mukta Arts were delighted. They told Ghai not to spend time on a small Chandni Chowk film. 'You are *the* Subhash Ghai,' they said. Distributors opened their purse strings.

The buzz got to Ghai. 'All right,' he said, 'let's make a grand film.'

On the side, though, he kept working on *Black & White*; it would release in 2008 as well.

It is only with the lapse of time that Ghai can analyse what might have gone wrong with *Yuvvraaj*. The initial response, from some viewers at least, was positive. The legendary painter M.F. Husain phoned Ghai from Dubai to say he had watched the film on the opening Friday and liked it so much that he had booked a bunch of tickets for his friends for the Sunday. Newspapers quoted Husain as saying: '*Yuvvraaj* is the kind of movie we get to see once in many years ... I feel it is a beautifully made film with extremely melodious music and some brilliant performances.'

Being a painter, he would have liked the form of the film. Form was what Ghai had ended up focusing on—to the detriment of the content perhaps.

Yuvvraaj's original story was set in Jodhpur, Rajasthan. Under pressure from distributors and their fat cheques, the revised screenplay shifted the scene to Europe, placing the family in London and Salman Khan as a chorus singer in an orchestra in Vienna. Every location, every costume, every frame had to be beautiful.

Ghai had shot all his earlier films in schedules of eight days to two weeks each. After each schedule, he saw the rush prints, studied the characters, held discussions with his creative team, and then shot the next schedule. For *Yuvvraaj*, Salman Khan gave bulk dates, making Ghai shoot without allowing him his usual creative breaks to analyse how the film was progressing.

After the first schedule in Austria, Kamlesh Pandey, who was writing the screenplay with Sachin Bhowmick, asked Ghai how the narrative was coming along. Ghai admitted that the main characters were not really flowering, but they had to try and make things work while immediately moving on to do more shooting. He put in more money, decorated the frames more and made the scale larger and grander. And he thought Khan's star power would carry the day.

He realized much too late that having Khan play the central character of Deven Yuvvraaj Singh was not the best use of the actor's talents. Deven is a person who believes he has been wronged and uses that to justify and rationalize his ignoble deeds. This was a role that had many shades, positive and negative. It needed a delicate performance to walk the razor's edge and retain the viewers' sympathy.

It probably wasn't the right role for Salman Khan. *Yuvvraaj* was one of the last films in the string of flops he gave till 2008. The following year, *Wanted* came and he found his groove in the role of an action hero tinged with comedy.

When *Yuvvraaj* was ready, Ghai found that it was less than coherent, although it was packed with striking visuals. The focus was too much on grandeur, to the exclusion of emotions. Ghai wanted ten days of extra shooting and reshooting to tie up the loose ends and asked for the release date to be deferred by three months. He did not get either.

This was when the global financial crisis was brewing. The market was weak. Distributors were bargaining for lower prices and pressing Mukta Arts to release *Yuvvraaj* as soon as possible. When Ghai said he needed more time, the distributors said they would pay less. That would have hurt Mukta Arts.

Ghai was still hopeful that *Yuvvraaj* would sail through on the strength of its star cast and masterful music. His confidence was high. *Black & White*, made on a shoestring budget, had released a few months ago and earned twice as much as its cost. *Yuvvraaj* was a grand film and Ghai thought it would, at the very least, recover its cost and turn in a small profit.

The film hit the theatres on 21 November 2008. The reaction from audiences was mixed, but critics called it a visual delight and a musical feast. Five days later, Mumbai was hit by the worst terror attack the country has seen. Theatres emptied out. *Yuvvraaj* fell well short of recovering its cost.

'Every film comes with its own luck,' says Ghai.

'Filmmaking is nothing but storytelling,' says Ghai. 'A film should have a new thought, a new emotion.'

That is why films that are made as projects targeted at a big initial often do not work. Some of them might be successful, but they are not memorable. Memorable films are those that tug at the audience's heartstrings or make them think.

That needs the kind of dedication and focus that Ghai brought to his films as a pure creative person. Now, he was juggling too many balls in the air, as a writer, producer, director and a businessman. To compound matters, the profile of the theatre audience was changing rapidly.

'Nothing lasts forever,' Ghai says. 'Sunil Gavaskar cannot open the batting for India today. His time has gone, as has mine.'

22

Whistling Woods: A New Innings

Just as Sunil Gavaskar morphed into one of the world's most successful cricket commentators after his playing career came to a close, Ghai is playing a new innings as an educationist in the film arena with Whistling Woods International.

The process of setting up Whistling Woods started in earnest in 2001 and Ghai was completely engaged in every aspect of it. 'Establishing Whistling Woods was equal to making twenty films,' he says.

Like a good film, the school had its own plot twists.

Ghai visited some thirty film schools in different countries over six months to study their courses and assess their relevance to the Indian film industry. He was determined to make his school market-friendly and job-oriented, and meet international benchmarks.

He identified forty acres in Panvel, on the outskirts of Mumbai, for the school. Word about this reached Govind Swarup, who was the chairman of Film City Corporation. He got in touch with Ghai and wanted him to meet the state minister for culture, education, youth affairs and sports.

The minister, Ramkrishna More, had earned a reputation for taking bold decisions. He had introduced English as a subject from the first standard in all government schools and compulsory board exams in standard 6 to measure the quality of education. (The latter decision was overturned by the government that followed.)

'Why don't you set up your film school in Film City?' More asked Ghai.

'I am wary of working with the government,' said Ghai.

'But we are the government,' said More. 'Work with us.' He offered Ghai twenty acres in the heart of Film City. In return, the state would take 15 per cent equity.

This was tempting. The government had created Film City in Goregaon in 1977 to give a helping hand to the film industry. It was full of shooting locations, such as a lake, a temple, a prison, a village, a haveli, and even a man-made waterfall. Expectedly, it had become a hotbed of film-related activity.

Having Whistling Woods in Film City would mean placing students in the lap of the industry they aspired to join. They could get practical experience just by turning up at the right place. Visiting faculty would be easy to get. The country's biggest entertainment companies were within a 20-kilometre radius. No other professional school in the world had such access to the industry it served.

Ghai decided to make do with the twenty acres More offered. The land was allotted in 2000. Chief Minister Vilas Rao Deshmukh and senior politician Praful Patel attended Whistling Woods' bhumi pujan (groundbreaking ceremony) in 2001.

Over the next few years, Whistling Woods became the focus of Ghai's life. He invested somewhere in the vicinity of ₹100 crore to make it Asia's largest institute of its kind and one of the world's best. The industrialist Anand Mahindra agreed to head its governing board, which also had stalwarts such as Kiran Karnik, Pradeep Guha and Manmohan Shetty. The institute drew its faculty from among film industry luminaries such as Shyam Benegal, Shabana Azmi, Vishal Bhardwaj and Anjum Rajabali.

In an unorganized and chaotic industry, a graduation certificate from Whistling Woods became a stamp of quality and a catalyst for career progression—similar to what an IIM degree does in the more organized world of corporate management. Its alumni started to work for the best film, media and entertainment organizations not only in India but also abroad.

In parallel, however, trouble was brewing. In 2003, the Comptroller and Auditor General of India said the Maharashtra government had undervalued the land given to Whistling Woods. Based on the CAG report, the Bombay High Court said in 2004 that the state government was 'desirous' of shifting from a joint venture to a lease model. The institute, which already occupied 5.5 acres, was told not to construct over the remaining 14.5 acre, where hostels and studios were to come up.

In 2009, a few farmers from Latur and Osmanabad filed a public interest litigation saying Vilas Rao Deshmukh, whose son Riteish was an actor, had misused his position as the chief minister to allot land to Whistling Woods. The government had changed. Ramkrishna More had died in 2003.

A long battle of legal attrition ensued, pushing Ghai, who was already balancing many things, further into a corner. His health suffered; he needed a heart surgery in 2010.

In 2012, The Bombay High Court told Whistling Woods to pack up and leave; the land would go back to the state government by August 2014. This led to review petitions and appeals.

Along the way, Ghai's team persuaded him to make a new film—*Kanchi: The Unbreakable* (2014)—about a young woman's quest for revenge and justice. This was a film that Ghai directed with his lawyer almost always on the sets. So deep was he in the legal wrangle that he had to be constantly running from the courts to the offices of ministers and bureaucrats. He released *Kanchi* without a final edit and was least surprised at its fate. The film was received with disappointment by viewers and critics alike and did nothing for Ghai's reputation.

Finally, when all seemed lost, the Bombay High Court gave interim relief to Whistling Woods in its review petition in 2014.

'Those five or six years when the legal battle was raging were the worst of my life,' says Ghai.

Discussing Whistling Woods seems to perk Ghai up.

'We do not teach classes, we interact with the students,' he says.

Whistling Woods has 3,200 alumni across media and film companies. Some of them are already names to reckon with. Shashank Khaitan, who was in the first batch, is now a producer at Karan Johar's Dharma Productions and has directed films such as *Badrinath Ki Dulhania*. Abhishek Jain is redefining the Gujarati movie industry. Anand Bansal and Aikeshwar Chaudhary worked as the cinematographer and associate editor, respectively, for *The Elephant Whisperers*, which won Best Documentary Short Film at the 95th Academy Awards.

But how is Whistling Woods different from the many other film schools?

The biggest difference is Subhash Ghai himself. The school was conceived and set up by the filmmaker, producer, director, writer and storyteller. He put together the best of teams. For instance, Naseeruddin Shah, one of India's finest actors, helped with the acting stream. He brought people from Los Angeles to Mumbai to meet Ghai's people in the initial years.

The faculty, says Ghai, is based on ability and experience, not just qualifications. And the school is self-funded, allowing it a fair amount of freedom in how it is run. One of its tenets is to let students do what they love. If they are inclined towards world cinema, they can pursue it. If their interest is in mainstream cinema, so be it.

'Cinema is a democratic art,' says Ghai. 'We must train and educate our children to tell our stories. We have all the stories. The hidden wealth in India is its wisdom. Those stories should be told.'

Today, Ghai is a contented man. He has left his Showman days way behind. It was a prudent thing to do.

The unstructured nature of the Hindi film world had done much damage. It was not uncommon for chartered accountants to tell producers not to worry about tax payments: 'we will manage' was their mantra. Distributors wanted to pay in cash, the stars wanted to be paid in cash. Theatre owners in some states would pay no more than 10 per cent by cheque. People felt bad if you asked them to sign written contracts. 'Don't you trust me?' they reprimanded anyone who wanted to be a stickler for contracts. It was okay for actors to write the dates of their availability for shooting on a random slip of paper.

This left many cracks in the system, into which stepped bad elements. Things worsened in the 1990s and touched a nadir with the hit on Gulshan Kumar. Three assailants pumped sixteen bullets into Kumar, the owner of T Series, on 12 August 1997, as he came out of a temple in Juhu. He died on the spot.

Ghai was not left untouched. When *Pardes* was ready for release, he received a call asking for the film's overseas distribution rights. Ghai said he had already sold those rights. This resulted in threats to murder him. Ghai went to the police and was given security for two years.

Things took a few years to change, but the industry cleaned itself up with rising corporatization and regulatory interventions. However, Ghai stopped hosting the big parties and Holi bashes, the invitations to which had become status symbols in the industry. Instead, he is happy now spending time with the young students at Whistling Woods.

In 2010, just four years after it opened, the institute came to be ranked among the top ten film schools in the world. More than two thousand of its alumni are working in top media and entertainment companies in India and outside.

'This is good,' says Ghai, 'instead of making movies, I am making moviemakers.'

Ghai wakes up at seven every morning, averages ten hours of work a day, and sleeps well. His daughter Meghna and her husband Rahul Puri manage the institute's day-to-day affairs. They have grown it from 200 students to 1,100, taught by 125 teachers.

Muskaan, Ghai's younger daughter, turned twenty-two in December 2023. She and Ghai have a one-on-one session every Sunday. Adopting the message of *Yaadein*, Ghai has become Muskaan's friend. 'You have to choose your destiny,' Ghai tells her. 'We are here only to finance your journey.'

During the Sunday sessions, they each come with questions that the other has to answer. The questions can be about anything—from studies, people, movies and television to politics and life in general.

The industry remains aware of the significance and impact of Subhash Ghai's cinema. *Hero* and *Karz* have been remade. In these remakes, Ghai and Mukta Arts have of course had no involvement.

Ghai writes poetry every morning and spends a couple of hours every day with the students of Whistling Woods, where they discuss anything and everything. He has set up a story lab in Mukta Arts, where he works with half a dozen writers: two youngsters, two mid-career, and two veterans. They have already developed several movie scripts and are working on programmes for OTT streaming platforms. Ghai frequently goes to other institutes to share his knowledge and experience. He also makes short films on social issues from time to time.

Raj Kapoor, the original showman, is famous for the song '*Jeena yahan marna yahan, iske siwa jana kahan* (It is here that I will live and here that I will die, where else is there to go)' about circus life in *Mera Naam Joker*, which became a parable for the film industry. Ghai, who took over the mantle of the showman from Kapoor, follows a different philosophy.

'For me, it is not "*jeena yahan marna yahan*",' he says. 'For me, it is: *zindagi har kadam ek nai jung hai. Jeet jaayenge hum, tu agar sang hai.* (Life is a battle on every step. We will win, if we are together.)'

Afterword

BY SUVEEN SINHA

The first time I met Subhash Ghai was in October 2016. He was toying with the idea of writing his memoirs.

I had grown up watching Ghai's blockbusters and had for years harboured a nagging feeling that would just not leave me, an itch I could not scratch. I repackaged that feeling as my take on his story, which I presented to him on the following lines.

Ghai was not only the biggest filmmaker from the middle of the 1970s to the end of the century, not only the man who started many trends and discovered several new faces, but he was also the biggest anti-hero maker, I said.

Look at his oeuvre. He began with *Kalicharan*, whose title character is an illiterate criminal and an imposter. He followed it up with *Vishwanath*, which features a criminal lawyer who takes to crime. Govinda of *Gautam Govinda* is a village goon, a gaon ka goonda. Jackie of *Hero* is a city equivalent, a sheher ka goonda. *Vidhaata* is about a train driver who becomes a crime lord. The 'heroes' of *Karma* are three convicted criminals on death row. Lakhan of *Ram Lakhan* is a corrupt police inspector. The two larger-than-life granddaddies of *Saudagar* have their own militia.

Besides, the villains in Ghai's movies are legends in their own right. Starting with the fabled Lion in *Kalicharan*, Ghai created the mute bad man of *Karz*, the chilling Dr Dang of *Karma*, Pasha in *Hero*, and many more. The culmination was in making a movie dedicated to the villain: *Khal Nayak*.

Yet, Ghai never made a film with the biggest star and anti-hero of his time: Amitabh Bachchan.

As we sat and chatted in Ghai's sprawling office at Whistling Woods International, he heard me patiently, thought for a moment, and said, 'Suveen ji, *chaliye karte hain*. Let's do the book.'

That was it.

Later, as I sat with Chaitanya Chinchlikar, Ghai's trusted lieutenant, he told me that he was dazed at the swiftness of Ghai's response. It turned out he had rejected several people who wanted to be his co-author. I had no background in film writing, except for the occasional foray to fill an empty slot in my publication, or just for the heck of it, if something took my fancy. Now that I look back, that may have worked in my favour. To take on a co-author who inhabits a world far removed from his own is the kind of thing that would appeal to Ghai.

The closest Ghai came to explaining his working relationship with me was when he introduced me to a visitor during one of our sessions in Delhi. '*Main sunata achchha hoon, Suveen-ji sunte achchhe hain* (I am a good storyteller, Suveen is a good listener).'

The first thing that struck me at our first meeting was the twinkle in his eyes, which on no occasion in the intervening years have I found to be missing. The twinkle, in many ways, captures the essence of his personality.

I have found him to be a remarkable person in being devoid of guilt and regret—feelings that usually trouble people who have had extreme highs and terrible lows in their lives, of which Ghai has had his fair share.

He has a natural light touch to the way he deals with life. You will rarely see him bogged down. Remarkably, for a man in show business, he does not take himself too seriously. At no point did I feel he wanted this book to be a paean to himself, or a hagiography. Never did he want to paint himself as a giant cut-out looking down upon his worshippers.

Nothing symbolizes this more than Ghai's relationship with the Almighty. When he prays, it is like he is chatting with God. I can imagine him saying things like, 'Bhagwan, I am going for this big thing today, please look after me. *Zara dekh lena*.'

He is equally comfortable with the current state of things in filmdom, when a new generation of filmmakers is rewriting the grammar of Indian movies.

'Generations now change every five years; it used to be fifteen earlier,' he says. 'Technology changes every year. We have moved from television and video to OTT and YouTube. New mediums bring in new people, new talents. We have to adapt to the current scenario to communicate our story.'

These stories can be of India's villages, towns, metros, or of society in general. The Western world tells their own stories, we must tell our own, says Ghai. And these stories must be told in today's language.

In the 1980s and 1990s, when Ghai was the biggest filmmaker in India, the stories were emotional and family-oriented. Today, they are less about emotions and much less about faith, he says. Ghai uses the term 'analytical communication' to describe today's relationships and bonds, without finding anything wrong with them.

'The bonds are different, not good or bad, and they are analysed. A young girl has the freedom to select, choose her career, and express her thoughts,' he says. 'Earlier, the father was always right. Father's aagya (instruction) was God's will. Now, the father is expected to be like a friend once the son or daughter turns sixteen.'

Movie watchers were more orthodox earlier, and more family-oriented too, according to Ghai. He notes that back in the day, summer vacations were spent with relatives; now you see relatives' vacation pictures on social media. It was not unusual for relatives or friends to turn up at your door without notice, and they were treated with warmth and respect. Even a total stranger could knock on your door and ask for a glass of water. Now, you had better phone your next-door neighbour ahead of time to ask if it was okay to drop in for a quick visit.

Nowadays it is all about the individual, Ghai points out. Youngsters are questioning the institution of marriage, questioning so-called truths. As relationships have changed, so have the movies. You will struggle to make a movie today about Shravana Kumar, a legend from the Ramayana, who embodies devotion to parents, he says.

It is more about superheroes now than obedient children, he adds. Some Indian filmmakers are following the Marvel Comics model of big heroes and big spectacles, creating the so-called 'universes' in India. Some others are focusing on good storytelling about real or rural issues. The middle path of family emotions and relationships is virtually gone.

In Ghai's heyday, films provided the common folks with a much-needed escape from their daily cares. They came looking for a feast for their senses, and filmmakers such as Ghai served them a full thali, with rice, roti, dal, several vegetable dishes, curd, pickle, poppadom, and a sweet dish. The audiences were least troubled by the fantastic and illogical elements of the screenplay as they laughed and cried with their beloved characters and had a gala time. They clapped when two little flames emerged from Sai Baba's eyes in *Amar Akbar Anthony* and restored Nirupa Roy's vision.

The new audience, especially in the cities, live a life very different from that of their parents. The new lot is more aspirational, more aware, and more exposed to the world. They do not immerse themselves in films and characters, they observe and analyse from a distance.

Raj Kapoor's *Sangam* created a sensation for taking viewers on a tour of Europe in 1964 while making them sit through two intervals. That wouldn't work for today's audience—many of them already know what Europe looks like, through travel, television, or the internet. Few would get enthralled by the helicopter shot we see when Ganga in *Pardes* first arrives in the US. Today, the audience does not want a thali. They go to the small auditoriums of multiplexes looking for a specific cuisine and you can serve them pasta, or pizza, or burgers, or just popcorn or nachos and a soft drink.

And increasingly, they don't go to the theatres at all. They prefer to watch in the comfort of their homes, on OTT platforms, enjoying a film on a large LED television screen. Or they watch movies on their smartphones.

As the audience has changed, so has filmmaking. A new generation of filmmakers has changed the narrative of cinema and made it non-linear. In Ghai's time, the audience were the masses who often did not understand non-linear narratives. *Karz*, for instance, suffered because its many flashbacks confused viewers.

Shot-taking has changed; camera movements have changed. Films like *Sholay* and *Karma* made a huge visual impact on the viewers in theatres. Now, shots are short, the cuts from scene to scene are much quicker. Earlier, if music had to fade out, a series of shots had to be planned, frame to frame, with sound effects. The fadeout effect was created during mixing, with a stay here, a bird sound there, and then the fade out. Technology and digital enhancements mean that a film can now pretty much be created out of the 'raw stock' of what has been shot, on the computer.

The atmosphere of filmmaking has also changed, as actors and technicians have become more professional. It is more of a business now. In the big studios, MBAs sit in creative meetings and stars dominate the show. Actors have managers. Public relations have replaced human relations.

'We lived an entire lifetime during the making of each film,' says Ghai. 'Our films possessed us, and went with us everywhere, to a party as well as to the bathroom.' Relationships between unit members did not take a pause when pack-up was called. There was invariably dinner together or a night on the town. People made friends not only with their colleagues but also with colleagues' families.

Still, you would never ever catch Ghai saying, 'It isn't like it used to be. In our time...,' etc. He accepts the changes with equanimity and good humour, though he does sometimes sound envious of the freedom today's filmmakers have to experiment—without ever being jealous.

'We cannot say yesterday was good, today is bad. We should see how wonderfully our children are making films. The good, the bad, and the ugly have always been there. They were there in the 1950s, when I was watching movies, and they are there today, when I am still watching movies,' he says.

Ghai wants the Whistling Woods students to reshape the industry and also influence the audience taste.

Is that possible. Can a filmmaker really change the audience?

'Of course,' says Ghai. 'Look at *OMG 2*. People are shy talking about sex and masturbation. It is part of education in Europe, but a moral issue here. There is hardly any sex education in India. The film teaches us there is no harm in it: this is part of a process of growing up. Do not be afraid or think you have committed a sin. *OMG 2* told the story in such a way it convinced the viewers.'

Could a movie about masturbation have been made in the 1980s?

'It could never have been made in the 1980s. People would not have accepted it.' Indeed, I think. *OMG 2* could not have been made back then in the same way that a movie about a race between a bus and a tonga cannot be made today, though it was massively successful in the 1950s in *Naya Daur*.

'Similarly, *Taare Zameen Par* changed people's attitude towards children with dyslexia,' Ghai continues. 'It taught parents to let children follow what they want. I met so many families who, after watching the film, allowed their children to pursue what they wanted.'

What about *12th Fail*?

'Yes, *12th Fail* says you can always restart. You never really fail. The thing is, it should be a good story and good storytelling. It should also be entertainment for the viewers.'

How has the role of songs changed in storytelling? Ghai's movies used songs that usually took the story forward, while also pleasing the senses. They were so hummable it was difficult to get the tunes out of your head. Most of them had simple lyrics: '*Ding dong, O baby sing a song*'; '*One two ka four, four two ka one*'.

Such simple hummable songs were also the hallmark of the great Raj Kapoor, whose mantle of 'The Showman' fell upon Ghai in the1980s.

Now the focus is more on having the characters talk. Ghai used six-minute songs as tools of the narrative. Now, songs are shorter and fewer, sometimes playing only in the background and sometimes missing in the actual film altogether.

Again, Ghai has nothing adverse to say about today's film music.

'My father loved K.L. Saigal. I liked Laxmikant–Pyarelal and R.D. Burman. My father thought my generation spoiled music. Thoughts change. Visuals change. Sound also changes. Today's sound is different. Earlier, melodies were taken from classical ragas, rural and folk music and bhajans. Now, sound is coming from a universal energy. Earlier, songs were usually composed on a harmonium. Now they are composed on the guitar. The melodies are bound to be different.'

It may be because of this acceptance of change that Ghai has turned composer too. On 24 October 2021, his fifty-first wedding anniversary and Mukta Arts' forty-third anniversary, he announced that *36 Farmhouse* (2022), a Mukta Arts production, would have three songs written and set to music by him.

This was an unexpected result of the Covid pandemic.

'I had a year at home. I said to myself, let me try. I wrote sixty to seventy poems. A few of them became songs. I held video calls with some of my students. They sang, I played music. We composed together. The pandemic taught me new things.'

Ghai also wrote the story for *36 Farmhouse*. Did the time at home also revive the filmmaker in him? Can we expect a return of Ghai the filmmaker? And if he were to make a movie today, what would it be like?

'People want me to make sequels to movies such as *Khal Nayak* and *Karma*. I feel excited, but it is a challenge,' he says.

The real challenge, he adds, is to take the narrative forward.

'I cannot remake a film that exists, but I can take a story further, with modern audiences and technology. The biggest challenge is to make sequels with new narratives and sensibilities.'

So, can we make a film about Ballu Balram, the titular Khal Nayak, about his life after he is released from jail?

'Let me see. We will announce something very soon. We need a new body, a new soul, a new story.'

Why not remakes? Some remakes have been money spinners in Hollywood as well as in India. But Ghai waves the thought away.

'Let others remake my movies. I have made what I had to make.'

He is more excited by the possible story of what happens to Ganga of *Pardes* after she marries Arjun. The story of Mansi of *Taal* after she goes back to Manav. And the life of his first anti-hero, Kalicharan, after he is fully reformed.

In all this, should they go ahead, Ghai will stay true to his connection with the audiences.

'Raj Kapoor was an institution, as was Bimal Roy; so was Mehboob Khan. What was their basic approach? Connection with the common man. That is why I became a mass director with aesthetics,' he says.

And music?

'Music is the only tool with which you can direct a story,' Ghai says. 'Our epics were kavyas, they were meant to be sung. I cannot think without music, I cannot write without music. Stories can be narrated better with music than with dialogue.'

Is anyone doing that today?

'Sanjay Leela Bhansali directs through music.'

Ghai also deeply appreciates the work of Rajkumar Hirani, Rakeysh Omprakash Mehra, Vishal Bhardwaj, Anurag Kashyap, Kabir Khan, Rohit Shetty and many others who have defined their own genres and made their own grammar.

Finally, is Ghai the last great showman of India?

'No human being can ever be the last,' he replies at once. 'Even if you look at incarnations, first came Ram, then Krishna, then Buddha. You do a bit of good work, make people happy, make the world happy. What matters is the satisfaction of doing good work. I am still a child, in action as well as in thought.'

This reminds me, inevitably, of a song, penned by Sahir Ludhianwi for *Kabhi Kabhie* (1975): '*Kal aur aayenge naghmo ki khilti kaliyan chunne wale, mujhse behtar kehne wale, tumse behtar sunne wale*' (Tomorrow there will be others to choose the pretty blossoms of words, they will say it better than I, and people will hear better than you do).

'You said it,' says Ghai. 'There will be greater filmmakers than me. There already are greater filmmakers than me.' But what satisfies me today is that I could set up a school in film and media arts as Whistling Woods International to enrich the creative minds of the generations to come. I feel blessed.

Maybe, but I believe we have only one showman: whose heart will go on.

This is his story.

Subhash Ghai's Filmography

As Writer (Ghai–Bhalla)

Khan Dost (1976)

Mama Bhanja (1977)

Akhri Daku (1978)

As Director

Kalicharan (1976)

Vishwanath (1978)

Gautam Govinda (1979)

Karz (1980)

Krodhi (1981)

Hero (1983)

Meri Jung (1985)

Karma (1986)

Ram Lakhan (1989)

Saudagar (1991)

Khal Nayak (1993)

Pardes (1997)

Taal (1999)

Yaadein (2001)

Kisna (2005)

Black & White (2008)

Yuvvraaj (2008)

Kaanchi (2014)

As Producer–Director

Hero (1983)

Karma (1986)

Ram Lakhan (1989)

Saudagar (1991)

Khal Nayak (1993)

Pardes (1997)

Taal (1999)

Yaadein (2001)

Kisna (2005)

Black & White (2008)

Yuvvraaj (2008)

Kaanchi (2014)

A s Producer/Presenter

Ram Lakhan (1989)

Prem Deewane (1992)

Trimurti (1995)

Rahul (2001)

Badhaai Ho Badhaai (2002)

Ek Aur Ek Gyarah (2003)

Joggers' Park (2003)

Aitraaz (2004)

Iqbal (2005)

Shadi Se Pehle (2006)

36 China Town (2006)

Apna Sapna Money Money (2006)

Good Boy Bad Boy (2007)

Bombay To Bangkok (2008)

Sanai Choughade (Marathi) (2008)

Paying Guests (2009)

Right Ya Wrong (2010)

Hello Darling (2010)

Love Express (2011)

Noukadubi (Bengali) / *Kashmakash* (2011)

Nimbehuli (Kannada) (2014)

Double Di Trouble (Punjabi) (2014)

Vijeta (Marathi) (2020)

36 Farmhouse (2022)

As Co-Producer

Valu (Marathi) (2008)

Samhita (Marathi) (2013)

Index

Aag, 6
Aakhri Daku, 31–32
Aandhi, 100, 163
Aankhen (1993), 221
Aap Ki Kasam (1974), 40
Aashiqui (1990), 222
Aatish (1994), 201
Aatma Balam (1985), in Telugu, 89
Abbas, K.A., 19
Abbas–Mustan, 38, 246
Abodh (1984), 163
actors, 15, 26, 46–48, 59, 103–105, 114–115, 118, 121, 133–134, 136–137, 148, 171, 173–174, 176–181, 185, 200, 235, 209, 240, 249, 255, 267–268, 275–276
Agashe, Mohan, 245
Agneepath (1990), 211
Agnihotri, Apurva, 221
Agnihotri, Rati, 107
Aitraaz (2004), 38, 246, 282
Ajanta Arts, 41
Ajit, 46
Akhtar, Jan Nisar, 11
Akhtar, Javed, 9–11, 14, 42, 72, 124–125, 127–129
Akhtar, Sardar, 158
Aman, Zeenat, 68, 71
Amar Akbar Anthony (1977), 145, 248, 274
Amritraj, Anand, 195
Amritraj, Ashok, 195
Amritraj, Vijay, 195
Amrohi, Kamal, 11, 72
Anand, Dev, 80, 116
Anand, Mukul, 208, 210, 212, 245–246; directing for Ghai's film, 211
Anand, Vijay, 197
Anand (1971), 144, 193
Ankhen Barah Haath (1957), 132
Ankhiyon Ke Jharokhon Se (1978), 69
Ankur, 23
Ankush (1986), 197
Apna Sapna Money Money, 2006, 246
Apsara Apartments, 23, 35
Aradhana, 23, 76
Ardh Satya (1983), 216
Arora, Vijay, 23
Arun, Ila, 206
Ashadh Ka Ek Din (1971), 39
Asrani, Govardhan, 15
assistant directors, 9, 34, 48, 62, 98
'attitude,' 25–26, 215
audience, 24–25, 29, 55, 75, 84–85, 112–113, 137–138, 140–142,

192–193, 216–217, 243–244, 252, 254–255, 262–263, 274–276, 278
auditions, 17–20, 115, 182
Aunty Ka Adda, 9–10
Aurat (1940), 158
Aur Pyaar Ho Gaya, 239
Awara Baap (1985), 163
Azmi, Shabana, 23, 265

Babita, 18–19
Bachchan, Abhishek, 249
Bachchan, Amitabh, 66–67, 82, 88, 92–93, 120, 125, 132, 138, 144–155, 158, 161; Ghai meeting, 27; Ghai on, 144–145, 152
Bachchan, Jaya, 92, 151
Badrinath Ki Dulhania, 267
Baharon Ke Sapne, 19–20
Bairaag (1976), 177
Bajaj, Tolu, 156–157
Bakshi, Anand, 77, 111–113, 128, 130, 136, 159–160, 175–176, 204–205, 213, 223–224, 228–233
Balachander, K., 107–108
balcony movies or 'class cinema,' 57
Balraj, Anand, 169–170
Bandit Queen (1994), 216
Bandra, night-time addas in, 9, 12–14, 21
Bansal, Anand, 267
Banu, Saira, 20, 151, 190
Barjatyas, 175
Barsaat Ki Ek Raat (1981), 161
Barsaat Ki Raat (1960), 249
Bedekar, Shivam, 27
Bedi, Kabir, 119
Be-Imaan (1972), 43
Benegal, Shyam, 23, 137, 265
Ben-Hur (1959), 140
Betaab (1983), 124
Bhagwan Dada (1986), 250
Bhalla, Bharat, 30–32, 36, 38–39, 280
Bhansali, Sanjay Leela, 279
Bharat Ke Shaheed, 23, 27
Bhardwaj, Vishal, 265, 279
Bhatt, Mahesh, 138, 192, 208
Bhonsle, Waman, 55, 215
Bhosle, Asha, 216, 232
Bhowmick, Sachin, 69, 76, 80–81, 134–135, 138, 147, 175, 227, 261
Bhuvan Shome (1969), 39
Bindu, 82
Bipin, 27
Black & White, 76, 259–262, 281
blockbusters, 5, 9, 52, 89, 92, 108, 209, 256, 260
Bobby (1973), 40, 43, 174
Bollywood Calling (2001), 246
Bombay Dreams, 244
Bombay to Bangkok, 2008, 246
Brahmchari, 24
Bulundi (1980), 177
Burman, R.D., 77, 109–110, 154–155, 157, 159, 230, 277

Censor Board, 93, 207; against fight scenes, 60
Chaalbaaz (1989), 175
Chacha Bhatija (1977), 25
Chakraborty, Mithun, 161
Chandiramani, Poonam, 64–65
Chandra, N., 166
characterization, 53–54, 103, 105, 240
characters, 41–42, 52–54, 58–59, 95, 102, 133–134, 139–140, 158–160, 168–169, 175–176, 178–179, 181–182, 245–247, 261, 274
Chatterjee, Moushumi, 68
Chatterji, Basu, 249
Chaudhary, Aikeshwar, 267
Chaudhary, Ritu. *See* Mahima
Chaurasia, Hari Prasad, 111–112
Chinchlikar, Chaitanya, 272
Chitralekha (1964), 249
Chopra, Aditya, 224
Chopra, B.R., 16–17, 19, 128

Chopra, Vinod, 208
Chopra, Yash, 92, 158, 192, 197, 248, 257
Choraria, Vijay, 257
choreographer, 107, 109, 113, 166–168, 206, 230, 239
Chor Machaye Shor (1974), 33, 58
cinematographers, 79, 140, 171, 174, 197, 221, 241–242, 267
cinematography, 15, 174, 240
computer-generated imagery (CGI), 140
Contractor, Mickey, 241
Coolie (1983), 120, 145
corporatization, 256, 268
co-writers, 76, 196
creativity, 132, 174, 219, 247–248, 258

Damini (1993), 222
Darbar, Ismail, 255
Datta, J.P., 208
Dave, Mohanlal, 22, 28–29
Dave, Ravindra, 18
Dayavan (1988), 166
debates, 6, 9–11
Deewana (1992), 222
Deewar (1975), 9, 92, 158
Denzongpa, Danny, 46
Deol, Sunny, 124
Desai, Mangesh, 50
Desai, Manmohan, 25, 145, 248
Deshmukh, Riteish, 266
Deshmukh, Vilas Rao, 265–266
Desh Premee (1982), 145
destiny (*taqdeer* in Urdu), 9–11, 18, 21–22, 143, 167, 269
'Devaa,' 147, 149, 171; mahurat, 150–151; shelving, 154, 157, 171, 174
Devdas (1955), 163
Devdas (2002), 255
Dhamkee, 23; Gai in, 26–27
Dharma Productions, 267
Dharmatma (1975), 43
Dharmendra, 16, 22, 24–25, 32, 67–71, 80, 132, 138, 146, 152, 161; and Hema Malini's love story, 70
Dhawan, Anil, 27
Dhawan, David, 235, 246
Dhillon, Poonam, 124
Dhondy, Farrukh, 254
Dhund (1973), 46
dialogues, 40, 47, 56, 60, 76, 97, 104–105, 127, 129, 187–189, 215
dialogue writers, 40, 76, 156, 175, 190
Dil Hai Ke Manta Nahin (1991), 192, 222
Dilip Kumar (Yusuf Khan as) 8, 11, 94–95, 97, 99–102, 124, 127, 133–134, 136–139, 142, 146, 148, 150–152, 176–181, 187–192; and characters, 102; Ghai on, 103–104, 123
Dil Se (1998), 229
Dilwale Dulhania Le Jayenge (DDLJ, 1995), 215, 217
directing, 34, 38
director–writer, 62
distributors, 41, 48, 50, 56, 91, 93, 95, 118–121, 149–150, 170–171, 185, 209, 214, 251–252, 258–262
Dixit, Madhuri, 163–167, 172, 183–184, 204, 206, 219, 221; 'Ek Do Teen Girl,' 166; 224; Ghai on, 165–166
Dixit, Rupa, 163
Dixit, Snehlata, 163
Do Bachche Dus Haath, 22–23, 25
Doctor Zhivago (1965), 196
Dolby sound, six-track, 141
Don, 9
Dost (1974), 32
Dutt, Guru, 28, 167, 260
Dutt, Sanjay, 94, 97, 101, 109, 119, 199–200, 211, 257; arrest, 201–202
Dutt, Sunil, 28, 41, 94, 158, 199, 257

Ebert, Roger, 243
editing, 15, 87, 104, 167, 236, 247; Avid, 216
education, 2, 147, 264–265, 276; schooling, 3, 6; Vaish College, 7
Ek Aur Ek Gyarah (2003), 246
Ek Duuje Ke Liye (1981), 107–108, 174
The Elephant Whisperers, Best Documentary Short Film, 267
Enakkul Oruvan (1984) in Tamil, 89

Fakira (1976), 58
family: father (Krishan Dayal), 1, 6–8; mother (Subhadra Ghai), 1-4, 7-8, 66, 71; Premnath on, 48; ran away from home, 4; stepmother, 4, 7–8
Farooqi, Pravez, 258
Farooqui, Akhtar, 11, 72, 106
Fellini, Federico, 16
film, as director's medium, 105
Film and Television Institute of India (FTII), 7, 12, 14–18, 27, 61, 63, 65, 106, 136, 151, 197
Film City, 265
Filmfare talent hunt, 16, 26
film industry, 5, 10–11, 13, 18, 36, 43, 63, 65, 210, 239, 243–244, 248, 265, 270
Filmistaan studio, 97
filmmakers, 5, 41, 48–49, 51, 57, 60, 240, 248, 267, 273–276, 278–279
Film Makers' Combine, 209
filmmaking, 54, 72–73, 121, 126, 133–134, 179, 182, 247–248, 258, 263, 275
film schools, 257, 264–265, 267, 269
film writing, 17, 22, 28, 31, 35, 76, 147, 272, *see also* screenplay writer
final cuts, 71, 83, 232
financiers, 56, 72, 118
first film, 51, 65, 73, 106, 117, 250
first house, in Cliff Tower, 104
flautist, 112
flops, 5, 35, 50, 64, 89, 92, 105, 107, 120, 212, 214
French Kiss, 212, 214
friendship, 26, 52, 63, 181, 217

Galaxy theatre, Bandra, 50
Gandhi, Indira, assassination of, 131
Garewal, Simi, 82–87, 89, 146
Gaurav, Kumar, 109–110, 199
Gautam Govinda (1979), 5, 51–52, 57, 59–63, 68–69, 71–72, 76, 80, 92, 271, 280
Ghai, Ashok, 3, 61, 157, 159
Ghai–Bhalla stories, 32
Ghai, K.D. (father), 106
Ghai, Muskaan, 104;
Ghai, Subash: as actor, 15, 22–23, 26; audition, 17–18; and Bhalla, becoming writers, 32; birth of, 1; brought his mother home, 7; death of baby, 63; Filmfare Best Director trophy, 192; first payment for direction, 39; fleeting appearances of, 80; meeting Premnath, 44; 1962-model Fiat, 36; Sinha on, 41–42; wedding of, 144
Ghatak, Ritwik, 15, 24, 54, 197
Ghazab (1982), 124
Ghosh, Rituparno, 246–247
Gill, Amrik, 251
Gill, Sonika, 169–170
global financial crisis, 262
Godard, Jean-Luc, 16
Gol Maal (1979), 76
Goswami, Rajiv, 116
Govinda, 109, 236
Grahan, 22
Grover, Gulshan, 169–170
Guha, Dulal, 32
Guha, Pradeep, 265
Gulzar, 260

Gumrah, 23, 25, 27, 30, 47
Gunga Jumna (1961), 188
Gupta, Neena, 206
Gupta, Sudesh, 185–186, 221, 225, 258

Haasan, Kamal, 107–110
Haath Ki Safai (1973), 82
Hariharan, 233
Hema Malini, 25, 32, 69–70
Hero (1983), 106, 111, 138, 140, 145, 162, 269; Golden Jubilee of, 5–6; mahurat, 118–119, 122; party, 5–6; Silver Jubilee, 121; 'Written, Produced and Directed by Ghai,' 106
heroines, 20, 75, 77, 80, 114, 116, 119, 126, 184–185, 198, 241–242
Hesse, Hermann, 82
Himalay Putra (1997), 234
Hirani, Rajkumar, 279
HMV, 203–204
Holi parties, 122
Hollywood, 108, 140, 195–197, 209, 243, 278
hostels, 7, 266
Hum (1991), 211
Hum Dil De Chuke Sanam (1999), 255
Hum Hain Rahi Pyar Ke (1993), 222
Hum Kisise Kum Naheen (1977), 80
Husain, M.F., 261
Hussain, Nasir, 16, 19–20
*Hyderabad Blue*s (1998), 246

Ilzaam (1986), 235
income taxes filing, 64, 258
Indian Motion Pictures Producers' Association, 257
Irani, Aruna, 69, 113
Irani, Manik, 117
Iruvar (1997), 239
Iyer, Meena, 183

Jaane Bhi Do Yaaro (1983), 210, 216
Jaanwar, 24, 76
Jaffrey, Javed, 125, 127
Jain, Abhishek, 267
Jain, Jainendra, 40
Jain, Sheetal, 148–149
Jalal, Farida, 18
Jawar Bhata (1944), 177
Jeans, 239
Jeetendra, 110, 112, 161
Jeevan Jagriti complex, 35
Jha, Prakash, 246
Johar, Karan, 267
Johny Mera Naam (1970), 91
Joshi, Pallavi, 193
Junglee, 20

Kabhi Kabhie (1975/1976), 83, 279
Kagaz Ke Phool (1959), 28
Kaho Naa... Pyaar Hai, 250, 252
Kaif, Katrina, 167, 260
Kalicharan (1976), 29–30, 34–35, 42, 44, 46, 52–56, 58, 62–63, 74, 145–147, 203, 242, 271–272, 278; as crime drama, 66, 227; release of, 50
Kalyanji–Anandji, 106, 111
Kashmakash, (2011), 246, 259
Kanchi: The Unbreakable (2014), 266
Kanoon, 128
Kanwar, Sohanlal, 43, 82, 163
Kapadia, Aatish, 251
Kapoor, Anil, 109, 124–127, 130, 136–137, 139, 146, 148, 159–161, 164, 166, 198, 209, 212, 257; threat calls from Pancholi, 211
Kapoor, Annu, 169
Kapoor, Boney, 148, 184
Kapoor, Kareena, 249, 252
Kapoor, Karisma, 183
Kapoor, Om, 90
Kapoor, Pinchoo, 94
Kapoor, Prithviraj, 6

Kapoor, Raj, 6, 8, 14, 16, 28, 33, 40, 270, 275, 277, 279
Kapoor, Randhir, 25, 31, 183, 192, 208, 249
Kapoor, Rishi, 80, 82–83, 87–90, 146, 161; as director's actor, 88–89
Kapoor, Shakti, 116
Kapoor, Shammi, 5, 11, 24, 95, 97, 100–102; Filmfare Best Supporting Actor award, 100
Kapoor, Shashi, 33, 58–59, 68, 71, 158
Kapur, Shekhar, 184, 208, 243
Karan Arjun (1995), 171
Karma (1986), 132, 138, 164–165, 198, 271, 275, 278; Diamond Jubilees, 143; release of, 142, 145
Karnad, Girish, 127
Karnik, Kiran, 265
Karz, 5, 7, 9, 74–75, 77, 77–80, 82–84, 87, 89–92, 94, 106–107, 111–113, 157–158, 210, 213; 'Dard-e-dil,,' 88; opening song of, 79; remake of, 89
Kashyap, Anurag, 279
Kaul, Mani, 39
Kaushik, Satish, 89, 162, 206
Kelkar, Ram, 40, 115–116, 156–157, 159, 163, 198–199
Khaan Dost, 32–33, 52
Khaitan, Shashank, 267
Khal-Naaikaa, 208–209
Khal Nayak (1993), 198, 208, 225, 278; music rights, 204; release, 208
Khan, Aamir, 182, 185, 220; Ghai on, 181–182
Khan, Amjad, 96–98, 125, 132
Khan, Anwar, 156
Khan, Arbaaz, 260
Khan, Feroze, 166
Khan, Iqbal, 50, 246–247, 259, 282
Khan, Kabir, 279
Khan, Kadar, 97
Khan, Mehboob, 16, 28, 50, 157–158
Khan, Salim, 124
Khan, Salman, 183, 219, 221, 260–262
Khan, Saroj, 107, 113, 118, 165–168, 206, 239; Filmfare award for best choreography, 206–207; Ghai on, 168
Khan, Shah Rukh, 90, 200, 211–212, 216–218, 224, 253
Khan, Shakir, 220
Khan, Zayed, 260
Khanna, Akshaye, 234–235, 249
Khanna, Ashok, 114
Khanna, Jatin, 18–19; *Filmfare* on, 19
Khanna, Prabhat 'Kuku,' 97–98, 114–115, 118, 165
Khanna, Rajesh, 9, 19–20, 22–23, 41, 80, 163, 251
Khanna, Vinod, 31, 41, 80, 82, 132, 234
Khari Baoli, 2
Khatoon, 163, 221
Khel Khel Mein (1975), 76
Kher, Anupam, 124, 137–138, 162, 193, 200; Filmfare award for, 163
Khilona (1970), 28
Khote, Durga, 84–87
Khuda Gawah (1992), 211
Khudgarz (1987), 249
Khurana, Jagjit, 63, 72–73, 106
Kiran, Raj, 80, 89
Kismet (1943), 42
Kisna (2005), 59, 76, 253–256, 260, 281
Koirala, Manisha, 166–167, 183–184, 186, 193
Kolhapure, Padmini, 95
kotha, 14
Kranti (1981), 177
Krishnamurthy, Kavita, 160
Krodhi, (1981), 66–68, 146
Kukunoor, Nagesh, 246
Kumar, Ashok, 42–43, 128; as Dadamoni, 42–43; Sagar on, 42

Kumar, Bhushan, 89
Kumar, Dheeraj, 18
Kumar, Dilip. *See* Dilip Kumar
Kumar, Gulshan, 268; killing of, 122
Kumar, Hemant, 16
Kumar, Kishore, 78–79, 145
Kumar, Manoj, 53, 116, 167, 197
Kumar, Pawan, 30, 32–33, 52–53, 55, 64, 91
Kumar, Rajendra, 109–110, 128, 158, 199
Kumar, Sanjeev, 34, 88, 98–99, 101–102, 138
Kumar, Shravana, 274
Kumari, Lalita, 169

Lal, Kabir, 221, 241–242
Lal, Kishori 215, 217, 219
Lamhe, nominees for Best Director for, 192
Lawrence of Arabia (1962), 196
Laxmikant–Pyarelal (L-P), 76–77, 79, 127–128, 135, 148, 155, 159–160, 176, 213, 230; and Bakshi, 112; Ghai reunion with, 111
Love Story (1981), 109, 174
Ludhianwi, Sahir, 279
Lulla, Neeta, 241
lyricist, 9, 128, 136, 175, 228, 230
lyrics, 77, 128, 130, 134, 205–206, 228, 230–232, 260, *see also* songs

Madhubala, 163
Madhumati (1958), 90
Mahabharat, 76
Mahajan, K.K., 39, 174
Mahal, 11
Mahasati Anusuya, 22
Mahima (Ritu Chaudhary as), 166–167, 220–221, 224–225, 242, 253. *See also under* Mukta Arts
Mahindra, Anand, 265
Main Tulsi Tere Aangan Ki (1978), 136
Malavankar, Dilip, 111
Mamta (1966), 163
mandali, 44, 47
Mandre, R.N., 95
Mangeshkar, Lata, 160
Manohar, Murli, 239
Manohar, Sunanda, 239
Mard (1985), 145
market rates, 110, 121–122, 139, 209
Mashaal (1984), 124
'Mass cinema,' 57
Matondkar, Urmila, 200
Meghna, (daughter), 167, 249, 257, 269
Mehboob Theatre, 50
Mehra, Om Prakash, 5, 14, 31–32
Mehra, Rakeysh Omprakash, 279
Mehta, Ashok, 174, 221
Mera Gaon Mera Desh (1971), 132
Mera Naam Joker (1970), 83, 210, 270
Meri Jung (1985), 53, 126–127, 130, 133, 136, 138, 145, 162, 280; Silver Jubilee, 130
Milan (1967), 28
Mohan Studio, 92
Mohra (1994), 91
Monto (friend), 12, 21
morality, 29, 64, 96
More, Ramkrishna, 264–266
Mother India (1957), 50, 158, 199
Motherland, 253–255; shelving of, 253
Mughal-e-Azam (1960), 113
Mukesh, 78
Mukherjee, Hrishikesh, 192–193, 249
Mukherji, Joy, 20
Mukherji, Subodh, 16, 19–21
Mukta (wife /Rehana as), 5, 11, 23, 35, 37, 61–62, 72, 104, 106, 146, 152, 154, 167; Ghai meeting in Pune, 11; marrying, 23; running household, 61; suffering miscarriages, 62
Mukta Arts, 89, 116–117, 121–122, 141–143, 156–157, 165–166,

184–185, 202–203, 207–208, 211, 213–214, 219, 224–226, 245–248, 257–260, 262, 278; Gayatri mantra, 119, 142; listed at stock exchanges, 258; as private limited company, 106; Shah Rukh Khan signing three-film contract with, 216; story lab in, 269; three-film contract with Mahima, 224
Mukta Arts Workers' Welfare Trust, 164, 225
Mukta Cine Insurance, 258
Mukta Films, 72–73, 89, 106
Mukta Searchlight, 259
Mumbai: first time in, 6–7, 15–16, 21, 139, 142, 163, 165, 176, 180, 204, 208, 229, 231; lingo of film industry, 35; terror attack, 262–263
Murad, Raza, 169–170
Murphy, Eddie, 195–196
Mushran, Vivek, 185–186, 193
music, 75–77, 109, 111, 118, 120, 127–128, 130, 134–135, 204, 213, 226–228, 230, 232, 238, 278–279; Disco, 79; with HMV, 203; orchestration, 77, 213, 222–224, 261
Muskaan (daughter), 167, 249

Naam (1986), 199
Nadeem–Shravan, 222
Namak Haraam (1973), 82
Nanda, Rahul, 252
Narasimha (1991), 200
Nargis, 101, 158
Naseeb (1981), 145
Natak, 23, 82
Nath, Amar, 2
Nath, Rakesh, 164, 166
Naya Daur, 277
Neela Tota, 1, 4
The Negatives, 195, 197; shelving of, 209
new actors, 185, 235, *see also* actors
New India Assurance Company, 257–258
Nigam, Sonu, 224
Nischol, Navin, 23
Noukadubi, 246–247, 259
Nutan, 127, 135–136, 139, 175

Odeon theatre, New Delhi, 141
OMG 2, 276
Om Shanti Om, 78–79, 90
Operation Blue Star in Punjab, 131
Osho, 226, 241
OTT platforms, 269, 273, 275
'Overseas,' 45
'owning the ship,' 72

'package,' 97–98
Paigham (1959), 177
Paintal, Kanwarji, 15
Painter Babu (1983), 117, 120
Pancholi, Aditya, 211
Pandey, Kamlesh, 175, 190, 198–199, 261
Pandit, Kulbhushan. *See* Raaj Kumar
parallel cinema movement, 24
Pardes (1997), 210, 215–222, 224, 226–227, 241–242, 249, 253, 268, 275, 278, 281; Golden Jubilee, 224
Parekh, Asha, 19
Parinda (1989), 216
Parivartan, 28–29
Parvarish (1977), 145
Parvez, K., 26
Patekar, Nana, 197–198
Patel, Praful, 265
Pathak, Neeraj, 215
patriotism, 132–133
Paudwal, Anuradha, 160
Peter Proud, 76
Pheri Bhetaula, 184
Phir Wohi Raat (1980), 124
Phool Aur Kaante (1991), 222
photography, 55, 70, 174, 183
poetry, 269, 278

Police Public (1990), 177
Prada, Jaya, 107
Prakash, J. Om, 16, 250
Pran, 52–54, 68–69
Prasad, L.V., 28–29, 75, 107
Prasad Lab in Chennai, 141
Prashanth, 239
Prem (1995), 184
Prem, Manik, 25, 27
Premnath/Premnath Malhotra, 43–48, 52, 54, 68–69, 81, 97; in Gautam Govinda, 58; Sippy on, 43
Prem Rog (1982), 95
producer–director, 18, 24, 43, 50, 166, 208, 253, 281
producers, 61, 72, *see also* financiers
product placements, 252
Puri, Amrish, 96, 126, 138, 162, 169, 193, 245
Puri, Madan, 96, 103
Puri, Rahul (son-in-law), 269
Pushkarna, Baldev, 25
Pyar Hi Pyar, 24

Qayamat Se Qayamat Tak (1988), 174, 182
quickies, 52, 156
Qurbani, 89, 96

Raaj Kumar (Kulbhushan Pandit as), 176–181, 186–190, 193–194
Raaz, 18–19
Rafi, Mohammad, 62, 77–78
Rahman, A.R., 213, 221, 227–233, 244, 255, 260; Ghai on, 228
Rahul (2001), 246, 259
Rai, Aishwarya, 167, 220, 238–239, 241–242, 253
Rai, Gulshan, 91–92, 94, 97–98, 105, 107, 118–120, 139
Rai, Rajiv, 120
Raja (1995), 222
Rajabali, Anjum, 265
Rajinikanth, 165
Rajnish, Acharya (Osho), 226
Rajshri Productions, 175
Rakhee, 161–162, 171
Ram, 72
Ramayan Chitra, 32, 52, 64, 67
Ram Lakhan, 155, 157–162, 166, 169–170, 172, 174, 176, 178, 200, 206, 209, 242, 280–281; mahurat, 170; under Suneha Arts 159
Ram Teri Ganga Maili (1985), 122
Rangeeli (1952), 177
Ranjeet, 54–55, 169
Ranjeeta, 69
Ranjit Films, 68
Rao, Kamalakar/ Kamlakar, 79, 118, 140, 174
Rathod, Shravan, 222
Ratnam, Mani, 229, 239
Rawail, H.S., 16
Rawal, Paresh, 169
Ray, Satyajit, 15, 24
Raza, Rahi Masoom, 76
Rehana (as Mukta). *See* Mukta (wife)
The Reincarnation of Peter Proud (1975), 74, 76
relationships, 51, 63–64, 147, 219, 259, 273–274, 276
Reshammiya, Himesh, 89
Reshma Aur Shera (1971), 41
R.K. Studio, 122, 256; Holi bash at, 33
Rockford (1999), 246
Roja (1992), 213
Roshan, Hrithik, 250–252
Roshan, Rakesh, 249–250
Roy, Ashok, 33, 36
Roy, Bimal, 16, 279
Roy, Nirupa, 158, 274
Roy, Reena, 25, 47, 52, 54, 62–64

Saajan (1991), 222
Saaransh (1984), 138

Saat Hindustani (1969), 144
Sadak (1991), 222
Sagar, S.M., 42
Saifee/Saifi, Nadeem, 222
Saigal, K.L., 277
Saigal, Mohan, 16
Salaam Bombay (1988), 197
Salem, Abu, 268
Salim–Javed, 9, 32
Saluja, Radha, 43
Saluja, Renu, 216
Samanta, Shakti, 16
Sangam, 275
'Sangeet' was shelving of, 109
Sanyasi (1975), 43
Sargam (1979), 107
Sarika, Baby, 18
Saudagar (1991), 173–174, 177–178, 181–182, 184–195, 198, 203–204, 221, 225, 227, 271, 280–281; Filmfare Best Director trophy, 192
Sautela Bhai, 260
Screen magazine, 166
screen names, 167, 221
screenplay, 54–55, 76, 81, 95–97, 125, 127, 129, 188–189, 191, 197–198, 212, 215, 255
screenplay writer, 40, 115, 159, 196
scriptwriter, 40, 128–129
Sen, Aparna, 174
Sen, Mrinal, 15, 24, 39
Sen, Suchitra, 163
Sen, Sushmita, 239
Seshadri, Meenakshi, 116–117, 119, 126, 163, 166–167
sex education, 276
Shagird, 20
Shah, Kundan, 210
Shah, Naseeruddin, 124, 136, 139, 146, 267; Ghai on, 137
Shahar Se Door, 22
Shakti (1982), 161
Shamim, Mohammad, 17–18
Shantaram, V., 28, 132, 167
Sharada (1957), 28
Sharif, Omar, 195–196
Sharma, Gorakh, 79
Sharma, Naresh, 222
Shatranj Ke Khilari (1977), 215
shelving of projects, 85, 108, 110, 153–154, 255; Devaa, 153; Motherland, 255; *Shikhar*, 222
Sherni (1973), 43
Shetty, Manmohan, 265
Shetty, Rohit, 279
Shikhar, 212, 222, 228, 253; mahurat, 213, shelving of 214
Shirali, Gurudutt, 55, 215–216
Shivdasani, Shyam Sundar, 58, 60, 63, 71–72
Shivpuri, Ritu, 167
Sholay, 9, 25, 60, 68, 71, 96, 99, 125, 132, 138, 275
'Showman,' 6
Shrestha, Rakesh, 183
Shroff, Jackie, 114–120, 124, 126, 136–137, 139, 160–161, 164–165, 171, 183–185, 200–201, 209, 211–212, 251
Siddhartha (1972), 82
Siddiqui, Javed, 215, 227
Singh, Jagjit, 208
Singh, Sukhwinder, 229–231, 233
Sinha, Shatrughan, 24–27, 30, 32–33, 40–42, 47, 49, 52–54, 58–60, 63–65, 67, 69, 144, 146; and Ghai, 49, 65; and Reena Roy as real-life lovers, 63; voice, 54
Sippy, G.P., 16, 18, 20, 201
Sippy, N.N., 33–38, 58, 124–126; introducing Ghai as director, 36; invitation to home, 36; as distributor of Hero, 119; signing contract with, 38
Sippy, Pravesh, 129
Sippy, Ramesh, 25, 124

Sivan, Sangeeth, 246
song, 63, 77–80, 88, 90, 111–113, 117, 127–128, 159–160, 164–168, 189–190, 204–208, 218–219, 222–224, 231–233, 240–242; 'Bol baby bol,' 127; 'Chhaiyya chhaiyya,', 29; "Choli ke peeche", 203–208; Dard-e-dil, dard-e-jigar,' 77–78, 88; 'Do dil mil rahe hain,' 218; 'Ek do teen,' 166; 'Ek haseena thi,' 113; 'Ek ritu aaye, ek...,' 71; 'Jeena yahan marna yahan,' 270; Kahin aag lage lag jaye, 231–232, 240–241; 'Kariye na kariye na...,' 230; 'Laila mar gayee,' 165; 'Mohabbat ye mohabbat,' 113; 'My name is Lakhan,' 159; 'Nahi saamne,' 232–233; 'Om shanti om,' 79; 'Paisa ye paisa,' 79; 'Pyaar ka imtehaan,' 113; 'Pyar karne wale...,' 112; situations, 77, 111; 'Taal se taal mila,' 230; title, 118, 176; 'Tohra bitwa jawan...,' 62; Tu dekh le bhai, 237; 'Ye dil deewana,' 218
Sonie, Bhappi, 24–25
Sridevi, 112, 124, 139, 164, 183
stardom, 16, 70, 145, 195, 200, 217, 251
stars, 16, 23, 25, 41, 43, 67–68, 91–93, 109–111, 121–122, 163–164, 170–171, 173, 182, 185–186, 221; Ghai on, 111
story, 25, 27–35, 39–44, 52–55, 58–59, 66–68, 73–75, 80–86, 93–95, 97–98, 111, 123–125, 158–159, 173–176, 178–182, 226–228, 245–247, 268, 273, 276–279; narration the, 30–31, 34, 36, 44, 67, 70, 82–83, 93, 98, 111, 115, 176, 178, 263, 277; of 'Sangeet,' 107; songs in, 167; of Taal, 227
Suhaag (1979), 145
Sunita, 3
Suneha Arts, 157, 159
Sutradhar, Tabun, 158, 222–223
Swarup, Govind, 264

Taal (1999), 76, 224–226, 228, 237, 242, 244, 248–249, 251–253, 257–259, 278, 281; at Chicago International Film Festival, 243; Variety on, 243
Taare Zameen Par, 277
Tabu, 184
Taj Mahal (1963), 249
Tak, Saawan Kumar, 208
talent hunt, 16, 18, 22, *see also* Filmfare talent hunt
Talpade, Shreyas, 246
Tandon, Sirjang Lal, 214
Tandons, 214–215
Tandoori Nights, 254–255
Taneja, Roshan, 15, 54; acting school of, 125
Taqdeer, 22
Taurani, Ramesh, 203–204, 268
tax raid, 121, *see also* income tax filing
technicians, 6, 9, 122, 147, 195–197, 226, 240–242, 275
televisions channels, 253, 256
The Ten Commandments (1956), 140
terrorism, 131–132, 207
Tezaab (1988), 166
Thackeray, Bala Saheb, support of *Khal Nayak*, 207
theatres, 2, 5, 27, 29, 55, 57, 127, 129–130, 132, 140–143, 208–209, 224, 242–243, 262–263, 275
3 Deewarein (2003), 246
36 China Town (2006), 38, 89, 246, 282
36 Chowringhee Lane (1981), 174
36 Farmhouse, 278, 282
Tina Munim, 80–81, 94
Tips Music Company, 203
title, 27, 45, 55, 74–75, 94, 175, 198, 208–209, 219–220, 246
Tiwari, Anuradha, 251

Tridev (1989), 91
Trimurti (1995), 213–214, 216, 221, 245, 253, 257, 281
Trishul (1978), 92, 100
Trivedi, Arvind, 207
12th Fail, 277

Umang, 22–23
Umrao Jaan (1981), 215
United Producers Combine, 16, 19, 21
Upkar (1967), 52–53
Uski Roti (1970), 39
Uttar Dakshin (1987), 165

Variety, 243
VCP (video cassette player)/VCR – the VHS rentals, 131–132
video parlours, 131–132, 140
video piracy, 121, 132, 140, 143
Vidhaata (1982), 7–8, 11, 91, 93–94, 96, 100, 103–107, 111, 113, 133, 145–146, 161–162, 165, 173–174, 198–200
Virk, Ranjit, 68
Vishwanath, 51–56, 63–64, 67, 71, 74–75, 80, 88, 91, 96, 271, 280; crime drama, 227
Vyjayanthimala, 24

Wadia, Shashi, 168, 185, 190–191
Wanted, 262
Waqt (1965), 248
Webber, Andrew Lloyd, 243–244
Whistling Woods, 264–267, 269; film school, 154; legal battle, 267
writer–director, 9, 22, 248, 257
writers, 22–23, 25, 27–29, 31–32, 34, 38, 62, 125, 127, 195–196, 199–200, 248, 251, 267, 269, *see also* co-writers; dialogue writers; screenplay writers; scriptwriters

Yaadein, 250–253, 269
Yaadon Ki Baaraat (1973), 46
Yagnik, Alka, 206
Yaqoob, Lala, 158
Yash (cousin), 13–16
Yash Raj Films, 224, 257
Yogi, 27, 30
Yuga Purusha (1989), in Kannada, 89
Yuvvraaj (2008), 53, 59, 76, 254–255, 261–262, 281

Zanjeer (1973), 145
Zinta, Preity, 253

About the Authors

PHOTO BY SOUMIK KAR

Subhash Ghai is a renowned film writer, director and producer. He is the chairman and managing director of Mukta Arts, his production company that was set up in 1982. Over a career spanning four decades, Ghai has directed and produced a great many memorable and successful films. He is the founder–chairman of Whistling Woods International, India's premier film, communications and creative arts institute, which was started in 2006.

COURTESY OF SUVEEN SINHA

Suveen Sinha is an award-winning father, according to his ten-year-old son, Sahir. Suveen is also a non-award-winning journalist and an author of non-fiction books. He grew up on a steady diet of Subhash Ghai's films, alongside those involving Yash Chopra, Gulzar, Salim–Javed, Ram Gopal Varma, Francis Ford Coppola, Martin Scorsese, Aaron Sorkin, Quentin Tarantino and Christopher Nolan. This is his third book.